BUSINESS/SCIENCE/T
DIVISION

D1418146

By the same author

Highliners: A Documentary Novel About the
Fishermen of Alaska

The Mallore Affair: a novel of India

FISH DECKS

Seafarers of the North Atlantic

with photos by the author

WILLIAM McCLOSKEY

PARAGON HOUSE
NEW YORK

TO KARIN
my daughter

First Edition, 1990

Published in the United States by

Paragon House
90 Fifth Avenue
New York, NY 10011

Library of Congress Cataloging-in-Publication Data

McCloskey, William B., 1928-
    Fish decks: seafarers of the North Atlantic / William B.
McCloskey, Jr. — 1st ed.
      p.   cm.
    ISBN 1-55778-076-5
    1. Fishers—North Atlantic Ocean.   I. Title.
HD8039.F66N575   1990
331.7′6392′091631—dc20   89-39054
                                                          CIP

Manufactured in the United States of America

*The paper used in this publication meets the minimum requirements of
American National Standard for Information Sciences—Permanence of Paper
for Printed Library Materials, ANSI Z39.48-1984.*

Contents

Acknowledgments

Where to begin, when so many people have taken me fishing, helped me get to the boats, and encouraged me in writing this book? I want to thank especially those who offered me friendship besides.

In Gloucester there were Joey and Joanne Testaverde: Joey is now the skipper of the wooden dragger *Nina T* since the *Peter & Linda* sank beneath him, an open-hearted man with a taste for innovation within a most traditional fishery. In Myre, Norway, there was gracious Kaare Hagerup, acknowledged father of modern Vesteralen fishing, who in his youth during the occupation had been clever enough to find ways of supplying Norwegians with more fish than the German army allowed; and Captain Oddmund Bye, the man to shake down the newest trawler of the company fleet before striking out on a bold private fishing venture with his brothers. In the Lofoten Islands of Norway, there were my rorbu mates headed by Edmund Sandholm, skipper of the *Arsteinvag*, who now fishes closer to home on the mainland while running a dairy farm in the traditional Norwegian fishing-farming pattern. In Lofoten also were the husband-wife fishing team Artur and Sigrun Nilsen—Sigrun who raised her eyebrows, commanded me to speak only Norwegian, rode herd on my intonations, and thus taught me—who now live in busy retirement with grandchildren trooping through the house.

In Canada there were Frank and Mary Clarke of Charlottetown, Labrador, whose summer fishing station on the outer rocks always had a bed for me and a place in the boat. John and Judy McGrath of Goose Bay, he the Labrador provincial minister in charge of northern development and she a restorer of native textile crafts as well as co-editor of the Labrador oral history magazine, *Them Days*, gave frequent hospitality along with their unique insights into the ways of north Atlantic Canada. In St. John's, Jim and Sharon Winters' hospitality always included seal meat from the freezer along with perspectives and lore on the whole range of Newfoundland society. There was sealing Captain Frank Puddister who took a chance on an "American writer fellow" aboard his ship. And Alex Saunders of a respected old Labrador fishing family who, sometimes holding tight for dear life as head of the tenuous new Torngat Co-op, still looked out for needs of mine that ranged from a bunk at his home and hitch-hikes on chartered planes to shared strips of caribou jerky.

But there were so many others besides, whose generosity extended beyond the sharing of information. In New Bedford, Captain Peter Jacobsen of the trawler *General Patton*, who altered sleeping arrangements to his own discomfort in order to accommodate me. In Myre, Tor-Erik Bye and Asbjorn Wolden, captain and bosun respectively of the trawler *Myrefisk Two*, and the young mate Jon Danielsen aboard *Myrefisk One*. Closer to home in my own Chesapeake Bay country, Bill Sieling of the Maryland Department of Natural Resources, who introduced me to watermen and often advised me on the accuracy of information; Lester Lee, Wadie Murphy, Earnest Delano, John Dize, Lewis Cain, Russell Dize, Jack Webster and other fishermen who took me aboard their boats; Betty Duty, the one-woman force that helps keep the Maryland Waterman's Association in shape from day to day; and Eugene Cronin, distinguished marine scientist who headed one of the leading Chesapeake Bay research organizations, now campaigns for public and political awareness, and intelligent management, of the Bay's problems.

In Newfoundland/Labrador Dr. Tony Paddon of Northwest River, second-generation torch bearer of the Grenfell missions; Jack and Florence Troake of Twillingate, he the center of three generations who have sealed and fished from their own boats all their lives; Bart Higgins, the imaginative new headman of the Smokey station who looks out for his people as he works alongside them; Wes and Leah

Hurley, light-spirited summer stationers along with the other Hurley brothers and their families on the remote rocks of Emily Harbor; Mrs. Eva Mouland, widow of Hughie who survived a famous 1914 sealing disaster, who kept me in warm home-knitted boot socks; young fisherman and sealer Winston Fowlow whose reedy voice out on the ice delivered ballads that brought back the sealing days of old; Canadian fishery officer Wilson Kettle, a man with whom to share a laugh as you hopped the dangerous ice pans; Don Linfield, sealing mate, coastal boat skipper, and fisherman, who with a sympathetic grin drove nails into my boots when he saw me slipping like a waterbug on the glassy ice.

For permission to reprint written excerpts I am indebted to author Elliott Merrick and his wife, the former "Northern Nurse" Kate Austen, for their reminiscences of days working at the Grenfell Mission hospital in Indian Harbor, Labrador. I am also grateful to *International Wildlife* magazine and to *Them Days* magazine for their permissions to reprint portions of articles on sealing and other Newfoundland/ Labrador activities. Some material in the book was taken from my own articles in *Smithsonian, National and International Wildlife, National Fisherman, Pacific Fishing, Oceans, Fishing News International*, and the *Johns Hopkins Applied Physics Laboratory Technical Digest*. I am grateful to the editors of these publications for their good counsel over the years.

The fishery attachés of the Canadian and the Norwegian embassies in Washington, D.C., were invariably helpful. These included George Béchard and later Harry Adams of Canada, Finn Bergesen and later Semund Remøy of Norway. Finn, who now heads the Norway-wide fisherman's organization Norges Fiskerlag, has also rendered aid in that capacity as well as Torlief Paache of the same organization. In the United States Richard Roe, northeast regional director of the National Marine Fisheries Service, gave perspectives on the fishery management process, as did Douglas Marshall, executive director of the New England Fishery Management Council.

An editor's cold hand on a book after it is written can bring an author heartache and despair. The sympathetic (not soft) touch with which Paragon handled *Fish Decks* was a noteworthy enough experience to warrant thanking Ken Stuart, PJ Dempsey, Ed Paige, Peter Borten (a freelance editor), and Bennett Paris for the parts they played. Among longtime friends there was my agent Julian Bach who had faith in the idea of *Fish Decks* before anyone else, Josephine

Brennan whose cool eye ferreted out rogue errors of syntax, and Ken and Jean Haviland whose huge private marine library was always available.

The book is dedicated to my daughter Karin, a physician in the rigorous new field of pediatric critical care transport, who exemplifies the grit in one area of endeavor that I have found consistently among fishermen in another. There is also my son Wynn, lawyer and wreck diver, who has been a fellow-crewman on fishing boats and a sounding board for things nautical from facts to yarns, as well as my parents, Bill and Evelyn, still here in spirit. And finally my wife Ann, who holds it all together.

Introduction
The Shadow of Ishmael

D own at the fisherman's hall, someone obligingly scribbled a
note that certified me to be a fisherman in search of a boat. On
the strength of this, I was able to turn my back on hotels along the
city streets of New Bedford—streets with functional old buildings
mixed among the new in nobody's dream of urban beauty—and to
ignore the bright motels that lined the outskirts of town. The Mariner's Home would accept me, a lodging house beside the historic
Seamen's Bethel, where Ishmael himself had attended a service.

Whaling built the foundations of New Bedford, but today, long
after any American threw his last harpoon or flensed blubber and
tried it out, the city harbors a fishing fleet that often delivers a higher
annual value of sea products than any other in the United States. In
days bygone, a would-be whaler found his way to New Bedford; then
as now it was a logical place to start pounding the docks if you
wanted to go hunting the products of the sea.

I entered a segment of town apart from the burgerhouses and
stores—no more than a hill—where cobblestones still paved the
streets and the buildings had a subdued colonial unity. Since this
was November, the tourists were gone. A chilly drizzle swept around
the old-time street lamps and glistened on the stones. If this had
been a movie, the time would have come for voices of the past to rise

on the sound track: loud fishermen's voices competing in a tavern with others thickened by grog, then a whalerman at sea bellowing, "She blows, she blows; thar she blows!" Up the music, and wiry untrained voices would start to sing, "Jack was every inch a sailor, five and twenty years a whaler. . . ." But I needed no sound track. The voices roared and sang for me without it.

On top of the hill, three solid buildings faced each other. The largest was the whaling museum, a cupola-topped structure relatively formidable for the narrow street, through whose big arched windows showed a silhouette of sails and ships' rigging. I knew from guidebooks that this was the celebrated half-scale reproduction, fully rigged, of the whaling bark *Lagoda*.

Directly across the street stood the equally famous Seamen's Bethel Church, built in 1832 for the spiritual edification of the reputed ten thousand seafaring men who once crowded the New Bedford docks, inns, and bawdy houses. The church was only eight years old when Herman Melville attended a service there. The great American author transformed the experience into a part of world literature by leading his hero Ishmael to a pew where a thundering mystical sermon washed over him before he shipped with Captain Ahab on the fateful quest for Moby Dick.

Alongside the bethel stood the brick and clapboard Mariner's Home, its entrance flanked by steps leading up from both sides. A bronze plaque on front anchored the home's location at Lat 41° 38′ 08″ N, Long 70° 55′ 26″ W. I knew nothing about the place except that the cost was supposed to be reasonable, and that to be handed the key one needed to prove a bona fide relationship to a boat or a ship.

Despite the glow of street lamps, historic Johnny Cake Hill grew dimmer by the minute. Through the shuttered windows of the Mariner's Home only a small light shone from far inside. Suddenly, in the twilight with slippery wet leaves underfoot and no other living person on the street, things looked unpromising. Shadows of the past make lonesome company on a wet evening.

I knocked on the door, half hoping that no one would answer and I could escape to a bright motel room. After all, life aboard a fishing boat when I found one was going to be Spartan enough. But a man answered—a friendly, quiet, sandy-haired man of about forty— glanced at my seabag, and beckoned me in. We walked unhurriedly into a carpeted living room, discussing the dreariness of the weather.

Introduction

The room had a smell of old fabric and old wood. From somewhere in back came the odor of stew. He gave me a pen to register, accepted my money, and handed over a key to the front door and another to Room Five on the third floor.

He wore a plaid shirt and loose work pants, under which his frame had the appearance of softened muscles in a body built for heavy work. I ventured that he must once have been a fisherman. Yes. But he had been grounded by a kidney transplant. A fisherman ashore is indeed a man grounded, but at least Ron Hansen's work now helped look out for others on the beach. The New Bedford Port Society, founded in 1830, maintained the Mariner's Home, he explained, as a lodging for fishermen and other seafarers away from home. The mansion itself, built as a private residence in 1787, assumed its present function in 1857. Both the bethel and the home, while funded in part by income and contributions, derived much of their support from endowments left by old New Bedford whaling families. A great harbor always needed a clean haven ashore for its men, and at a reasonable price. It was as true a century and a half ago as today. A night's lodging cost three dollars in 1978, at the time of my first visit, and a decade later the price had only doubled.

Seeing my interest, Ron took me over to the bethel and turned on a few lights. Can a place have the odor of quietness, and the look of old silences? The wood was plain, the air chilly. There it was, suspended in an ocean of space, the pulpit shaped like a ship's bow from which the fictional Father Mapple had preached the earthy, mighty sermon heard by Ishmael. Old rubbed cenotaphs along the walls listed names of men lost at sea. There was silent witness everywhere to the perils of life on the water: "This worthy man, after fastning [sic] to a whale, was carried overboard by the line, and drowned May 19th 1844 in the 49th year of his age." Another "fell from aloft, off Cape Horn, Feb 10, 1850 and was drowned."

Some cenotaphs (the word means "empty tomb") had the shine of recent years, and the dates they bore were not from the distant past but rather recorded fishing boat tragedies with the names of men who had walked the streets of New Bedford within heartbreakingly recent memory. Ron Hansen pointed to his father's name among six who died on a single boat in 1951. The dates continued to the immediate present.

Back at the Mariner's Home, I climbed stairs that had the comfortable creak of weathered boat timbers. The accommodations were austerely plain, so plain that few obstructions such as furniture existed to collect dust. No one else seemed to be in residence. The emptiness gave an echo to the hall, where a single light at each end reflected off shiny new gray paint on the wide floorboards. Most rooms contained three beds, privacy not being a luxury expected by most seafarers. The doors had no locks, only latches. For a hall light, I sneaked to another floor and stole the bulb from an unoccupied room. A box in the hall contained a Jacob's ladder in case of fire, and as an added nicety there was a knotted rope tied to a bar by the window in my room. (Historic buildings and ugly exterior fire escapes do not mix in New England.) Directly across the street, I could look into the high windows of the museum, straight at the whaling bark Lagoda.

Thank goodness, I had not lost heart, and had knocked on the door! Looking out, I felt myself to be the chosen custodian for this night of all the men who for a century and a half had left their homes to fish on the sea.

In truth, I was only a sometime fisherman. My workplace was usually an office. By the time of this recounting, however, I had begun to quit this security for periods, with the acceptance of a wife who understood more than many would have, to work as a crewman on salmon seiners and king crab boats in Alaska. By now I knew what it was like to do wet labors on a pitching deck. I had worked long enough for it to cease being adventure, through the time of such aches and fatigue that nothing appeared more desirable than the shore, to the point where aches tapered and fatigue came only as a normal part of the day's sequence.

It might have started when my dad took me at age nine to see that wonderful 1937 movie of Captains Courageous, thinking it might do me some good. Lucky Freddie Bartholomew, to fall from a mere ocean liner and be rescued by Spencer Tracy in a fishing dory! All this might be termed dilettantism, since I had never owned a boat nor committed myself beyond a fishing season. Yet to work as a fisherman had become my pleasure, my consolation even. When I went to a fishing boat and saw nets stacked in wait, oilskins hanging together on hooks by the cabin, the wood and metal on deck scraped white from a thousand abrasions; or when I smelled grease and salted rust combined with the faint sour odor of fish long scrubbed away, it was like a homecoming, an atavistic return to another incarnation.

Perhaps one carries baggage from the past. In my father's effects, I recently found a book on seamanship under sail, inscribed by one "Capt James D. McCloskey, Nov 1st 1853." I think that he was my great-grandfather, but no one left in any family generation can confirm it since my late granddad left home at an early age, taking little of his history with him. The book is well-thumbed rather than one bought for a library shelf. It links me back. I can daydream a reincarnation without wading too deep into theological waters.

Did I once, as a young fellow starting out, stand on a wooden deck with fingers clawed into net, pulling with all my back, or did I row a dory into twelve-foot waves to haul a mile of baited line hand over hand? Did I work my way to the command of a fishing smack, a coastal schooner, a naval frigate, a whaling bark, a great clipper ship? Did I finally drown with a roar, or fade ashore with a crusty tongue that was the despair of those forced to live with me? I (in the present) enjoy all kinds of ships and seafaring, but my blood pounds only at the sight and smell of fishing boats. My ancestor Captain James is therefore declared to be a fisherman, since I feel it and there is nobody around to contradict.

It turned out that I was not alone after Ron Hansen closed the door to his own apartment. Three glum older men occupied a room down the hall. They only nodded when passing to a common lavatory. In them, all the sweat and smells and shouts of the past seemed distilled away. I was after all only a passer-through in an occupation that wore men out and made them old before their time.

But the wet breeze that merely soaked the leaves off the trees ashore had been making itself felt as a northeasterly roar on the ocean beyond the breakwaters. Suddenly, a collective stomp and buzz began downstairs, punctuated by bursts of laughter. Sixteen fishermen had checked in, from Maine herring seiners in the harbor that had decided not to fish in the bad weather that night. Most were bearded young men with clear eyes, fellows whose chests filled their jackets. Their cheerful noise and feet thumping on the floorboards, even a bit of horseplay, made the halls of the old building come alive. This was a place of the present.

The present continued early next morning, because just down the hill and across a busy street lay the fish auction house. If you wanted to meet New Bedford fishing skippers and talk yourself into a site aboard one of the boats, this auction—at least in 1978—was considered the place to start.

1

Georges Bank

The present New Bedford fish auction house, visited in 1989, did not seem a convivial place at 6:30 in the morning. The buyers from local fish houses, glumly nursing coffee in paper cups, paced inside the central enclosure that only they could enter. On a platform flanked by blackboards, house employees were silently chalking the names of boats and the poundage of their "trips" by species. Skippers and mates stated gruffly their "hails"—the fish they were putting up for sale—to clerks at the side of the enclosure who wrote out the tickets and handed them up for posting on the blackboard. Many of the fishermen had the scuffed, red-eyed look of men just in from days on rough water.

Fortunes hung in the balance, at least the income for a crew's labor at sea for a week or more, and a buyer's ability to remain competitive in a shifting, cutthroat marketplace. The posted rules were terse and simple:

"It is the responsibility of the captain or mate to make sure the hail posted on the board is correct." . . . *"Only two representatives from each vessel allowed in exchange at a time."*

In former days, at a publicly owned auction house, fellows looking for a site on a boat used to hang around, as well as crewmen watching their payday transpire, and mere spectators. Now it is easier to crash the Harvard Club than to attend a New Bedford fish auction without credentials. The fish buyers own the place and pay a stiff fee, and they feel no obligation to entertain nonmembers.

"*Scallopers. Trips posted by* 7:00 A.M. 7:10–7:12 *two-minute bell warning to decide whether to sell or not. Trip sold to highest bidder at* 7:15." The draggers' trips then were posted at 8:00 A.M., with a few minutes more allowed since their trips dealt in multiple species, but the bell rang down the final bid at 8:22 sharp by the big clock on the wall.

On the board, each of fourteen draggers, named along with the skipper and assigned a number, had its trip listed in a long vertical of abbreviations: "3.5 *had*, 2.5 L *cod*, 5.5 *market*, 7.5 *sd*" translated to 3,500 pounds haddock, 2,500 pounds large cod, 5,500 pounds market-sized cod, 7,500 pounds scrod (small cod). Other abbreviations showed the variety of the harvest: Ls = lemon sole, bb = blackback flounder, sab = small blackbacks, pw = peewee-sized blackbacks, sand = sand dabs.

Each buyer had a permanent assigned letter, and capital letters at the bottom of some trip postings indicated buyers to whom the boat would not sell. In a place where boats and fish houses dealt with each other year after year, there were bound to be enmities.

The skippers and mates retired to a room separated by glass from the main floor. When the bell rang to start, the floor erupted in a gunfire of bids from about twenty buyers. The auction boardmen scribbled, erased, scribbled. Buyers clutched individual phones connected to their market sources, muttering in low enough voices not to be overheard. Quickly, the price structure of the day emerged: haddock, $.75; large cod, $.35; markets, $.45; scrod, $.30; lemon sole, $1.40; and so forth.

The accents of the region were evident. "Foahty-eight on the mahket, boat seven," called an older buyer. He wore a tie and had a dignified paunch. "*Fifty*," shouted a muscular buyer in jeans who had not shaved that morning.

Numbers and instructions popped from everywhere as the boardmen scribbled furiously. During the two-minute bell, the bidding stopped. One skipper consulted his mate and they withdrew their catch from the board, evidently hoping to make a better deal privately. The withdrawal raised the price for the remaining boats when bidding started again.

"Dollah fifteen on the small."

"*Twenny* on that, one foahty on the large yellow."

The clock second hand moved, the final bell rang, and the auction ended. The last bid on any species had bought the boat's entire trip. Skippers left to move their boats to the piers of the buyers.

My own New Bedford tale began at the old auction house, which burned in the mid-1980s during a bitter union strike that altered the structure of the local fishing establishment. The old house, public property and open to anyone, seemed a more sociable place, although the same tight rules governed transactions.

I had been given some names of owners and skippers, and I asked around until I found them. Nobody had a site for a stranger. A classic way to start a fishing career, if you have not gone to the boats with your dad and uncles since an early age, is to work without pay—or, as a writer or photographer, to ask yourself aboard as a passenger, giving the strong impression that idleness is not your goal.

"Maybe," said Leif Jacobsen, a large, balding older man who no longer fished himself but owned more than one boat. He told me to look him up in Fairhaven across the bridge in two hours. Mr Jacobsen conducted his family-sized waterfront enterprise from a little office built into the corner of a warehouse. A spur of the road led to a pier that had withstood the scrapes of many boats, where a mast and superstructure rose behind a pickup truck.

Leif Jacobsen introduced me to his brother Peter, skipper of the *General George* S. *Patton*. Peter Jacobsen, a large-boned man like his older brother but less relaxed, perhaps more volatile than placid, looked me over as we talked. He had a deep voice and an energetic manner. "Okay, if you want to come out," he said at length, in the same slight Norwegian accent as his brother. His gray-white hair had an offhand sweep with just a touch of the comb, and the sweep seemed to characterize his nature.

The *Patton*, eighty-four feet long, lay moored at the end of the pier. Its winches may have shown the old browns of daily salt abrasions, but its white and gray hull, barely chipped or rusted, had a proud panache alongside the wooden draggers in other parts of the harbor. This was a stalwart young prince among aging courtiers, a new boat built in response to dramatic new hopes.

Only the year before, in 1977, had the United States and Canada assumed control of the marine resources within two hundred miles of their coasts. The territory included one of the greatest stretches of the world's sea wealth, from Georges Bank and its adjacent grounds

[3]

north to the Grand Banks off Newfoundland. These resources had for two decades been fished predominantly by large factory ships from the Soviet Union, Poland, the two Germanys, Spain, Bulgaria, and other European nations. The situation had permitted very little of the area's legendary marine abundance to come ashore in the holds of boats from adjacent New England and the Canadian Maritimes. Local fishermen had simply been outclassed and bullied away from their traditional grounds. To add to the injury, the efficient large factory trawlers also intercepted most of the fish that would have migrated inshore where the smaller boats might have taken some gleanings. During this time, as the inshore fisheries of the northern Atlantic coast withered and frequently appeared to be gasping their last, few Americans invested in new vessels or gear. This, of course, widened the gap of competitiveness still further.

But now there was hope. The United States and Canada controlled their resources at last. While the foreign ships had not been sent home from the waters of either nation with the decisiveness local fishermen were expecting, and while the United States government had begun to impose some infuriating restrictions on the quantities of fish its boats could land even if it found them, fishermen saw reason to invest for the future.

Leif Jacobsen had earned the reputation of an innovator by introducing new gear technologies to the conservative New Bedford fleet. He recognized the signal when the two-hundred-mile law first started to gather momentum in the U.S. Congress. With the steel-hulled *Valkyrie*, he took the leap from old wooden hulls that still serve some of the New England fleet, and with the *Patton* leapt further with a boat that had the speed and deck power to fish, on a smaller scale, in the efficient manner of the slowly vanishing factory trawlers.

At 11:30 A.M., Captain Peter listened to the weather report. This was November, and the meteorologists reported a northeaster on its way from Canada. However, its course was still uncertain and the predicted arrival still hours away. He decided to put to sea, and phoned his crewmen to get ready.

Six men arrived one by one with their gear, most of them driven by wives rather than sweethearts to judge from the orderly kisses they exchanged. I threw down my seabag, and greeted them soberly since they appeared to be sober types. They looked me over as a group, and nodded politely. The men ranged in age from their early twenties to about sixty. Each had his own characteristics, but there were too many to sort out all at once.

Their conversations jumped between English and Norwegian. Ron Hansen at the Mariner's Home had confirmed the night before that New Bedford crews were predominantly Norwegian or Portuguese, many first generation. In like manner, Gloucester crews answered to names that found their origin in southern Italy and Sicily (and two generations ago also to Portuguese and Finnish names). Throughout New England, Yankees still fished from smaller harbors like the two Rockports of Maine and Massachusetts, and Point Judith in Rhode Island, but they no longer dominated the scene. The attrition of men drowned in the fogs and storms on the banks (little Gloucester once lost more than two hundred of its men in a single terrible year) had steadily opened the way for adventurous fishermen from nations with less productive grounds.

The *Patton* had a long work deck aft and a ramp cut into the stern. The forward housing contained the wheelhouse above crew quarters at deck level. The quarters were spacious by the standards of a New England dragger, with separate two-bunk cabins, mess room, and galley. Peter started the diesel engine, which throbbed with a vibration that hummed through the deck plates. We cast off lines and soon passed beyond the shoreside buildings of New Bedford, through the breakwater, and into Buzzard's Bay. Peter gladly showed the route on his charts as he steered past West Chop Island and through Quick Island Pass. At each point closer to the sea, the boat rolled and pitched a bit more, until it came alive. The sun shone brightly and sparkled on the waves.

Since the others made the trip routinely, it had no charm or history for them, but nevertheless they turned cheerful as they stowed gear and went inside. Peter in the wheelhouse began to sing under his breath. Leaving the shore behind can do this, on a lively day, despite any stress that may lie ahead. We dipped past Martha's Vineyard, with its bluffs and big old houses, and the sea opened wider and wider around us until a breeze began kicking wisps of spray across the deck. I drew breaths of the salty air, and would not have changed places with the president of IBM.

Georges Bank is one of the most abundant fishing grounds in the world. We were headed there to trawl, or to "drag," as fishermen call it, for cod and flounder. The trip would last a week or more. Georges

Bank is a submerged plateau of ten thousand square miles that begins about sixty miles off Cape Cod. Its depths, ranging between ten to fifty fathoms—the irregular fifty-fathom line delineates the bank—contain a legendary concentration of marine life. Georges may be only a portion of the seafood-rich continental shelf system that extends along the North American coast from Florida to Newfoundland but its abundance makes it special. The place has accumulated histories and traditions, evoked by such names of specific bottoms as Cultivator Shoals, the Leg, Billy Doyle's Hole, and Outside Hole.

Jacobsen was a practical fisherman, and when the wind began to change toward the predicted northeaster he chose Nantucket Harbor for the night rather than a buffeting in seas that would probably be too rough in any case for setting the nets. Storms may be a fact of life, but Georges Bank fishermen respect them. Too many men have lost their lives in terrible seas that can knock a boat to pieces against the shoals—ironically, the same shoals that attract fishermen because they provide habitats for the fish that the men are chasing. Boats are lost even in summer out there. Most men I know who fish the region do not brood about the fragility of their rough life, but they do consider it.

The detour into Nantucket provided a glance at two other fishing fleets so different from our own that they dramatized the variety of fishing options in New England. We tied alongside a boat with an extravagantly raked bowsprit. It, too, had decided to treat itself to a calm haven for the night, in the course of cruising for swordfish. Like the old whalemen, the swordfish men hunted with harpoons that they flung by hand. The man I talked to, rail to rail, had a remarkable suntan for November. Well sure, he said with a southern drawl, they'd just been off the coast of Florida last week. Their grounds ranged over thousands of miles.

Another variety of the fishing scene appeared next morning, when in sunny, frosty calm we headed back to sea. Bobbing in Nantucket Bay were sixty open workboats anchored to lines that miraculously did not get tangled. One or two men stood in each boat, their yellow slickers showing arms and backs brightly against the gray-green water and shore as they reeled up dredges and emptied out piles of scallop shells. According to Peter, this was a limited inshore fishery licensed for Nantucket residents only. The scallops taken here were little

|6|

fellows compared to the big ones that the scalloping fleets out of New Bedford and the Nova Scotia ports landed on Georges, but many people preferred them for their sweetness.

At last we reached Georges Bank, and with loran and depth readings Peter located the grounds that he wanted to try first. Fish never guarantee their presence, but fishermen gather their own experience of fathom curves and knobs and trenches where they have been fortunate before. He gave a shout from the wheelhouse and slowed the engine. On deck, Øivind (pronounced approximately "Ervind") switched to power takeoff (you can do this only with the main engine idling or the shaft would turn too fast and burn out the mechanism), opened the hydraulic system, and pulled a lever to start unwinding the big drum of net down the stern ramp.

The steps of shooting a trawl are basically the same aboard fishing boats and ships of all sizes, although the functions performed by the drum and the stern ramp have several variations. First the flattened cod end floated astern. The bag had heavier mesh than the rest of the net since it needed to bear the strain when full of fish. A confetti of rope-strand chafing gear covered the bag to protect against seafloor abrasions that could range from rocks to ships' jettisoned cables and cans.

Others in the watch unbolted the two otter boards or "doors" chained against the boat, and lowered them. These large, slightly curved flat structures, basic to all trawling, plane in the water like kites to hold open the net. The sea had turned rough, so that the horizon twisted in all directions. The deck plummeted beneath us and then rose, scooping in cold seawater through the scuppers to hit against our legs. A fisherman soon learns to balance and absorb some of the motion with bent knees in order to keep working, but this motion in itself becomes work. With the brutelike steel doors freed from their cradles, where they had merely bumped back and forth ominously, they slammed against the side of the boat until they reached the water. Each of them weighed 1,100 pounds. Any hand (or any person) caught between would have been crushed.

The two winches on the afterdeck payed out parallel cables, or warps, attached to the doors. A man controlled each to keep their lengths exactly the same and prevent a snarl. At every twenty-five fathoms (150 feet), a distinguishable patch of paint or entwined wire marked the length. Øivind shouted out each mark above the wind and engine noise so the skipper could gauge the progress of the set. As a thumb rule, a boat lays three times as much cable as the depth of the tow. In the wheelhouse, Peter kept the boat moving forward despite the heavy sea, to maintain strain on the warps so that the doors would plane apart in the water.

The tows each lasted about two hours. They came back with disappointingly small loads. We gutted and iced the dozen or so cod of several sizes and the flounders and haddock. But there was also a zoo of other twitching and flapping sea creatures—flat triangular skates, sandpaper-skinned dogfish of the shark family that some of the men slammed against the gunnel to kill before returning to the sea, other fishes flat and round, lobsters, spiked sea urchins, scallops, spiny little crabs, squid, shrimp, ugly flaccid catfish, and slimy brown-green things that answered to no easy description of plant or animal. Most of it went back over the side, much of it dead or moribund from the pressure of the net, since it had no value on the auction board.

Kris shucked the few random scallops and shared them around to be eaten raw. We saved the occasional legal-sized lobsters to sell privately ashore for the beer money that New England crewmen call "shack." (Wives who pay the bills are not supposed to know about this.) The lobsters went into a drum of seawater, their claws secured by tight rubber bands so that they would not fight each other. Every now and then, someone would freshen the lobsters' seawater with the deck hose.

The variety was impressive enough, but not the quantity for men with bills to pay. "You makin' any money up there?" boomed a heavy voice over the wheelhouse radio.

"Nope," replied our skipper. "Nope, nope, nope."

We moved to other locations as Peter searched the grounds he knew. There were always a few fish. The slow pace did give an opportunity to settle in with the others. New England draggers usually work around the clock by staggering watches: six hours on and six off; twelve on, six off; or, in our case, eight on, four off. This meant never a full expanse of sleep, but our watches all changed in some fashion that insured noon and 8:00 P.M. meals together. A sixteen-hour workday gave lots of time with each other on deck. The men were taciturn, as Norwegians tend to be and hence also those of recent Norwegian descent, but just as it appeared that their conver-

The helmsman-fisherman of the famous harbor statue by Leonard Crask gazes toward the breakwater through which generations of Gloucester fisherman have passed on their way to sea. A wreath in the snow, containing the photograph of a boat lost recently with all hands, reaffirms the danger in fishermen's lives despite the protections technology provides.

Spray crashes over the side on Georges Bank.

The sun rises, deck lights go off for the day, and the 24-hour "clockaround" dragging and hauling of nets continues.

Crewmen on one of the night watches start cleaning a load of cod aboard the *General Patton*.

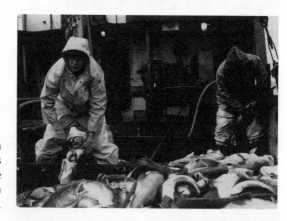

Øivind Ullang takes a stance with knees bent for balance while gilling a high binful of cod.

The watch lines up with needle and twine to get a net torn by rocks back over the side quickly. Mending with gloves is virtually impossible despite the November chill on Georges Bank.

sations covered nothing but fish and gear someone would make a comment that roused a general chuckle.

Everyone but the skipper worked routinely on deck, but some had ancillary duties for which they received an extra percentage above the standard five percent crew share. The mate, Kaare (pronounced Cora) Hemnes, held the bridge for the initial four hours of his watch while Peter slept or ate. On deck, with a cigarette between his lips, his hands flew while mending nets or performing any other seamanlike job. His pace changed when he ventured a joke in English. He told it as carefully as if his words were picking their way through briars. Kristoffer Birkeland, Kris the scallop shucker, was a heavy, slow-walking man of about fifty, with a scowl that had nothing to do with his dogged, easy nature. As engineer, he kept the oil changed and the engine in working order.

Øivind Ulland, as gear man, saw to the maintenance of the deck machinery. Øivind had a Norwegian type of clarity to his eyes, which were both tired and merry. Divorced, in his late thirties, he was the second youngest aboard, at ease with all the fishing skills because this was his career. Then there was Ingolf Josang, quiet even by Norwegian standards, so lean that his face had lines imposed over lines. In a rare moment of communication, he volunteered that he had once fished king crab off Adak in the stormy Aleutians of Alaska. Captain Peter's son Pete was the junior crew member. In his early twenties, Pete had not yet finished college and he was unsure of his eventual direction. He knew firmly, however, that it did not include a career gutting cod on a pitching deck. Guided by this reservation, he worked as hard as the rest, but without the same sense of purpose.

The cook, Erling Sjoen, was the oldest man aboard, calm and paunchy. But never judge a fisherman by age or by the size of his belt alone. Erling could stand on deck, his back locked in a half-crouch, and gaff cod and flounder so rapidly, pronging accurately in the head each time so as not to tear the meat, that the fish flew in a blur. He worked the four-to-twelve watch on deck, which allowed him to hurry in and prepare meals between sets. He also stayed in the galley to clean up after the noon meal, so perhaps he was the hardest working member of the crew. (The cook often is, aboard a fishing boat.) Erling prepared solid old-country meals and delivered them in heaping quantities: salt cod and boiled potatoes with pork rind gravy, cod fried heavily in butter but flaky inside, and corned beef and cabbage.

I am not immune to seasickness, although I learned long ago to fight it by staying on deck in the fresh air and working as hard as possible rather than taking to bed. Erling watched with mother-hen concern as I picked over his sturdy meals with a bird's appetite. He concocted a thick pudding for me, so thick that my eyes rolled inward when I saw it. I gulped it down to show how much I appreciated his trouble and then, it being dark, managed to stroll to deck and lose it over the side without hurting anyone's feelings. Erling insisted that I look through his refrigerator at any time to take whatever I fancied. And there on the second night lay a plate of cold peeled and boiled potatoes. It is amazing how comforting and flavorful they were, and how they brought me around. By the end of the trip, I was wolfing down fish balls and fried cod like a deck man from Karmøy or Hammerfest itself.

During that second night at about 1:00 A.M., we had shot the net, hosed the deck after dressing and icing the modest haul, and headed for the galley, when the signal came from the wheelhouse to haul in. The thirty-fathom tow had lasted only ten minutes, but a thrumming strain on the warps indicated the kind of load we had been waiting for, assuming it wasn't a pile of rocks. The thick cables—one on each side—wound in slowly, mark by mark.

The doors came back aboard, heavy sinister flats of welded steel that banged against the side with each roll of the boat until we secured them. A door swinging out of control in bad weather can wreck and kill, but the men handled the job so neatly there hardly seemed to be danger involved. They shifted a series of shackles and steel straps, all of it slippery heavy stuff, and then began rolling in the net on the drum.

The bag surfaced a few feet aft. The higher it rose, the fuller it appeared. At least it was not merely filled with rocks if it floated! Deck lights caught the promising gleam of fish bodies so thick they protruded through the mesh. Suddenly, the seabirds converged, their screeches and white shapes a frantic presence. Day or night on any northern fishing grounds, there might be only a single one of them in the sky, but suddenly they will gather by the dozens and then the hundreds.

The bunched mouth of the bag started up the stern ramp, gradually becoming fatter, like a python that has swallowed mice and then rabbits. By attaching a series of straps, we boomed part of the bag

[10]

high and dripping, then made more adjustments because of its size to bring it aboard safely. At one point in the operation, Øivind needed to crawl onto the bag, balancing over the water that foamed threateningly against the ramp, to correct a snag that developed. Kris held him by the seat of his pants. We were working so close to the gulls that their wings swished a breeze around our heads and their beaks occasionally delivered a peck. To a man positioned under the furiously dripping bag with oilskin hood snapped tight, the pounding wetness beneath the strings of chafing gear felt like the inside of a car wash.

It was a real bag of fish! Ingolf tugged loose the pursed rope that held the mouth of the bag shut, and they poured out around our legs with enough pressure to make us stagger. There was a mountain of sea life. Some of the cod weighed forty pounds, their dull green backs and gray-white undersides gleaming like porcelain vases under the deck lights. Big two-pound and three-pound flounders flapped against each other layer upon layer. Only a few skates and dogfish marred the purity of the haul. We shot the net again at once, then waded into the pile and started honing knives. The splendid cod went into the largest bin set off by boards (fishermen call these bins checkers), blackback and yellowtail flounders into a smaller one, the rest of it "trash" over the side.

Peter came from the wheelhouse to enjoy the sight. "Ha, see that, 2,000 pounds at least!" he shouted. (Actually, this haul of cod turned out to be closer to 2,500 pounds.) The wind whiffled the bushy gray sideburns that protruded from his watch cap. Lines in his face that had deepened during the search for fish no longer showed.

The flounders were the easiest to dress, because all their vital parts are concentrated in a "poke" on one side that can be cleaned with a single flick of the knife. We separated yellowtails from blackbacks since the sweeter-tasting yellows, identified by an ochre edge around the white of their tails, brought a better price. Nature camouflages flounders, flat bottom-dwelling fish, with a light side and a dark side. Their white underbelly blends them into the general surface light when viewed from below by predators, while their dark, green-brown backs enable them to lie unseen on the seafloor waiting for prey. (This does them little good when caught in the trawls of man, their biggest predator.) Fishermen pay attention to the contrasting sides because storing flounders dark side up discolors their snowy meat.

[11]

We took care to throw them into wire baskets with the dark side on top so that the basket need only be overturned when they were iced below.

Cod look as different from flat, poke-intestined flounders as they possibly can while still being fish. They are round as tubes, and so packed with organs that there is no way to avoid a mess when cleaning them. Two of the four-man watch opened the gills, then cut from inside straight down the belly, which released a red and ochre tumble of inner parts. The gill-cuts hit cartilage so that blades needed frequent honing. We all stood in a slurry of blood and intestines that shifted with each roll of the boat.

We sorted the cod into three general groups with some necessary overlap, the big ones in one area, the fifteen- to twenty-pound "market size" in another, and the three- to four-pound "scrod" in a third. The other two men on watch cleaned the carcasses, running hands down the open bellies to eviscerate them. The water was as cold as it could get without turning to ice, and so were the fish intestines. Since we needed free fingers, we wore only tight cotton gloves to provide some grip on the slimy fish backs.

Out over the water, a small northeaster had settled in at twenty knots, enough to kick up a routine-sized sea that coughed in through the scuppers and bubbled persistently around our ankles. Some of the water on deck began to turn ice-white and slippery. It made little difference to men at last into the fish. Suddenly, Peter in the wheel-house gave the signal to haul in again. At this rate, we'd fill the hold and be home in another night! We'd have to forget watches and call all hands if this kept up. We began to grin and speculate as two of the watch stepped out of the checkers, hosed the gurry from their oil-skins, and started the winches while the others cut and gutted with concentration to keep ahead of the work.

Up the ramp came the next bag of fish. "Sonofabitch, fuckin' dogs!" someone declared, and the others whistled through their teeth.

The bloated bag of fish resembled a fantastic mine set to blow up the ocean. From every one of hundreds of meshes poked the gray, elongated nose of a dogfish. Junior members of the shark family, the hated dogfish even bear the unlovely slitted lower mouth. None of this would matter but for their sandpaper skin, and the fact that they lack commercial value. You can slip an ordinary slimy fish eight or nine inches thick through a five-inch mesh, but try pulling a four-anda-half-inch dogfish through the same opening. He sticks in the twine, while the flaring gills make it impossible to push him back the way he entered. You must cut him in half to clear the net.

With the bag suspended the better to work it from all sides, we sliced with a high reach that kept fish blood dribbling steadily down our sleeves. According to notebook scribbles that night: "Wrists ache from sawing through several inches of dogs and bone, over and over. Knuckles raw from net chafe. Cut a dogfish throat, you get first a gush of water, then blood. Severed snouts like big bullets. Blood and snouts all over deck. Hundreds. Then, when job looked finished, lowered bag into water, turned it, hundreds more goddamn snouts sticking through." The knife sometimes slipped and cut the net, while the unfortunate creatures' fins had a sharp edge that also severed twine. We took two hours to saw loose the dogfish, and then spent more than another hour mending.

Net mending is one of a fisherman's baseline skills, his most important one in trawl and seine fishing where a net hole can open an escape hatch for all the fish inside. The mending skill follows enough geometric logic to please a professor, because each mesh must be rewoven to become again a square with equal sides. Anyone can reconstruct the shape of one or two torn squares, but what of twenty-odd squares ripped asymmetrically?

Kris, Øivind, and Ingolf mended by second nature, Øivind with the knife in his teeth pirate fashion to keep it ready for paring ripped strands. The process involved tying a succession of knots with twine wound around a thick, flat needle, done by forming loops that the fingers held in place until the needle passed through. One knot connected each leg of mesh, starting and ending on a "three-legger," moving back and forth from "sider" knots to "half-mesh" or "pick-up" knots. Each type of knot tied differently to conform to the weave of the original net which had been designed to absorb stress in all directions. It required a remarkable mind's eye to envision the pattern and keep it straight.

Despite bad luck with dogfish, the hold filled steadily. Winter storms to come would make this weather a picnic, but nevertheless the sun had disappeared and the sea snapped with crested waves as cold rain and spray swirled together in the wind. The deck was never still. Day after day, the gloomy sky reflected its gray on rails, spars, rusty winch casings, anything that held a film of water. The watches came and went, eight hours on deck followed by four off in which to eat and sleep, so that soon the world became a continuum of chilly fish intestines, straps and cables, dripping nets, mended rips.

A skipper in the wheelhouse has his rewards when the nets come in full, and often otherwise a tight stomach and a headache. On a boat the size of the *Patton* he pitched in when the need arose, but nevertheless he spent hours alone each day watching his crewmen expend their energies on deck. The radio was his line to all the other skippers, or at least those he considered part of his own fleet. (The Norwegian and Portuguese boats of New Bedford did not appear to intercommunicate.) Most wheelhouses had at least two radios, one of which stayed tuned to an emergency frequency. The other was the party line. The talk rolled on, from information to trivia, and everybody listened.

The accents on Georges Bank had a heavy New England overlay that incorporated some of the European roots of its participants. "Monday and Tuesday," said one unseen skipper in the seventeenth minute of his conversation, "I think there's goin' to be a lot of boats in, so, I don' know, I think I'm gonna prob'ly go home and come back out Sad'y. Sad'y night prob'ly. So, why don' you give a call then, gimme a call tomorra night then, gimme a call any time tomorra night."

Or another: "We fished yesterday. I guess we been fishing about thirty hours now. I don't know what the hell to do. I can't find any fish around heah."

"We hung up there again this tow and I didn't do any damage, so I set her right back out to finish the tow, you know, so we gonna take back in about five minutes."

"Gettin' late, gettin' late, y'ain't goin to get no more good weather less you go way south."

Peter gossiped his part, commenting once, cheerfully: "A rotten life out here." His usual closing was "Ja, finest kind, out."

In the middle of the best steady fishing, one day there came over the wheelhouse radio from the skipper of a boat fishing in sight of us: "I'm losin' my shirt every haul." We had just watched him through binoculars bring aboard at least 1,500 pounds of fish, and from the gutting activity on deck a good share of it was cod. "Shoulda quit the other day," he continued in a glum voice. "Just give me two decent sets, I'd be happy. All day got forty-five fish; that's all we got."

Some of us shook our heads and laughed. That old game of hard-luck talk has probably been around as long as fishing itself, something that Norsemen and Chinese and South Sea Islanders and Galileans were practicing two thousand years ago. Tell the world and bring a fleet of other boats to pick the site clean? Ha.

"That is no good," said Kaare gravely. "I have always told the truth."

Peter chuckled. "Sure, me too."

We carried tons of crushed ice, stored below in bins separated by movable boards. The duty of one man on watch, cook exempted, sent him down through a narrow hatch after dressing each set, to arrange the fish between layers of ice. The icer shoveled bin by bin, making room for fish in the spaces he cleared.

It was not bad duty, especially in nasty weather. With water bubbling across deck, the men up top bolt shut the hatch as soon as the fish go down, and there you are protected from the wind and cutting spray, warmed quickly by the heat of your exertions. A sealed, pitching hold, of course, is no place for any poor fellow prone to seasickness or claustrophobia. A bare, gurry-flecked bulb (in the old days a swaying lantern) furnishes the only light. Ice combined with fish in good condition generates a sharp, somewhat metallic, very fishy smell. This odor is the good smell of money to most. The ice and fish in the bottom layers, however, might smell less sweet at the end of a trip of several days.

It is impressive how a wash in clean water can freshen a week-old fish that has received proper icing originally. Nevertheless, just in the last few years, the most progressive American and Canadian fishermen have followed the lead of the quality-conscious Norwegians and Japanese by icing their fish in plastic tubs that prevent cumulative pressure and gurry at the bottom of the pile.

The boat's expenses included ice. The *Patton* carried about twenty-five tons of it each trip. Fuel, however, was the biggest expense, since the engines consumed seven hundred gallons an hour steaming and five hundred gallons an hour towing. ("And it's close to fifty cents a gallon," said Peter in 1978, shaking his head at the unconscionable price.) Then you had to buy grub for a week, several hundred dollars' worth. This all came "off the top" before calculating shares.

The boat drew a forty-two percent share, the skipper ten percent, and each crewman five percent before adding extra for special duties. Before the year ended, the boat would have made about thirty trips,

with layovers in between for rest and for engine and gear maintenance.

We filled the hold steadily. By the fourth day, we had taken our
entire fourteen-thousand-pound weekly quota of cod, so Peter
moved to deeper, rockier grounds where flounder schooled in the
greatest concentration. This meant routine snags and more time
spent mending torn nets despite larger fish. One night I kept the
helm for hours—I was the novice with needle and twine compared to
the others—as the skipper joined the rest of the watch patching vast
tears from a disastrous tow over sharp rocks. Lights of other boats
bobbed around us, glinting on the crests of the choppy water. We
were not the only ones forced to seek grounds away from the cod. At
daybreak, their hulls and rigging took gray shape around the lights. It
brought home the fact that, while isolated in our own tight world, we
remained part of a community.

The change of grounds brought another consequence. While without question we had left behind the abundant cod grounds, one or
two-hundred pounds of the big fish still tumbled from each netful.
They might have been dead or dying, but the law required us to throw
them back. And when we moved to less rocky bottom to avoid ripped
nets, the hauls of flounder fell off and the number of cod increased. It
was an upsetting, shameful, infuriating waste of resource and income, and we railed against the politicians who had drafted the two-
hundred-mile law so that it delivered the management of American
fish into the hands of Commerce Department bureaucrats.

"They should let us catch fish. That quota's a lot of baloney,"
declared Peter with great restraint. None of the men were comfortable with excessive profanity, even in the face of outrage.

Gradually, the weather turned rougher and colder, as if nature had
decided to take it out on us by degrees. The wind began to cut
through my oilskins despite an extra suit of thermals. It was impossible to keep hands and feet warm. Waves rose sullenly above the
gunnel where we worked, and the wind spat bits of cold spray from
their crests into our faces, leaving a perpetual taste and sting of salt.
Sometimes the deck would fail to rise with a wave, and water would
sweep across the deck as Peter or the mate in the wheelhouse
shouted a warning. The water had a frightening force that under-
mined the legs and urged you toward the open sea.

We worked watching that water, our enemy now, to grab hold somewhere against the force of a maverick wave. It became exhausting just to maintain balance on the pitching deck. In routine procedure with the rest, I had fastened thick rubber bands around the legs of my oilskins to tighten them against my boots, but when water came bubbling knee-high the water pushed open the seal. Soon my socks were sopping and cold. There was no way to stay dry. Below-decks duty shoveling ice became attractive enough to do it in turns.

Over the radio came the sobering message that a man had been washed overboard, about thirty miles away. "Never pick him up in this kind of sea," said Peter sorrowfully, "except maybe with luck."

The others all knew the man. They said little. Øivind shrugged. "If it comes, it comes."

We did not wear life jackets, which would have posed an even surer danger if they caught in the running gear. The swelling water was dark even in daylight under a gray sky, and on the late watches as black as the surrounding night. We had enough fish that we might have headed for home, but this would have been too dangerous in high seas, pitching over shallows where the hull might crash on an exposed shoal. We waited it out.

By the afternoon of the seventh day, the weather had changed, and our hold was full enough with dripping layers of ice and fish to take home the catch in time for next morning's auction. After the final tow, the net went back into the water for a washing. Then we wound it clean and dripping onto the drum, and tied it secure. With hatches battened, Peter backed the boat into waves that crashed up the stern ramp and swept over the deck. It saved hours of hosing and scrubbing to dislodge all the fins and bits of intestine that a fishing boat necessarily accumulates.

Erling produced a large fried meal and then scrubbed his galley and closed it. Anyone who drew coffee after this, or picked through the refrigerator, was expected to clean up. Kris and Kaare opened a cribbage board on the mess deck table, and soon became absorbed in the game. Peter as skipper had the duty of bringing the boat home through the lights and buoys. The others washed up, and then slept.

The homecoming past famous landmarks might have beguiled a newcomer to the coast, who, now that the last cod of the present trip had been readied for sale, could ruminate on the millions of cod salted and fresh that had filled New England holds for more than two centuries. To men who repeated the trip every ten days or so year after year, it was a simple commute from the place they worked.

With bad seas calmed and your boat heading home, the hold reasonably full, it is easy to forget the cold, wet, danger, and fatigue for a while. Best to think about it when the time comes again, not before. Fishing is, after all, a job.

2

To Fish for a Living

Several thousand years ago, Homo sapiens evidently progressed from grabbing at fish with his hands to spearing them with a stick. In time, he improved the job by using sharpened stones lashed to the end of a pole. Later (and the order of this is all conjecture), he carved bone hooks, and then twisted fibers into a line from which to dangle them. Then, much later, he bent metal into hooks, meanwhile weaving fibers that could be knotted into meshes that became nets and traps. Though millennia have passed, and man has perfected machines that propel him across water and land, into the air, and through space, it is still with those basic nets, hooks, spears, and traps that he harvests fish.

Fishing—the hunt and capture of sea creatures—remains a basic occupation for coastal peoples around the world. With man's other sources of animal food neatly domesticated, fishermen have become the last of the hunters.

The occupation has the finest pedigree imaginable. According to the *Encyclopaedia Britannica* (1954 edition): "Fishing is probably the earliest form of hunting, and, as men were surely hunters before they were cultivators, is actually the oldest industry in the world." The Britannica article continues with even grander speculations: "It is not generally recognized how great a part fisheries have played in the destinies of nations. . . . When the first man ventured to sea in a dugout, it is probable that his purpose was the better to pursue fish,

[19]

and not only the modern deep sea trawlers, liners, and drifters, but the merchant and fighting navies are lineal descendants of the prehistoric fisherman in his dugout. Thus fishing may be presumed to have prepared the way for sea trade, without which modern civilization is inconceivable."

Ancient fishermen probably had no more notion of the mighty part they played in civilizing the earth than those today who go out on the water to make a living from its resources. If they see themselves in any role it is as a food provider—like a farmer, although one with a more adventurous spirit, since after all a farmer's turf does not roll and pitch underfoot. These two historic occupations both depend on the patterns of nature with all her extremes. Here the basic similarity ends. A farmer can watch the progress of his wheat and livestock, but the fisherman's harvest remains invisible and unassessable until its capture.

No single account of men and women who fish for a living can tell their entire story. They fish by themselves and collectively, in oceans and estuaries warm and cold during all seasons, in every manageable sea state from calm to roaring, wherever the waters support edible marine life. They cast from shore; they pull nets and lines by hand from open skiffs under oar, balancing themselves inches from the water on slippery thwarts; they labor aboard old gurry buckets that house little more than an engine, a single-burner stove, and tight bunks curved along the inside of the bow; and they work big nets and traps from boats spacious enough to have a separate galley and head, and sometimes even private cabins and a washing machine.

The social condition of fishermen is extremely varied. Some in the big-money fisheries of the moment wear gold watches, and can afford million-dollar mortgages on the latest in boats and equipment so that they can follow wherever the fish choose to go. (However, the larger the investment, the deeper the tumble if things go wrong.) Other fishing lives remain primitive, because just as some soil may be arid and stony, some waters lack the ingredients to support a large marine population. Since subsistence fishing does not provide the means for investment in the latest gear, the poor tend to stay close to shore and take only what comes their way.

The majority of the world's fishermen now go to sea in gas/diesel-driven craft for a day to a week or two, and most live in the communities where they tie their boats. Some, however, travel in ships that roam distant fishing grounds for months at a time. The nets of all these modern fishermen, some of them weighing tons, come aboard with the help of engine and hydraulic power, as do their longlines (some three miles long), dredges, and pots (some weighing eight hundred pounds empty). A part of the sophisticated gear cycle may still require locking hands into web or around steel for a heavy pull, but technology now spares men the worst of back-killing labor while also expanding their options for success and survival.

However, even in prosperous areas—or on the fringes of them—live fishermen whose gear would have been recognized by other fishermen ten centuries ago. There are still Labrador fishermen who row out in open dories and pull up heavy nets by hand like their great-grandfathers. Japanese villagers still bend huge oars to reach a collective fish trap and haul manually. This is sometimes merely practical, rather than a sign of poverty. Watermen on the Chesapeake Bay in Maryland, a few miles from the mills and commerce of Baltimore, dredge for oysters under sail by law in order to limit catches. They also harvest oysters throughout the cold winter with hand-scissored tongs whose heavy wooden shafts rise as high as thirty feet.

Much of a fisherman's fortune depends on geography. The luckiest ones work from coasts that drop only gradually into the deep sea, for it is the continental shelves of the world that determine the abundance of fish. Continental shelves are those portions of the landmass that extend out from some shores for miles at relatively shallow depths of less than one hundred fathoms before plunging thousands of fathoms down to abyssal plains. In such shallows, surface winds cause a circulatory motion that draws bottom water to the surface often enough to bring it in touch with light and oxygen. These are the necessary ingredients for the growth of plankton, the tiny vegetable and animal matter of the sea on which other creatures feed.

Abundant plankton at the beginning of the food chain nourish small fish, which in turn become the prey of larger ones (which eventually provide food for man, the greatest predator). Some shelves can be extravagantly fruitful, such as those around the east coast of North America that reach the height of their richness in the legendary Georges Bank off New England and the Grand Banks off Newfoundland. In contrast, the deep ocean is a dead place, over the surface of which tuna may migrate, but where very few creatures live.

Shallows in cold water provide the optimum conditions for generating the food that fish eat. Therefore, most of the world's edible fish—at least those that school in the vast numbers needed for a commercial harvest—come from northern waters. The cold allows plankton an orderly growth cycle, compared to the choking overstimulation that in tropical waters so accelerates the cycle that the planktons die as quickly as they generate.

The species of fish (by which I mean all marine creatures) that pass through a fisherman's hands have a wonderful variety. They range from slick deadeyed cod and haddock and flat flapping flounders that must be gutted at once, to thousandfold herring and menhaden and capelin that travel these days by suction hose to and from the hold without ever being touched, to heaps of mud-blackened scallops and oysters dredged aboard to be culled apart from seafloor rocks, to huge tunas and halibuts and swordfish that must be fought aboard and then subdued before being hefted into storage like so many concrete blocks, to small snapping crabs transferred gingerly from pot to lidded basket, to sluggish purple king crabs the size and weight of old-fashioned alarm clocks, to little pandalid shrimps that need to be hosed and shoveled like gravel, to big brownie shrimp sorted one by one from piles of "trash," to brilliant reef fish and stolid conches gathered one by one, to claw-meat lobsters and skittery tail-meat crawfish, to glorious silvery salmon that pound against the legs, to tutti-frutti fish and sea-glops of all sizes.

There is hardly a coast of the world without some fishermen. Collectively, this last community of hunters caught more than 93 million metric tons (MT) of fish in 1987. (This and the following statistics were compiled by the U.S. National Marine Fisheries Service in the 1989 edition of the annual publication "Fisheries of the United States." Such statistics always lag years behind current time.) Asians are the world's heaviest catchers of fish, accounting for more than 41 million MT annually, of which the Japanese landed 11.8 million and the mainland Chinese 9.3 million MT.

The Asian harvest compares to 12.6 million MT caught by Europeans, 11.2 million caught by the Soviets alone, 12.2 million by South Americans, 9.2 million by North and Central Americans (5.7 million MT of it by U.S. fishermen), 8.2 million by Oceanans, and 5.2 million caught by Africans. In descending order of volume landed, these are the big fishing nations of the world, those that deliver at least one

[22]

million MT each year: Japan, the USSR, China, the United States, Chile, Peru, India, South Korea, Indonesia, Thailand, the Philippines, Norway, North Korea, Denmark, Iceland, Canada, Mexico, and Spain. Delivering nearly this much volume are the United Kingdom and South Africa. Of these nations, Japan, the USSR, Taiwan, and South Korea in particular catch much of their fish off coasts other than their own with fleets of high seas fishing ships.

Fishing lives have as many shades as there are varieties of fish. Some are bitterly poor, some merely humble, some isolated and lonely, others hard but apparently satisfying. A book attempting to portray the entire gamut would quickly become an encyclopedia. My less grand intent is to report on those representative fisheries along the great continental shelves of northern Atlantic waters which it has been my good fortune to observe. Most of these personal experiences concern the middle categories of fishermen, those who can rely more on machinery than on their own knotted arms for propulsion and hauling. But first, to round the picture, I would like to dip nets briefly into others of the world's fishing waters.

Along the sandy beaches of the state of Madras, on the southeastern coast of India facing the Bay of Bengal, fishermen and their families live in thatched huts so fragile that a monsoon flood can sweep them away. The men wear little else but white dhotis with a loincloth underneath, and when they go into the water they wrap the dhoti around their heads like a turban to save it from wear.

One hot day in October, a dozen men were setting a beach net through the warm, low breakers. Some paddled out, perched cross-legged in catamarans that were no more than logs planed and lashed together, to lay the net in a wide circle. When they brought the ends to shore, everyone formed a line into the water and heaved the net back in unison. A few sentences describe the work of two hours. The 110-degree sun glistened on their sweating backs. Slowly, the net came in. Made of water-absorbing local fiber rather than the latest in nylon, with stone sinkers attached to hold it open, the net had a certain weight no matter what its load.

When the bag finally emerged through the surf, the men hurriedly pulled it onto the sand to make sure nothing escaped. Women and children ran from the huts with baskets for the harvest. Everyone crowded around. Ten fish flapped inside, none longer than a few inches. The stoic faces betrayed little, but the catch represented both

[23]

dinner and the entire livelihood of the village. The men made another laborious set. After two hours, they caught enough small fish to fill a single basket.

There were also days when the net intercepted an entire school of fish, and the women had an abundance to carry on their heads to sell at the open-air market. The sea never guarantees a yield, although sometimes it delivers one.

Other fishing lives are equally humble, although not so desperate. In the forty-hut village of Buen Hombre on the northern coast of the Dominican Republic, there lives Tuba Pérez. Tuba is a lean, straight-walking man in his midthirties with a sensitive face that breaks easily into a smile. Following local custom, he always shakes hands politely whenever he meets a friend, even if it is for the fifth time that day.

Each morning, Tuba gathered with the other fishermen on the beach. Some of them loaded traps built with twigs and chicken wire into their skiffs, and others like Tuba and his brother-in-law Narciso tossed in their packets of mask, snorkel, spear, and flippers. The reefs they fished lay only a mile away, visible where the water changed color from turquoise to deep sea blue beyond the reef wall, but it was a long trip in the old leaky wooden boats. Water sloshed around our bare feet, and the small outboard motors—some boats had only oars—putt-putted at low horsepower with no urgency.

Buen Hombre people usually joked often and loudly, but on this morning the men spoke little. The day before, they had buried one of their number, a young man who had made a routine dive and then floated to the surface dead. In a village without running water or electricity, located thirty miles over a rutted dirt road from a town with a telephone, no one held an autopsy or inquest. Those who die on the reefs—perhaps from a burst lung, who knows—receive prayers and a burial like any other, and life moves on.

By the time the boats reached the reef, they had scattered along the horizon, since there was no sense competing for the handful of fish in each area. The boat I rode with Tuba rose on smooth surging crests that rolled in from the open sea just beyond the reef line. We peered among black-green coral heads beneath the clear water for a spot of sand that would hold the anchor, then threw it, jumped in, and began to scan the reefs. One of Tuba's flippers had torn at the strap, but he modified his kick to keep from losing it. The water was startlingly chilly for the tropics. Because of the cold, or perhaps with the thought of the dead fisherman, the world of fantastic multi-colored structures and swaying plants—a sight of endless beauty during a pleasure dive—seemed for once sinister.

The clear water abounded with fish, but most were only schools of little yellow clownfish or rudder-thin black tangs, too small to be anything but a nibble for a fish really worth catching. When Tuba saw one of any size, he free-dove straight down as deep as thirty feet, his body arched. Approaching the fish, he trailed to wait for a broadside target and then fired his rubber-powered spear gun. If the creature did not flit into a fissure, Tuba usually succeeded in spearing it, but the day's diving yielded only ten fish and one conch. By midday, Tuba himself admitted he felt the chill.

Tuba's wife met us on the shore. We walked home, barefoot for nearly two miles over a stony dirt road, past houses of thatch and sticks where people appeared in doorways to exchange banter and eye the stranger. The Pérez house had a metal roof, but like the others it consisted of two rooms with pounded earth floors. The family all slept in one room and cooked in the other.

We sat out front as Mrs. Pérez served heavily sugared black coffee in tin cups, laughing at the antics of a puppy while several Pérez children and their friends watched with friendly curiosity. Other men came to call and have a look at the visitor for themselves. They all had an easy, dignified, bantering grace about them. Dinner was the usual rice and beans. As it grew dark, the mosquitos moved in. Returning to the hut of a Peace Corps volunteer with whom I was staying (sleeping bag on the packed earth), the lights of kerosene lamps glimmered through the twigs and wattle of huts along the way.

Though the sea did not yield much, no one seemed to require more. Nevertheless, when a team from the Smithsonian Institution's Marine Systems Laboratory in Washington, D.C. came down to sponsor a self-help plan for the mariculture of giant herbivorous reef crabs, Tuba and Narciso were among the first in line. They began under supervision to build live-boxes that contained frames, beehive style, on which algae could grow to feed the baby crabs born in captivity. The project would take years to become self-sustaining, but everyone around Tuba's hut agreed that it was a good thing in life to look to the future.

At the other end of the fishing scale are factory ships and big trawler-processors. During the mid-1970s, while riding fishery patrols as a guest aboard U.S. Coast Guard cutters (I had once been a Coast Guard officer), I visited several of these fishing leviathans on the Atlantic and Pacific coasts of the United States at the time when none flew any but foreign flags. Nowadays, American ships and American crews catch and process fish at sea off United States coasts, while the foreign fleets do their far seas fishing off African and South American coasts where they can still negotiate quotas.

Factory ships, now as well as then, manufacture large quantities of finished fish product in the forms of fish paste (the Japanese surimi), canned fish, meal, or frozen blocks. As one nears any factory ship whose operation requires cooking, the acrid stench of steam-rendered fish is overpowering. But aboard, perhaps because the nose becomes stunned, but more likely because the cooking odors are blown seaward from stacks high above the deck, the smells are merely workaday fishy.

The Japanese factory mothership *Soyo Maru*, 566 feet long, carried a crew of 437 men. It produced surimi and fish meal from the fish delivered it by twelve catcher boats. We reached the ship in a small "kawasaki" workboat sent to fetch us from the Coast Guard cutter. The hull of the *Soyo Maru* rose from the water like a black cliff. On most fishing ships at sea, the crew puts over a Jacob's ladder, since everyone coming to visit is presumed to be agile and healthy, but our hosts on the *Soyo Maru* lowered a rope-and-canvas basket by crane instead.

The basket hovered several feet above the deck to reveal a stunning panorama of superfishing. Below stretched two field-sized bins loaded as thick as grass with pollock. Each bin extended more than a hundred feet along the length of the ship and filled out the sixty-eight-foot beam width except for a walkway. Men in glistening black rubber wet gear waded through the fish with wooden pushers, distributing the load and easing portions of it onto a continuous feeder belt.

A man in a red hard hat greeted us, distributed white cotton gloves, and led us into the ship as the men in the bins watched with polite curiosity. We clumped over wooden trestles with water gushing beneath, following the same course as a conveyor belt that moved invisibly under heaps of fish. In the factory proper, the belts carried the fish past twenty individual machines each tended by one man. The machines had a series of blades that decapitated, bobtailed, and eviscerated the fish. The attendants fed their machines by taking fish from the conveyor belt and lining them side by side with the fins all positioned neatly in the same direction. Each man handled approximately two fish per second. Their faces had that universal vacant expression of any assembly-line worker under the pressure of a quota. With the same rapidity, the machine disgorged limp fillets and transported them, in unending lines, to another area where rollers squeezed the skin from the meat. The men who supervised the roller machines were less tied to a single motion. Some watched us curiously, even grinned and discussed us among themselves.

The ship had left Japan in early April and would not return until November after more than eight months of continuous fishing in the Bering Sea off Alaska. Shipboard work continued twenty-four hours a day, with men divided into two shifts each working eight hours at a stretch. This meant a constant change of sleeping and waking times. Back home between seasons, the company continued to employ each worker at half pay, but he was free to work another job while receiving it.

After a long tour, the guide led us to the wardroom, where at the door we turned in our white gloves and traded boots for sandals. The captain and his officers waited to greet us in friendly, halting English. They all wore brown coveralls bearing the Japanese insignia of Taiyo Fisheries, one of the huge fishing conglomerates of the world. After refreshments, we passed photos of wives and children back and forth, watched Japaese kick-boxing on the VCR, and joked about the contours of Hollywood movie queens.

When I asked to see how everybody lived, the chief engineer showed me his cabin, a compact private room with a bunk and a desk. On a table stood a small electric stove with a pot of stew cooking. I then followed him through boot-lined passageways that smelled of food, to the crew quarters. The men slept sixteen to a room in adjoining compartments of four, separated by a central sitting area. Some were sleeping with curtains drawn across tiered bunks, while others played cards. A pot of food simmered on a hot plate. To my knowledge, mess halls existed, but the size of the ship apparently made individual cooking practical. The sanitary facilities included porcelain toilets set at floor level, and big adjacent tubs of cold seawater and hot fresh water for the hot soaks that are deeply a part of Japanese life.

Crews have a collective personality that differs from ship to ship whatever the flag. The *Soyo Maru* crew seemed more like factory workers than seamen. (In truth, these were not the men who caught the fish, although statisticians count them as fishermen.) My visits on other big ships have included one aboard a Japanese trawler where the fishermen joked raucously as they pulled nets, and another where the deck foreman screamed like a feudal lord and everyone was grim faced and sullen. Aboard a South Korean longliner, ingrained with rust and gurry, the utmost relaxed friendliness prevailed. On one Soviet BMRT (large stern trawler) everyone acted suspicious in the stereotypical manner of Russians toward strangers, while aboard another BMRT the fur-capped crew with its pet dog lined the rails to grin and shout friendly jokes as they snapped our pictures.

There has not yet developed a profession of far seas fishermen among Americans as among Japanese and Russians. The new U.S. factory ships tend to be staffed by young people who consider the dreary work temporary as they pass through to accumulate money.

One American vessel I visited during the early years of American entry into the factory ship business in the late 1970s had a crew of kids and misfits. They relied on drugs and rock music amplified to ear-shattering volume to see them through the wet, smelly, monotonous factory work. On another that I visited recently, with company rules now firm, everyone pursued his (or her) work in businesslike, subdued order, both handling nets on the icy deck and in the factory below. They comforted themselves with thoughts of the better times awaiting them ashore when they would have saved up enough money from the ship work to leave. However, the big American trawler companies now report a growing cadre of processor professionals among Americans.

The fishing village of Jimboran in Bali, Indonesia, is a collection of huts on the sand rather like those of the huts in Madras, although it has none of the latter's desperation. The fishermen beach their log canoes adjacent to the huts, and during the day mend nets under the shade of palm trees in a place apart from the women and children but within earshot. They all share the same buzzing flies, and communicate back and forth in good spirits.

At 10:00 P.M., by lantern light, I joined the crew of the head man, Embli Astara. Embli was a dignified, quiet man of about thirty-five who moved with authority on the beach. His nine crewmen dragged a canoe to the water and paddled a few at a time to Embli's boat. The thirty-five-foot boat, built of mellowed wood, had a gaily painted hull that erupted in curlicues around a high prow. The deck was entirely open. The mast, which still resembled a tree trunk, had a cross stick nailed near the top around which the lookout could wrap his legs. A big sputtering engine provided power, while delivering more noise and fumes than speed. A smaller, three-man purse boat joined us on the dark water.

We cruised with the noisy engine until the lookout spotted a school of fish by the phosphorus it stirred. Embli shut off the engine, and in silence, so not to spook the fish, we passed part of the net to the purse boat which encircled them. Then the shouts started between the boats as the crew gripped hands into the net to haul it in, their bare toes curled to grip the slippery deck. The hauls were not made up of the big fish found in northern waters, but the purse boat crew managed to take aboard a few brailsful from each set. We seined all night. Eventually, the air grew chilly under the brilliant profusion of stars overhead. The men wore sarongs that they wound around their heads like turbans while hauling, and then used as wraps during a doze on the open deck between sets.

The best haul came in around daybreak—a multiplicity of flapping sardine-sized fish. An hour later, with the sun already hot, Embli brought his boat to a beach within sight of the village, where some twenty boats our own size were assembling along with about fifty smaller ones. This was a daily convergence from several villages along the beach. There had been mild good humor during the night, but now everybody was in high spirits. The stranger in their midst furnished a special laugh when, fingering a breakfast of cold rice and curried things from a banana leaf like the rest, I bit into a raw chili and fanned my mouth elaborately.

The early light throbbed on the bright-painted hulls. We anchored gunnel to gunnel with other boats, positioned just outside the break point of the mild surf. The catch went off in baskets suspended on poles. It made for joking when a swell covered a man in the water and nearly swamped his load. Sociability flowed from the boats to the beach, where despite the early hour people had gathered in numbers.

On the sand, the basket men ran a small gauntlet of women and old men who picked out fish for themselves without challenge. The

remaining catch weighed in at 1,250 kilograms under Embli's watch-
ful eye. He now wore his bright-colored sarong wrapped around the
waist, and with bare muscular chest and straight posture he was no
mere net puller, shouting and sweating as during the night, but a
figure of dignity and command. The fish went from the scales to the
back of a truck, where a man with a shovel interspersed them with ice.
Their destination (I was dealing in sign language) appeared to be a
co-op fish plant.

Back at Jimboran village, the men napped on cots or mats in their
one-room huts until afternoon while outside the women and children
led their own noisy life among the flies and squawking chickens. Then
the men returned to their shaded spot around the nets.

In an enclosed harbor within the city of Xiamin on the southern
coast of China lay eighty large wooden fishing boats, waiting out an
October typhoon before returning to their fishing grounds in the
Formosa Strait. They had a sturdy, assertive look, with high, straight
prows painted auspicious red, and thick planking on their decks.

Fishermen in China must be half acrobats. A single long swaying
plank without rope or rail, laid from the quay to one of the bows,
served the entire fleet. Crewmen jaunted up the plank, even carried
heavy loads, as if they had a solid pavement surrounding them, and
then hopped from gunnel to gunnel to reach their boat.

Su Shau-er, a short man with shining metal teeth, who had lines
beginning to show on his face beneath spikes of youthful black hair,
conducted me over a dozen sets of boat rails to the seiner that he
skippered. Several crewmen watched with friendly interest. Most wore
wrist watches, a universal signal of Western-aspiring prosperity in
Third World countries.

The rails and siding were scuffed, but the main deck had a fresh
coat of dark red paint. She had been built less than a year ago in
the company's boatyard, Mr. Su said. The boat was rigged with a
heavy gray canvas jib and mainsail, now battened. Mr. Su confirmed
that much of the boat's propulsion came from the sails, but he
made it clear that his boat had a good engine aboard, one made in
China at that. Four skiffs lay on deck. When fishing, one carried the
seine and the others, with lights attached to stubby masts, were
used to attract the fish and then hold them mesmerized as the net
encircled them.

We walked forward on the main deck and climbed a straight ladder through a small trap door to the wheelhouse. The electronics were modest by current Western standards. They consisted of a very small radar (U.S. manufacture), a loran receiver, and a chart fathometer. There were thirty crewmen, a crowd these days on a ninety-foot fishing boat that stayed at sea for a week and more. It indicated that there was relatively little back-saving machinery to pull the nets.

There were other indications of a modest life-style. Throughout the boat, rain gear of a stiff oilcloth variety hung with other clothes on lines and hooks, along with hard hats and straw hats. (Summers along this coast are humid and blazing hot.) Overhead, each fitted into its grooves, hung an assortment of porcelain wash basins, some decorated, some chipped and plain. Each crewman had his own, and this appeared to be the extent of washing facilities. The galley was simply a space centered around a wood/charcoal stove, surrounded by big pots—no mess table or chairs. A woman, often the skipper's wife, rode aboard most boats in the fleet to do the cooking. Fresh seafood provided the staple, and the pots were used to boil the thin local noodles usually served with oil and garlic.

The single housing structure that included wheelhouse, galley, and engine space seemed to have no place for men to sleep. Gui Fang, the lean-faced bosun, showed me with a grin, sliding back a panel of what appeared to be one of many cupboard shelves built along the bulkheads. Inside was a cubicle with life jackets, two bedrolls separated by a center strip, toiletries suspended overhead in a plastic bag, and a few pieces of clothing. Gui Fang apologized shyly for the untidiness. They hadn't been expecting a visitor.

The Xiamin Number Two Ocean Fishing Company, which owned the eighty boats, had its office up the street from the harbor, and here I met with some of the officers. The company was a prosperous one, Mr. Goa, the director, declared. Besides having its own boatyard, it operated a plant that processed shrimp and other quality products for export to Hong Kong and Japan. Of course, the company, he said, owned all the high-rise apartment buildings I had passed on the street leading to the harbor—had I noticed all the television antennas on each roof?—and the company also maintained for its members a kindergarten, a free eight-doctor clinic, and a "Fishermen's

Theatre" that presented movies, staged shows, and special programs for the elderly.

It took awhile to realize that the "company" was in fact a former commune, renamed and democratized, and that here, a five-minute bus ride from the center of town, I was visiting a "fishing village." The commune had been founded in 1950, and the change took place in 1984.

The end of the commune system came in the wake of China's revolutionary (for a communist country) "responsibility" system, instituted in 1979. The enlightened central government under Deng Xiaoping, the man who ten years later ordered the supression of the student democracy movement, had with "responsibility" managed until the 1989 demonstrations to inject a touch of capitalism without opening the sluice gates. Workers were allowed to keep for themselves the fruits of their labor beyond a quota guaranteed the government. The effect on the economy was phenomenal. With the incentive of ownership, fishermen and farmers found themselves able to double or triple their production, which provided more food to the nation and also made them prosperous.

Direct food producers are the new rich of China, the ones who sport wrist watches. Salaried workers—the teachers, clerks, and civil servants, whose jobs the angry students knew would be their lot—are the new poor. From all reports, fishermen and farmers did not play much part in the May 1989 demonstrations against the government.

On another day during this visit to Xiamin in late 1988, I traveled with my interpreter, Wu Jiangming, to some small fishing boats near the harbor where men from a village a few miles down the coast were setting their nets. One of three men aboard an open boat, standing with big crusty bare feet gripping the rough wooden deck, shouted merrily at sight of the approaching visitors. Wu translated: "Hey, you and your friend think you want to be fishermen? Good, we'll put you to work."

Young Wu spoke idiomatic English that indicated years of study, but he had grown up in the countryside, where his parents, both teachers, had been sent to the fields for "rural reeducation" during the Cultural Revolution, and he bantered back with the dialect and humor of a country boy.

"Hey, you've got a soft job, taking rich foreigners around. You make much money?"

Wu must have answered honestly, because they all hooted. "Hell, we make four times that. You'd better come fishing with us." Even Wu laughed, but not as merrily as they.

There are few places in the world like Bristol Bay, Alaska, during the three-week July run of sockeye salmon. Norway's Lofotens resemble it during the great cold runs in late winter. Both are scenes of frantic fishing while the limited run lasts, by fishermen who count on making a major part of their year's stake and who therefore give no thought to sparing themselves.

The Bristol Bay terrain is level, mainly sand and tundra, broken by curling patterns of mud flat and water. Ashore during the time of the fish runs, the air is as thick with hefty mosquitos as the water is with salmon. At sea, the water runs brown, especially close to the beach where acres of mud shoreline bare at each low tide. The prevailing winds of June and July usually keep the rain blowing and the water choppy (the best fishing weather) with temperatures consistently in the fifties. At this latitude and time of year, night falls around 11:00, and it is light again by 3:30.

Alaska limits the fishery by law to 1,800 gill-net boats with a maximum length of thirty-two feet, and to half as many set-net sites. This means that in a few square miles of fiercely tidal water there might be 1,800 lines of bobbing white corks holding up gill nets each nine hundred feet long. Everyone hustles. The boats zoom everywhere, sometimes rushing in buddy-packs when someone passes word of a good strike.

But the fishing boats are gnats compared to the floating city of masts waiting to receive their fish and freeze them or carry them to one of the huge shore plants for canning. At the mouth of the Naknek River, the processor and tender ships appear like a wall of continuous hulls and masts by day, an unbroken mile of lights at night. Included in the conglomeration are dozens of big Bering Sea crabbers utilizing their circulating seawater tanks for tendering, plus all manner of scows and ships doing the same. Dominating the scene are freezer-processor ships, each carrying a crew of a dozen-odd young people who often work through the night, heading and gutting and freezing the salmon. Astern is tied a bobbing string of boats waiting to deliver, with one or two others alongside sending brailerloads of fish up to the deck bins. Close by on the open deck, the kids, in yellow oilskins, butcher the endless salmon straight from the bins, protected from the weather by plastic sheets. Down a chute go the slimed carcasses, to be flash-frozen and then stored in refrigerator holds.

Gill nets catch fish by entangling them, so that the daily work aboard the two-man and three-man Bristol Bay boats is a wrestle to disentangle each salmon from the tenacious nylon meshes. One day in Half Moon Bay on the west bank of the Kvichak River, we set on the right point of tide. The white floats bobbed out astern in the muddy water, and, after the few seconds it took for the leaded bottom line to unfold the net, the surface exploded with spray and thrashing tails. The nets were smoking! We whooped and slapped each other on the back, even though we knew that hours of picking drudgery lay ahead.

When it came time to haul in, we were soon panting with the effort of pulling a dozen five-pound fish at a time over the sluggishly powered roller. Periodically, we had to extricate our legs from the tangle to keep from being buried in fish. We deposited a mountain of the shining, flapping salmon in the stern bay, then moved forward over the midbay, then over the hatches, still pulling them in. With the final buoy aboard, we lay down in the fish to catch our breaths, then started picking.

When we had freed the first "shackle" of net, we set it again immediately, and into it poured more frenzied sockeyes. It was a nightmare of fish. Through the picking, we saw the last light of one day and the first of the next. And then, having delivered, we made another smoking set and it started all over again. A fever grips fishermen engulfed in such abundance. Our total sustenance was black coffee, occasional strips torn from a salted salmon, and one big fry of bacon, potatoes and eggs accompanied by a salmon boiled on the run. It was cold, blowing, and wet, our backs and hands hurt, and we were tired to the point of sickness, but it never occurred to us to stop fishing.

The day following, however, the nets were dead in the water, and the current badgered the corks into listless S's and circles. The great sockeye run had exploded through, and the survivors had gone their way. Other days followed with respectable catches, but that was the last exhilarating nightmare of the season.

Do men fish for any reason besides necessity? "It's a livin', boy, but ain't much of a life now, is it?" said a glum Newfoundland trawlerman on the Grand Banks, in the ninth day of working in cold water on a

Some fishing lives are poor and simple. Two village fishermen near Madras in southern India prepare a small dugout to take a net into the Bay of Bengal. Their larger community boat lies beached on the sand above the tide line.

Chow-down aboard a small Japanese trawler. The pan on the charcoal stove in the center of the galley holds curried squid.

"In the outports of New-foundland . . . old men fol-low the boats out through the breakwater with wistful eyes. Do retired accoun-tants yearn like that over ledgers?" John Kippenhuck, in his eighties, sits on the pier in sight of the boats and mends nets for his sons in Square Islands, Labrador, where he himself fished through all the years of his working life.

"Then there are the days, now and then, when nets or pots or lines come in exploding with life. The crew can hardly walk on deck for the abundance flapping around their legs." A Bristol Bay gillnetter brings a set aboard during the height of the sockeye salmon run.

wet deck. But fishermen take comfort in complaining, and you would need to have given him an alternative to know for sure whether he meant it. "Wouldn't have it no other way, don't have to answer to nobody but yourself," says another, voicing a sentiment heard in many places and languages, the deckhands among them forgetting for the moment the way an easygoing skipper can sometimes become a shouting tyrant on the grounds and the skippers forgetting knotted stomachs when they can find no fish. Working in cold and slime, of course, remains a powerful alternative to going hungry in places with few other options. Yet these are true fishing societies.

In the outports of Newfoundland and Norway, kids in pint-sized rubber boots and oilskins rush to the docks to lend a hand when the boats return. In the same communities, old men follow the boats out through the breakwater with wistful eyes. Do retired accountants yearn like that over ledgers? As for old fishermen, often a lifetime of pulling gear from cold water has caught up, and their twisted hands are so arthritic that they can barely hold a needle to mend the web ashore and remain part of the work. The kids never seem to notice this to project their own fate as they yearn for the time when they can haul a full share of the nets and lines.

I am convinced that many men—at least in those parts of the world that offer alternatives—fish because it is what they want most in the world to do. They say so, as do many born to it who are theoretically stuck with the fishing life unless they summon extraordinary effort against peer pressure. There is a pride in the self-sufficiency that comes from knowing how to fix a balky engine, mending nets on the run, and being able to repair any number of objects. To fish combines the spice of gambling with the excitement of the chase. Unique among ways to make a living, it depends on the pursuit of live creatures that remain invisible until they are caught, despite all the wonders of electronics. And then—call this atavistic, an urge from the animal subconscious—fishing requires the facing of primal forces as does no other occupation.

The work itself is repetitive, but the unexpected appears everywhere: in squalls, sunrises, empty nets and full ones, sudden towering seas or flat calms, breakdowns that challenge one's ingenuity, sparkling clear days when each breath is a pleasure. There are terrible icy days when, despite hours of working the gear with numb hands, nothing comes up but seaweed clotted around the lines and nets

[35]

ripped by rocks, nothing anywhere to pay for fuel and grub, much less the bills at home.

Then there are the times, now and then, when nets or pots or lines come in exploding with life. The crew can hardly walk on deck for the abundance of fish flapping around their legs; they must block the scuppers to keep it from escaping. They shout, dance, laugh, throw things (or grunt and humph to conceal any hint of pleasure, depending on their nature and nationality)—all the while knowing that now, instead of a stretch-out for a sore back between sets they will cull, shovel, gut, ice, bait, pick, and mend throughout the day and night and all the next day, near-dead with good fortune.

Fishing—at least beyond the subsistence level—may in truth be one of the few remaining occupations of great satisfaction. A sign aboard one boat declares: "The worst day of fishing is better than the best day of work." That's the spirit on the happiest of fish decks.

3

The Wooden Hulls
of Gloucester

Joe Testaverde steered his fifty-seven-foot wooden dragger, the *Peter & Linda*, into Gloucester Harbor near dusk. It was a cold day in the middle of February. Coming home the ice, already knocked from deck while the gear had been worked, began to form again in a new glaze over the windlass, nets, and rigging with every spray. The sun caught the clean edges and twin steeples of Our Lady Of Good Voyage Church on one of the low hills. Then, as we passed further in from the breakwater, the church disappeared behind masts, and the sun outlined the ornate tower of the city hall and some lesser towers rising among the old frame houses of Gloucester. Other draggers in the fleet of wooden day boats followed. Some were already unloading. The low tide exposed ten feet of slippery pilings that separated their decks from the tops of wharves. We headed for a wharf beside a two-story building and long enclosed shed, where some men stood high above us in the slush, working a crane that raised trays of shrimp and iced fish from a boat hold.

One boat the size and rig of the *Peter & Linda* had a deckful of snow blown against the forward hatch. We had shoveled our own deck fifteen hours earlier in the dark, before setting out to the grounds. The boards of the other boat's hull had a bleached, patched look, and the cabin needed paint. "She don't go out in bad weather, like we had today," said Joe. "She can't take weather anymore; look at her. That's a boat same age as mine, built early 1940s, same kind. If you don't put money back in these boats, they die."

Joe Testaverde, like most serious fishermen, appeared to spend more time caring for his boat than for himself. Both his beard and his clothes were heavily functional, the kind that needed no attention. His glasses would generally rate a wipe when a splash of seawater turned them opaque. His hands, bruised and pocked with scars, were puffy, like inflated gloves. A gray tractor cap imprinted with a red sketch of the *Peter & Linda* seldom left his head. When he removed it to wipe away the sweat, a high forehead was revealed, prematurely bald. A man in his late thirties with muscular shoulders and a torso starting to betray his taste for beer while ashore, he filled much of the space remaining in his crowded pilothouse where a stanchion rose exactly in the center of the deck. During the day he fitted a skipper's chair on top the stanchion, one that in the ripeness of its years sagged halfway to starboard. He lounged in this wobbly seat between hauls, talking to other skippers on the radio bands, calling New York and Boston for fish prices on a cellular phone, discussing the ways of fish and the Celtics team with his crewmen Frank Catania and Bobby Gross. He liked to talk and he had a lot to say.

The *Peter & Linda* was as functional as its owner. A grainy roofing material on top the deck boards provided traction. The wood of the rails and checkers was marked with the abrasions of constant hard use. But coats of protective paint covered the hull and housings, the cables on the drums had none of the frayed wires that would have betrayed employment beyond their time, and the windlass, sheltered under sewn canvas when not at work, glistened to the depths of its moving parts with the black of frequent greasings. Once a year, Joey put the boat up to wash, paint, and caulk it.

Nor was the *Peter & Linda* an object forgotten at the end of the day. Its mast, painted red, still had a big Christmas wreath secured halfway up, so that the boat faced gaily into the ocean. Red paint from the same brush decorated the white wheelhouse. During the holiday season, Joey and his men strung colored lights over all the rigging, as did other crews of the fleet.

We moored astern the *Linda B*, a wooden schooner similar to the *Peter & Linda*, skippered by Joey's older brother, John. Since it had been owned by their father, *Linda B* was the original Testaverde family boat. The *Sea Fox*, belonging to their younger brother, Tom, was tied alongside. Up on the pier stood Salve Testaverde, the Old Man himself, with a fine head of white hair and a solid expression of command on his square, healthy face. He wore a dark suit rather than oilskins like the others, and a gold chain glinted through a white shirt open at his collar. "I come all the way from Florida just for you," he barked cheerfully to Bobby, the crewman who was tossing up a line from deck.

"Yeah, if I only live," said Bobby, a breezy guy of twenty-seven with a black beard trimmed approximately three days before. He had joked all day about his hangover from the bachelor party just thrown him, and about the cold feet he was developing. The next day, Bobby was to marry one of the Testaverde nieces. Though Bobby was on the eve of his wedding, for now he remained the man who descended into the hold to break out the boxes of catch he had been icing all day. With delivery completed, the three men padlocked the wheelhouse and hatch, climbed the ladder to the wharf, and headed for their vehicles parked in a compound around the wharf.

"See ya two A.M. as usual," called Bobby.

Joey laughed. "*You* ain't going out tomorrow."

"Take my mind off things. You're coming in early anyhow. I *feel* like fishin', man."

"And something happen out there? You crazy? You think I want all the women down on me? Go home take a bath. Me and Frankie's manage fine without you, not even gonna miss you!"

"Ahh . . ." Bobby obviously preferred the idea of arriving at his wedding straight from the boat, the way a fisherman might be expected to do.

The *Peter & Linda*'s catch of shrimp remained in its plastic boxes for delivery to a local plant that would process it into frozen packs. The whiting and other finfish, iced in wooden boxes, were already being packed with other catches into a refrigerator truck that a driver would take overnight to the Fulton Fish Market in New York City. Several fishing skippers, all of Sicilian ancestry like the Testaverdes, had a decade and a half ago formed their own marketing organization that they called Fishermen's Wharf, Inc. (They did not call it a co-op.) Having an organization with facilities provided them guaranteed mooring and a place to wait out bad weather in their own good company but, more important, it made them a collective marketing force able to call some of their own shots. They could afford to truck fresh catches direct to New York, the highest-paying market in the region. The alternatives for Gloucester fishermen in the fresh fish trade were local buyers or the Boston auction. The Boston price, generally lower than that of New York, would be reduced another ten to twenty-five cents a pound by buyers in Gloucester plants.

Selling to New York meant that the Gloucester boats in the fresh fish trade now worked Sundays, but stayed Fridays in port. Fulton Fish Market was closed over the weekend, so that a Friday catch would have to wait too long. Boats could, however, fish on Saturday and hold over their catches, to travel with fish caught Sunday to reach the markets by the 2:00 A.M. opening Monday morning.

Joey talked awhile with his dad, whom he had not seen for several months. Then he drove home, where Joanna waited to serve dinner and his two older girls would be juggling homework and television. His comfortable house, with a painting of the *Peter & Linda* in the living room, was part of an old residential area located at the base of the ridge along which Gloucester stretches, in sight of water and within walking distance of the boats. The two-story frame structures had all been built close to each other, and neighbors could talk from porch to porch. Most were fishermen of Italian origin. Joey had grown up in the house just across the street, where now his brother Tom lived.

On the wharf, Salve Testaverde received general greetings from other fishermen. The Old Man had taught all his sons to fish and then, after fifty years of fishing himself in a career that started on his own father's boat, had sold his boat and house to his sons and retired, a widower, to Florida. He was no longer part of the daily scene, perhaps, but he had gone into the weather with them thousands of times, had helped pioneer the practice of icing daily fresh-caught fish in boxes as a quality product, and still owned a share in some of the boats. He had even written an expressive 150-page book about his half century of fishing, which the local bookstores carried autographed.

Salve's face, naturally swarthy, had a fine tan that extended to the neck and broad chest showing through his open white shirt. The gold chain that gleamed around his neck seemed to express the good feeling of how it all worked out for a kid who first helped out on his dad's boat at age five, and peddled papers and shined shoes in Boston during the depression to contribute food for the family table. He now had three sons who owned and skippered their own boats while the fourth, a Ph.D. marine biologist, worked for the National Marine Fisheries Service in town. "So I guess . . . I think we done pretty good." By "we" he meant his late wife, whose loss he referred to often.

I asked Salve the obvious question: do you miss fishing or are you glad it's over? He considered for a moment. "Yeah, in a way I kind of miss," he said in a voice hoarsened from years of shouting into the wind. "But no, what there is today? If I was on a boat fishing today and I see what comes in that net compared to what I was used to, what they bring up now . . . I think I commit suicide!" He had just watched our work of the past twelve hours weighed out on the pier in the hundreds of pounds. "You know, I use to bring in five, six *thousan'* pound of shrimp every day."

But then (transcribed as he pronounced it, in the pattern common to Boston-area fishermen of Mediterranean descent): "Twenny yeahs ago, five, six thousan' pounds of shrimp, I couldn't sell 'em." He couldn't even get four cents a pound, compared to the $1.20 a pound price that Joey expected for his shrimp. "Brokah took 'em off my hands says we done you a favah, foah cents a pound."

When Salve started fishing with his father, they worked longline in an open dory, using a very labor-intensive technique that requires placing bait by hand onto thousands of hooks. It involved, for them, twenty tubs of "trawl," each trawl consisting of eight forty-two-fathom lines. This amounted to more than forty thousand feet of line that needed to be baited, set, and hauled daily, hand over hand. "You was always busy, cause if there was fish around, you had to first catch 'em, then haul 'em in, take up the fish, cut 'em and clean 'em up. No fish, you still hadda overrun your travel line, bait up and start all over. That kept you busy all week long, workin'. Where *now*," he laughed, "when no fish come, guys sleep most of the day!"

Salve warmed to his subject. "We had *no* holidays except for Christmas, Easter, St. Peter, St. Joseph. We didn't know what vacations were. Young lad growin' up, like in school, I didn't know baseball, football, sports. No radio, no television like the kids watch now. We didn't know what the outside world was. All we had, a world of ourselves—the boat, the ocean. That was my life."

[41]

Undoubtedly, Salve Testaverde and his generation had times that would put most of the younger generation under. But during the worst of January a flounder still stiffens into a frozen board in mid-flip as it emerges from the water, while sea smoke blown off the tops of waves still covers the rigging with instant ice.

These days, during bad winter blows, the fleet stayed in port. Too many boats littered the bottom from disasters past. There had been terrible weather for more than a week. Two days before, restless with staying ashore, we had gone out at 2:00 A.M. to test the sea. In the black winter darkness, the boat pitched and rolled without visual reference to any horizon. Joey in the wheelhouse braced himself against a bulkhead, consulted his radar and loran, and commiserated by CB radio about the state of the weather with his brothers and other skippers. We could see some of their boats around us as crazily bouncing lights that vanished in swells for seconds at a time.

The *Peter & Linda* was a typical wooden-hulled schooner of the old-world fishing families in Gloucester. It resembled the ones in which Joey had learned to fish with his father. Although the boat was built in 1944, his ownership dated back only seven years. The design of these boats has not changed for generations, even though other fishermen have converted to steel and fiberglass. Insurance companies decline to cover wooden hulls anymore. They certainly require maintenance, as well as greater caution when the water ices over, but they remain strong and resilient craft for day-trip fishermen. Some of the larger ones still make the week-long runs to Georges Bank. The fleet around Fishermen's Wharf, skippered by families with names like Spinola, Aiello, San Philipo, and Testaverde, sticks with wood in part because wooden hulls scrape more kindly against other wooden hulls.

The *Peter & Linda*'s traditional "eastern-rigged" design placed the wheelhouse aft, the fish hold amidships, and the "fo'c'sle," the living quarters, forward under the deck. (Fo'c'sle, pronounced foke'-sul, is the contraction of "forecastle" that all English-speaking seafarers have used for centuries.) To reach the quarters, you climbed down a ladder after hunching into a shack-like "doghouse" raised on the main deck. The doghouse had a curved back to fend off the heaviest slams of water from the bow, and small shuttered doors facing aft. Depending on the weather, the doors could be closed, or left open to allow the close air below to circulate.

[42]

The wooden dragger *Peter and Linda* heads home to Gloucester after a day's fishing that began at 2 A.M. As crewmen cull keeper fish from the last set, skipper Joe Testaverde, in the wheelhouse, talks to his wife, fishing buddies or his New York marketplace.

Joe Testaverde, in the wheelhouse of his traditional "eastern-rigged" New England wooden fishing boat.

The bobbins and floats of a trawl net come aboard the *Nina* T. out of Gloucester. The stringy chafing gear around the men's feet is attached to the net to prevent tearing when it drags along the sea floor.

Emptying a bag of shrimp and fish aboard the *Peter and Linda*.

On this stormy morning, it was a wild, wet passage below decks from Joey's little hut. The cranky wheelhouse door handle had to be dogged just right to keep the door from banging back open in the wind with berserk force. On deck, you had to be careful not to slip on ice as you ran for shelter before the bow hit a wave and sent up an umbrella of seawater.

Below decks, it was chilly and damp. Bobby fired the stove and gradually some warmth crept along the bulkheads and filled the room. It was a bare place, some of it not painted as recently as the more income-producing surfaces on deck. A patched and welded stovepipe snaked along one side. Oilskins swayed on hooks fastened into gray wainscoting. Up forward, a double tier of bunks curved along the interior edges of the bow. A table occupied the center, with benches whose seats lifted for storage space. Boxes of food and gear had been crammed onto shelves.

Since the *Peter & Linda* was a "day boat" that returned to port every night, Frank and Bobby had no need to make a home aboard so long as they stowed objects tightly enough to prevent their slamming across the cabin in rough weather. It was different aboard the larger wooden "trip boats" that traveled to Georges Bank for a week at a time, as did the steel-hulled *General Patton*. I had ridden out of New Bedford. The men aboard these lived much of their lives in the fo'c'sle and required a different discipline.

Once I spent a while on Georges Bank aboard a wooden trip boat out of New Bedford. The boat had the same design as the *Peter & Linda*. Unlike the *General Patton*, which had separate two-berth cabins, galley, and mess straight off the main deck, the wooden boat combined all these functions in the cramped below-decks fo'c'sle which the six or seven crewmen entered through a doghouse. They kept the area scrubbed, but after several days on the grounds it had accumulated a collective odor of sweat, cigars, cooking, propane gas, and fishy boots. An old curtain on a cord separated the bunks along the bow from the mess table and stove. With staggered watches, some men were always sleeping. This was the way that New Englanders put to sea for generations, the way that many still do.

Aboard the *Peter & Linda*, Frank went forward to relieve Joey at the wheel. With two or three hours' cruise to reach the grounds, the skipper napped in a bunking space behind the wheel while the two crewmen took turns at the helm. Below decks, Frank and Bobby kept

[43]

their sleeping bags in two of the bunks and used the other two for storage. Bobby climbed up and slid into his bunk, and pulled a sleeping bag around him without removing his boots. "Keep my feet warm," he explained of the boots. "And one less thing I gotta do when Joey blows the whistle."

Frank gave me his bunk for the trip out. The sleeping bag was damp, but body temperature soon had it cozy. There is nothing like time spent in a bunk curved against the bow of a fishing boat in rough weather for contemplating the force of the sea. Only a wooden or steel skin a few inches thick separated me from tons of water slamming against the hull. The crashing sounds coordinated in brutal cause-and-effect with the plunge of the bow into heavy water after it pitched in the air. The plunge halted the boat for a moment and everything inside jolted forward. Water thumped against the hull as hard as a fist, sometimes a hammer. The sound was physical. It had force. Just let the hull puncture an inch and the force would become cold tearing energy. The skin of this bow had sustained millions of sea slams. With any kind of fisherman's odds, I told myself, the hull would continue to hold for many thousands more such knocks. This reassuring thought sent me quickly to sleep at three in the morning.

The pitching suddenly converted to a hard roll and then the motion everywhere increased. "We've turned around," said Bobby from under his cover. "Joey's goin' back home." Frank climbed down a few minutes later, his oilskins dripping, to confirm it. Some of the other draggers a few miles ahead of us and further from the lee of shore had reported that the weather was only growing worse, so the whole fleet had decided to turn around. As we sat at the table passing some buns, a wave hit an open seam around a deck vent and cold seawater rained over our heads. We joked about it and put on oilskins, while Frank and Bobby discussed where they had better caulk when the weather cleared.

Frank, a man with heavy, rounded Italian features and a deliberate efficiency that contrasted with Bobby's bounce, had fished for more than thirty years, since the age of twelve. A Gloucesterman all his life, he had long ago earned the nickname "Big Munza," or just "Munza." Nobody could remember why, but it started in high school, and that is how all those of his generation knew him. Munza's own pattern was set, a man happier being a crewman and leaving the skipper's head-aches to somebody else, but when he heard that I had fished in other places he wanted to know more, persistently. What was it like, say, on one of those Norwegian draggers? Like, what kind of chow, and how did they bunk? Did they ever get rich? How did they hang their nets? I answered as best I could while dodging overhead dribbles whenever a fresh sea hit.

Back in the harbor calm, we moored gunnel to gunnel, still in the winter dark, and wandered up the stairs of the building on the pier. The glassed-in office of the fishermen's collective stood to the right, and a large waiting room opened straight ahead. Several skippers and crewmen who had returned ahead of us lounged in an assortment of worn chairs probably cast off from their homes. The television set churned out an early talk show, but most of the men talked above the noise about the weather out there, its effect on fish prices, and whatever hints there might be in it all for betting the numbers.

An hour or two later in gray daylight—nobody seemed in a rush—several of us drove through early morning traffic to a diner at the end of the harbor. Other fishermen were already settled into booths with platters of eggs and pancakes in front of them. Everyone chatted with the waitresses about family affairs. Whatever the life represented by the traffic outside, the diner people were part of the same community as those from the boats. When the men left, they dropped fisherman-sized tips equaling about a third of the bill.

After breakfast, the men scattered on various errands. Some passed back through the office to lounge, follow prices, and exchange opinions. By noon, most had wandered into one of three dark, warm bars across the street to join around tables with a beer. At the Old Timers, we talked above a video movie that delivered a crash or an explosion every few minutes, paying no attention, and took turns in matches at the pool table that were hotly enough contested to raise occasional gleeful shouts. Later we changed to the relative quiet of Mitch's, the smaller bar.

An older generation—fathers and uncles of the men with whom I was fishing—congregated at the quieter St. Peter's Club a few doors away. When I had been seeking a site on a Gloucester boat several years before, people had advised me to find skippers there, but to go before eleven when the men would all head off to the betting games.

The barroom conversations of the young generation covered subject after subject, all related to fishing. There had recently been an unsuccessful herring joint venture with the West Germans. The men agreed that a faulty pumping system ultimately caused the project to fail. John Testaverde, Joey's older brother who skippered the Linda B, leaned back comfortably as he ruminated over the way fish came in cycles. One year you had lots of mackerel, and the next year the mackerel disappeared while you found squid and whiting everywhere. "You got to stay loose and be prepared," added Joey, leaning toward the others with elbows on the table. As for the sea itself, storming out there as everybody had just seen, Nimo Spinola, the relaxed, clean-shaven skipper of the St. Mary (who looked like a businessman on his day off), put it this way: "We punch her, she punches back harder."

Tom Testaverde, a confident, stocky man with a young face that had weathered into reds rather than browns like the rest, joined the other skippers, automatically bringing a new round of drinks from the bar before pulling up a chair. He and Joey started discussing their new pair trawl. The brothers had decided to experiment with a technique still virtually unknown in the area, which involved using two boats to pull opposite wings of the same net for a potentially larger collective catch. It would involve coordination, and had already resulted in a 25,000-dollar investment for the net and tackle in addition to hours of their own work welding and constructing. When the whiting hit in late spring, they'd give it the first try. Then in fall they'd be ready for whiting, mackerel, herring, whatever schooled from surface to bottom, a versatility impossible with simple drag gear. If they lost some fishing time getting the kinks out of the system, maybe they'd make it up in future hauls.

The group was a fluid one that came and went, but by 5:30 everyone had gone home for dinner. These were the fishermen of a community in which boat and family formed a dual nucleus.

That night, the weather report gave some hope even though seas remained high. Joe, like the other skippers, listened to the reports before he went to bed, and then looked around him when he rose at 1:30 A.M. He phoned Bobby and Munza to come down. By 2:30 A.M., half the boats had already headed through the breakwater, and the harbor stirred with the dark shapes and red/green running lights of others maneuvering from their slips. The water was rough, but not as bad as before. Aboard the Peter & Linda, we napped and alternated watches during the trip to the grounds. Since the storm had caused enough upwelling to disturb the bottom, no one knew where the shrimp might be, and the boats scattered to try different areas.

The *Peter & Linda* might have been a boat of another generation in its design and hull, but Joey had packed the wheelhouse with the latest equipment on the market for his purpose. "When I *can* catch maximum," he explained, "I wanna be able to catch maximum."

The radar and the loran had backup duplicates. A third loran fed information into a computerized video plotter that pictured in color the boat's course and location, with a record of present and past sets on the same grounds. Joey could see from this exactly where he had last fished before the storm, for example, or where he had made good sets at the same time a year before. One program in the plotter showed the location of wrecks, most of them fishing boats that had sunk over the years. There was a paper chart sounder of a type on the market for decades, whose stylus snapped back and forth like an inverted windshield wiper to sketch the depth and bottom configuration on a continuous drum of paper. A newer type sounder presented the same information in color on a screen. A different type color sounder stood idle for the moment, a new investment to be attached to the net itself during the season for fish that schooled in large masses.

At 6:30 A.M., just as the sky was turning light, Joey double-tooted the wheelhouse whistle. Other boats dipped and bobbed around us, their deck and running lights still shining. This was Ipswitch Bay, a place of varying mud, sand, and gravel bottoms (and dangerous submerged rock mounts in places) that attracted many species and many types of boats. Frank and Bobby pulled into their oilskins at once—one leg of Bobby's orange skins had a flapping tear—and climbed the ladder. Ice coated the deck. Only our faces were exposed under wool caps, but the wind cut them painfully. The cold seeped at once through lined waterproof gloves.

The men worked precisely step by step, as they had done hundreds of times before, "on automatic," as Bobby put it. The side-trawl gear consisted of a single net supported by two doors, all of it set from the starboard side. They dumped the net over by hand and the boat's motion opened it through the water in a narrow arc. Then, assisted by Joe, who hurried from the wheelhouse, they shackled the doors to the net. When some web snagged on one of the doors, Frank leaned far out over the water to free it while Joe stood ready to grab him. No job on a fishing boat is routine enough to be free of glitches, some with potential danger. The doors lowered free into the water, and the tow moved astern although it stayed always to starboard on the side where it would come back aboard.

At 50 fathoms depth, the standard rule of thumb called for 150 fathoms of cable. The cables attached to the doors payed out from parallel drums, controlled by Bobby at the windlass, while Frank called depth markings as they unwound. With the tow set and hardened, that finished the deck work until it came time to haul back, and left it up to the skipper. Now alone responsible for the payday, Joey needed to direct the weighted net along the unseen depth curves and bottoms, aided by electronic gadgets that could tell him much but could guarantee nothing in captured fish.

The Gloucester inshore fishermen in the group with Testaverde shrimped from January through mid-April, and then fished for whiting and hake through the fall. The shrimp that they caught were smaller than the jumbo whites and brownies in the Gulf of Mexico (a different species) but large enough that their meats when peeled had the thickness of a crayon. In recent years as fish stocks fluctuated, the little crustaceans had been the inshore fisherman's salvation from Massachusetts to Maine.

Shrimp are more ubiquitous in the world's waters than any other edible sea creature. Men fish them for a living in the tropical waters off India and Brazil, and in the frigid waters off Norway, Labrador, and Alaska. Most modern shrimp boats drag twin nets from an outrigger on either side of the boat and haul the bags up a ramp cut in the stern. The stern ramp design is safer and more efficient, but for an older boat it requires costly and extensive modification. Alabama shrimpers from the Gulf of Mexico had just begun introducing the double-rigged boats to Gloucester. Those comfortable with the old ways watched with consternation, both at the change and for the invasion. Despite Joe Testaverde's boldness in trying new electronic gear and experimenting with a pair trawl, he had no plans to alter his shrimp nets.

The heat belowdecks felt good. It had built to a high temperature, as enclosed fishboat galleys will, the kind of satisfying heat that men on cold decks dream of. The thud and bounce subsided as the pull of the tow held the boat steady in the water, but it remained rough. Bobby prepared breakfast, balancing a small pan over the burner until the eggs stiffened to prevent them slipping over the rim, and apologized for the broken yolk in one of his over-easy's. "I usually can do bettah than that, any weather," he declared.

Fishermen who would not be caught dead in their wives' kitchens ashore take pride in their ability to fix good meals afloat. Crewmen expect the best in the short time they give to shoveling down their food, since eating and a smoke are usually the only creature comforts available during the cold and wet of the day's work. But they have little taste for quiches and flurries. Once I hired aboard a small shrimp dragger as cook. (This meant, of course, working the deck besides—on small fishing boats one crewman cooks, one services the engine, another keeps the deck gear in shape, and the skipper steers, but all shoot the gear and wade into fish when the bag comes aboard.) As we cruised to the grounds, with no pressures yet for heavy labor, I prepared an admirable curry of lean beef augmented with home-baked bread (the dough bought frozen), lightly cooked vegetables, salad with oil and vinegar dressing, and a sensible fresh fruit dessert. Then I waited modestly for the smack of lips and the compliments.

The skipper tore off a piece of bread and picked through the curry sauce as the others said nothing. "Uh, Bill . . . the gravy's maybe in that pan on the stove? And the, uh, potatoes? And these string beans—they're kind of still bright green, you know?" I explained that I'd tossed the grease overboard, and overcooking vegetables took out all the nutrients, and with bread and rice who needed more starch?

"The gravy, *overboard*?" cried Andy the engine man.

We picked bravely through the meal. (These were polite young guys, although they had been fishermen for years.) Fortunately, a bottled dressing in the refrigerator provided something thick on the salad and a pecan pie lay buried in the freezer.

The skipper stayed behind for a pleasant talk as I did the dishes. For the next meal, I swirled flour into the grease until it became a thick brown muck, cooked the vegetables a dull green, and laid out steaming big pots of canned creamed corn, spaghetti, and boiled potatoes.

"Bill! This is good. It's *good*, man!" The others said the same. Their voices all echoed a common relief.

In the warmth of the *Peter & Linda*'s fo'c'sle, with the skipper far away at the wheel trying to outwit hidden schools of shrimp as he participated in the party-line conversations on CB radio (his break-fast served by means of a dash across the open deck), there could have been standard gripe-talk. Instead, the men volunteered that Joey never cheated them. "He says the old man taught his boys to give the crew fair share, and he does the same, not like some skippers around heah, they get sometimes prices and weights we don't see, maybe don't need to tell us about."

The accepted share system of Gloucester day boats these days, Joey told me later, started with all expenses off the top—the ice, grub, oil, lube oil, filters, everything. Then the boat took fifty percent, and the remaining fifty was divided evenly among everyone including the skipper. (The skipper pulled about a quarter share more from the boat share.) A Gloucester inshore crewman in the late 1980s made about thirty thousand dollars a year, a man on a trip boat to Georges Bank potentially about ten thousand more. Before "insurance went crazy," the boats worked on what they called an "Italian lay." Under this system, the boat never reached a full fifty-percent share, but always had a half share less than the crew. However, insurance raised the cost of maintaining the boat and did away with this.

A double toot two hours after the net entered the water signaled the time to pull it up. The bag came back over the starboard side, hardly filled enough to need the strength of one man to lift it from the rail to a bin formed on deck with movable boards. "Ahh . . . no morning glory this one," Bobby declared, using the local phrase for the frequent best catch of the day in early morning.

Worse, the net had a big tear. Frankie-Munza settled down at once with needle and twine to start mending as Bobby held the web taut. The tear was large enough to require cutting open a dozen other meshes before starting in order to provide a clean set of two-leggers (double attached strands) and three-leggers. Frank worked with bare hands, his teeth clenched, humming a tune, in cold that began to stiffen my own fingers through thick gloves.

In the wheelhouse, Testaverde talked to his brothers and his other buddy-fisherman, Ricky Beal of the Gannet, sharing the news of a poor catch as he headed to test another area. The storm had scat-tered the shrimp and no one could find them again. One of the voices on the radio observed glumly, "Fuckin' kelp, the bottom's all stirred up, gotta be the goddamned tide."

There was actually little heavy language over the radio bands among these inshore boats, far less than I had heard on Georges Bank. Among the Georges fleet, from boats identified as Boston-based, the profanity—FCC rules notwithstanding—echoed like sledgehammers. Cuss talk of the more homogeneous groups had a modifying down-East ease, a Scandinavian singsong, or a Mediterranean verve. Perhaps this reflects a difference in outlook between men who go home to fishing communities and those from heterogeneous city neighborhoods where fishing and its hardships are little understood.

Joe decided that if the shrimp were gone from fifty-fathom water they might have moved deeper. By the time a half hour later that we reached a sixty-fathom ground, the net was mended and ready to go back overboard. After making the set, we fitted a heavy wooden chute over the bin and sat sorting the previous haul as spray turned icy and rattled down our oilskins. The catch was a conglomerate batch of shrimp, herring, whiting, sculpin (an ugly toadfish of no commercial value, whose spiked fins could pierce a thick rubber glove), lobster, skate, and crab, none of it in any quantity. We filled sparse basketfuls of keeper species, and Bobby jumped into the hold to ice and store them.

The sixty-fathom set brought up more than had the one at fifty fathoms, but not enough to make the day's trip. Testaverde cruised and consulted his buddies, and eventually made a set at forty fathoms within sight of shore. By now the wind had abated, the water had calmed, and, under patches of sun that sent warmth through our oilskins and thermals, the ice had melted.

Joey delayed hauling in the third set by a few minutes because a Celtics game on the little fo'c'sle TV had reached a crucial point. It was a set worth waiting for. Munza yanked the draw cord, and shrimp and fish poured from the open bag like concrete from a hopper. "Yeah, now," he shouted appreciatively as the mass oozed around his legs.

Dozens of seagulls hovered in the sky, moving so in concert with the boat that they appeared to be suspended. Occasionally, a bold one swooped into the bin and flew away with a shrimp in its beak. "Robbahs!" yelled Bobby. We ourselves snapped open a few of the shrimp and ate them raw, in the fashion most expected of the Japanese. They had a soft texture and a sweet nutty flavor. The opportunistic gulls continued their squawking feed as we culled, catching small fish in midair that we tossed back over the side. The cull yielded four baskets of shrimp and a few lobsters, not enough to stop Salve Testaverde from talking cheerfully of self-destruction in light of bounties past, but sufficient to reassure Joey that he had found the schools dispersed by the storm.

When it came time to return home, we hosed the deck, secured the doors and net, covered the windlass, and stood for a while enjoying the good weather. The rays of a late sun, shining first amber and then orange, etched the lines of distant rooftops ashore and then the graceful shafts of the twin Cape Ann lighthouses. Radio banter in the wheelhouse had turned lively, since other skippers had also found the shrimp again.

Frankie-Munza on deck began talking about the presidential primary, which had taken place the day before in New Hampshire, just a few miles from Gloucester. What did I think of this guy Dukakis? And Bush, could Bush hack it?

"Ahh, who cares," said Bobby in good spirits.

Frank turned on him gravely. "You should pay attention. That's very important shit."

In the wheelhouse, Joey had stowed the sagging captain's chair, so that its bare stanchion in the middle of the deck made a good foot prop. He started to talk about his four daughters. In summer he took the oldest ones on the boat sometimes and they helped cull. "But I don't make 'em work unless they want to." He thought it over and pulled at his thick beard. "You'd never hear my old man say that. We *worked* on that boat, just young kids, like he did with his old man. The thing is, though, our kids, girls even, they work. Fishing's our life-style. They feel it, like we did."

The elder Testaverde had helped in his time to establish the type of inshore "box" fishing that his sons now pursued. Joey spoke of it proudly, how the Old Man and a few other skippers had decided to pack their fish in iced boxes and sell to a quality market in New York rather than just fill the entire hold with fish that weighted each other down layer by layer. "A lot of boats wouldn't go box fishing, said the work was too much," Joey remembered. "They says: lot of work, pack the fish, clean the fish, wash it, pack it in ice, then ship it every day. Be home at six or seven, then you got to be up again at two o'clock every morning doin' it again." But the price that New York paid for better fish worked out to be worth the time. And it felt good to be delivering a quality product. The three Testaverde brothers all stayed in the box fishery.

Salve Testaverde had once dreamed of a boat crewed by all his sons. Sal, the marine biologist, held to his desire to leave the deck and go to college. As for the other three, Joey explained, "My father always wanted us to stay together; he had the *Linda* B all free. I was at that time the engineer. But Tommy, he was younger, he was itchy, said I want my own boat." After accepting the inevitable, Salve helped his youngest son find a good boat. They traveled together as far as Florida and Maine before they settled on the *Sea Fox* that Tommy still skippered.

Joey laughed, as he often did, and said realistically, "We bought three boats to keep us separated so we don't kill each other. We work together but we're separate. If we were all the same crew, which God forbid . . . you know, we got different ideas, and different temperaments. My father's proud of us. It turned out okay."

Dr. Salvatore Testaverde, the marine biologist, now lives in Gloucester apart from the fishing boats and works for the National Marine Fisheries Service. He plays an active part in monitoring the health of the local fisheries, and testifies frequently before meetings of the New England Fishery Management Council. And, a bureaucrat working regular hours away from the cold winds and spray, he sometimes finds himself talking wistfully of the boats and the freer life aboard them. There is, of course, no turning back. As for his brother Joey: "He's a fleet highliner in fact as well as in spirit, because he's always ready to take on something new or more advanced."

There remained at least an hour before mooring and unloading. Down in the stuffy shelter below decks, Munza and Bobby had settled around the table. Munza kept a cigarette in his mouth, as he dealt from a deck of cards that stuck comfortably to his fingers from many previous games.

4

Boats That Go Down

The Pilgrim Fathers landed on Plymouth Rock in 1620. Friendly
Indians soon showed them how to take advantage of such near-
shore food from the sea as lobsters, shellfish, eels, and herring, and
the great New England fishing tradition began. Only three years later,
the settlers had taken their bearings enough to establish the village
of Gloucester seventy miles to the north, in order to avail themselves
of the rich seafood lode along the shallows just off Cape Ann. The
men who went to sea from there started close inshore within the
sight of land, harvesting from the waters that the *Peter & Linda* still
fishes. As Gloucester boatwrights built them stronger and faster
boats, the settlers also traveled further and further into the rich
grounds of the Atlantic, until they had established themselves as the
prime fishermen of the New World.

An account published in the early 1880s in *Century Magazine* presents the contemporary scene:

> Six sloops, one boat and one shallop comprised the Cape Ann fleet
> in 1693; now it has nearly five hundred sail, of almost 28,000 tons, and
> Gloucester is the largest fishing port in the land. Its fleet is manned by
> men of every clime. A tide of young men, mainly from the Provinces,
> sets steadily toward this port. Many have the characteristic reckless-
> ness of the sailor, and earnings of weeks are spent between sunset and

sunrise. . . . All haunts are prepared for Jack, and he is prepared for all haunts.

In the typically euphoric journalism of the time (which still manages to detail the business and social requirements of a fisherman's economy), the writer continues:

Here are no labor strikes. The sailor brings in a fare of fish, they are weighed off, the vessel is put to rights, and he goes up to the counting room for his check. The whole value of the fish is reckoned by the vessel owner or his clerk; then is deducted cost of ice and bait bought; then one quarter of one percent for the Widows and Orphans Fund; one half the remainder belongs to the owner, the other to him. From his part is then deducted charges for wood sawing and splitting, for water, medicine chest, condensed milk, and any charge for labor on the vessel which belonged for him to do, but which has been hired done. His check is then handed him, and he presents it in person, or it finds its devious way to the bank by other—perhaps not cleaner—hands.

One of the most exciting scenes imaginable is that of a fleet of hundreds making the port in a storm. In a northeast gale they must beat in. All day long, by twos and threes, they come. It is luff, bear away, or tack ship to avoid a smash. Crack, snap, goes a jib-boom off. Crack, snap, there is one main boom the less. Hoarse voices of the skippers howl in entreaty or command above the howling gale, and the shore is lined with listening lookers-on.

Despite the fact that Gloucester is now a town large enough to support more than one business, anyone sticking to the mile of road along the harbor would still associate all its activities with fishing. Masts cluster around the piers beside low boxy fish-processing houses, and boats stand exposed on dry-dock ways. Even the parallel shipping streets on the hill above the harbor give a view of water between the low buildings.

When the boats are in port, men in knit caps, boots, and oilskin pants stand among nets stretched flat along dockside spaces, talking quietly as their hands work needle and twine through torn web. Snow and ice may lie deep on the road, but steam pours from the fish plants where workers in white smocks and caps stand their shifts cutting fillets or sawing blocks of frozen fish into the shapes that, breaded, become fish sticks and fishburgers.

Tourists and artists converge on the town in summer, but these people play no part in the lives and economies of fishermen who pay as little attention as possible to clicking cameras and easels planted in the concourse of a wharf. The summer outsiders do make themselves felt when they usurp parking spaces that fishermen need in order to reach their boats. After early September when the weather turns raw, the competition, of course, vanishes.

Beyond the downtown harbor, dominating an esplanade along the sea, stands the famous green bronze statue of a fisherman in boots and sou'wester, crouched into the wind and spray as he grips the spoked wheel of his schooner. The sculptor, Leonard Crask, has depicted a clear-eyed man of grit. The inscription stirs anyone who knows the harsh fishing waters: "They That Go Down to the Sea in Ships." The statue provides a focus for a procession on Memorial Day, when the names are read of any lost that year at sea. At the time of the statue's dedication in 1923, tiny Gloucester had lost eight thousand fisherman since 1830. On a recent blowing February day, a wreath stood at the base of the statue, its stand buried in snow and its fresh ribbons flapping. The wreath enclosed the photograph of a boat lost with all hands during a gale ten years before.

Gloucester, population 27,800, is located on one end of an island that is only a bridge span from the mainland. Rockport, a smaller fishing community seven miles away, occupies the other end. Fishermen know the area collectively as Cape Ann, after the main seafarer's landfall, marked by twin lighthouses, that lies on the rocky coast between the two harbors. Within the limits of generalities, Gloucester fishermen are Italian-American and those of Rockport are Yankee. Finns and Portuguese used to be an important fishing element in Gloucester. Older Portuguese families remain around Our Lady of Good Voyage Church on Portuguese Hill, but most of their fishermen now work out of New Bedford. The Italian and the Yankee groups remain mostly apart, leading separate lives, not necessarily admiring each other. As one Yankee Rockporter, who works his gill nets alone, put it of the traditional Italians: "Those guys are Guineas; they're squash heads. They don't do nothin' but cling to the old ways."

Another Rockporter, Bob Beloff, shows his Yankee differentness in more than talk. A lean, quiet man of forty whose eyes keep track of everything around him, Beloff lives with his wife and kids in a house with a deck porch surrounded by woods. The construction of the house bears his hand, and he has always fished from boats he built himself, at least in part. The first was a twelve-foot skiff from which as a teenager he worked ten lobster traps. "You don't need to pay a ship's carpenter for something you can do yourself." He did the same for his present boat, the forty-five-foot *New Horizon*, for which he bought only the "eggshell," the bare fiberglass hull.

With a two-man crew, he works gill nets in season for cod, haddock, flounder, herring, and pollock. During the bad weather of January–February, he usually repairs gear and stays off the water, as do most other local gill netters, since it is also a time when the nets collect so much slime that it scares away the few available fish. Beloff carries good electronics on board, although he needs less than draggers do. When fishing, he sets three strings of seven or eight nets each, for a total length of about 2,500 fathoms, leaving them to soak on the bottom overnight. Lacking the family connections from which to draw crewmen as do the Testaverdes and their friends, he has a problem with turnover. "They jump around. Why bust your hump out there when just work at McDonald's gets seven bucks an hour?"

Although many Rockport fishermen work gill nets and also "trawl" lines (longlines), lobstering is the town's distinctive fishery. The open lobster boats with little raised cabins the size of outhouses, most of them less than thirty-five feet long, have the same simplicity as the crab and oyster boats of Chesapeake Bay. Tourism also counts in Rockport, because no harbor in New England has greater weatherboard charm. The main wharf with its pots and colored lobster floats has been painted and photographed as ferociously as the Grand Canyon, and even on winter weekends cars from Boston crowd the narrow curbs as their occupants stroll the wharf line of converted fish houses, where boutiques offer nautical-looking objects.

The draggers bring up lobsters as incidental catch, but formal lobstering is conducted with "trawls," strings of baited pots or traps, set in relatively shallow water. Wood and wire lobster traps used to be rounded on top, but these days a squared wire version has replaced them—to the disappointment of artists and tourists who mourn the infinitely more picturesque wooden ones. Like the shaft tongers in Chesapeake Bay, the New England lobstermen are quintessentially independent, since they can operate alone or with a single helper.

The lobstering scene has changed. Frank Mackay, a lumbering, friendly man who has now left the water to help his wife run a shop on the Rockport pier called "Through the Looking Glass," remembers that as a youngster transplanted from Brooklyn in the mid-1940s he worked as backup man on a Rockport boat that fished forty-five pots from a boat under oars. In those days, they considered a "big strike" to be seventy-five pots. Aboard the boat, one of the Grand Banks dories of legendary stability, Mackay would stand on the gunnel and haul in the pots by hand, helped only by a converted manual washing machine roller.

Now, in order to capture the same number of lobsters, a man needed to work about seven hundred pots to make a living, pots that cost forty dollars each, and he needed "a damned good hydraulic hoist" to do the hauling of the ever-lengthening trawls. He also kept one or two hundred pots in reserve against loss in storms or by vandalism. Along with tourists have come hordes of scuba divers whose pleasure is lobstering. (Legal sales of their catch undoubtedly also pay for their tanks and other expenses.) On weekends, according to Mackay, fishermen pull their gear from any area near the divers, to avoid repairing traps pried and ripped open with knives by the underwater sportsmen.

Diversity characterizes the New England fisheries. Another fleet that marches to its own beat is that of the herring seiners. Like cod and shrimp, herring is one of the great food crops of the world because it occurs in so many places and in such abundance. While herring has gone out of style on American tables except in pickle—American fishermen are in fact inclined to use it as bait to lure other fish—its flavor adapts well to the kippering, smoking, and sharp sauces that please the northern European palate, while the Japanese pay a good price (sometimes an extravagant price) for the roe. In Norway, where even modest hotels include a breakfast buffet, four or five herring preparations usually occupy the center of the table.

Herring schools travel in huge numbers through the Gulf of Maine and along the Massachusetts coast, and a small fleet of seiners follows them for the entire year. Gloucester sees the fleet during fall and winter. It is easy to find them when they deliver. Just home in on thousands of circling seagulls, who know from experience that scraps tumble everywhere when the fish being unloaded are small and

abundant. The boats cluster in a separate community along a concrete quay. One can recognize them by the huge aluminum skiff tied
to the stern atop a pile of netting and round white corks, by the
hydraulic power block suspended on an after boom, and sometimes
by the high net passed through the block like a sail when the crew is
mending it.

Aboard the seiner *Miss Vicky*, skipper Lee Riley and his six-man
crew from New Harbor, Maine, drifted to the wheelhouse around 3:00
P.M. of a Sunday in late October, ready to go to sea. The boat, eighty-
two feet long with a steel hull, looked strong and new, and in fact had
been built in an Alabama shipyard only a year and a half before. A
late, bright sun reflected its heat through the wheelhouse windows,
belying the chilly wind outside. The talk turned on how the wind
would develop during the night. Some men dropped by from others
of the four seine boats tied alongside. One was Riley's son, who
skippered his dad's older boat *High Chaparral*. The men were relaxed
Yankee types, trim, clear-eyed, slow to smile or to get excited but easy
and good-humored.

Within the hour, we had all cast off, and Willie the cook, an older
man turning bald, laid out supper. In the wheelhouse, Captain Riley
headed toward his grounds as the sea took us over with a gentle rock
and pitch, watching his depth sounder for the big smudgy masses
that characterized a herring school. Herring rise from the bottom at
night to feed, and this is the time for a seiner to catch them. Unlike a
dragnet on a trawler, which scoops fish from the seafloor, a seine
encircles them near the surface.

It had turned dark when Riley found a target on the sounder and at
once tooted a sharp signal. Everyone abandoned dinner and jumped
into oilskins—bright yellow and orange colors that throbbed under
deck lights—and in a moment gear started to clang on deck. The skiff
man climbed a hill of stacked net to reach his boat, whose sides were
so high that when he leaned down he disappeared. He pulled aboard
one end of the net and secured it, and started the engine idling, as
the others worked a boom to lower him. As soon as the skiff hit the
water, it headed off pulling the net, the skiff man in yellow oilskins at
the controls a disappearing spot of color in the dark. Web zipped over
the stern, pulling the attached strings of big white foam-plastic corks
that bounced in the air.

The crew needed to work fast before its quarry took fright and dashed away or sounded. Riley communicated with his skiff man by walkie-talkie, trusting his instincts and the picture on the echo sounder. To keep from spooking the fish, the Miss Vicky made the entire set in the dark. Only a little masthead light showed the movement of the skiff, while on deck the men used flashlights.

With a seine, corks keep the top of the net afloat while weights hold down the bottom. When the seine is brought into a circle, both ends of the bottom rope, attached by rings, are hauled back simultaneously while the top is left floating. This closes the net at the bottom like a drawstring purse, trapping the fish which before this have only been encircled. During the setting procedure, the two vessels holding the ends of the net can keep it open by moving in parallel with the net stretched between them. This allows fish swimming with a current to enter the wall of net. Or, if the skipper thinks that he has his fish at once, the two vessels can converge immediately to make a "round haul."

Aboard Miss Vicky, we round hauled. Within ten minutes of Riley's signal from the wheelhouse to the men at dinner, and within five from the lowering of the skiff, the skiff man had returned to the side and thrown aboard the line attached to his end of the net. In the dark, the crew wrapped the two heavy drawstring lines around winch heads and pursed the net. Meanwhile the skiff man moved to the outboard (other) side of the mother boat, and with a line thrown him used the skiff to pull the main boat sideways and keep it from drifting into the net.

When the pursing had been completed and the herring trapped, suddenly the deck lights blazed on. Now the herring could spook as much as they pleased. The haul-in proceeded by pulling aboard the net over the rotating wheel of the power block. The block, suspended from a boom, raised the net with its attached floats and weights high over the deck. It was huge, that net, as the power block drew it up, a cone of solid web the height of a two-story building. A torrent of water poured from it. As the net dropped back to deck the crew worked beneath—slime and bits of fish plopping on them from overhead—to stack it for the next set with the floats laid in coils on one side of the stern and the weighted end on the other. In another part of the stacking operation, Willie the cook gathered the large metal purse rings as they came aboard and slid them like donuts onto a heavy bar.

The circle of floats in the water tightened and became helter-skelter as more and more of the net came aboard. Some of the big white corks began to bob as the bag underneath tightened and the entrapped fish swarmed in eddies to the surface. The water around the corks became a frenzy of movement. Thousands of fish glinted silver and blue under the high deck lights, some leaping into the air, the bulk of them moving in a collective boiling motion. When it came time to haul the bag of fish aboard over a roller, everyone lined the rail, including the skipper, to lock fingers in the web and pull.

The fish tumbled aboard within the bag and slid in masses into the hold. Their scales flew everywhere like sawdust from a rotating blade. (You can tell a herring fisherman by the shiny little scales that inevitably glue themselves to his oilskins. Never get a herring scale in your eye.) That was the end of the set, a modest one that poured fifteen tons of herring into a hold with a capacity for one hundred tons. It was 7:30 P.M., an hour and a quarter since Riley gave the signal. Dinner resumed, for those who liked cold, dried-out pork chops.

The fishing continued through part of the night, then stopped abruptly when a blow came up that would have filled the raised net dangerously like a sail. That ended the lively part of purse seining for herring. Next morning in harbor, everyone had an easy breakfast of bacon, eggs, and pancakes. At 9:00, a tank truck pulled alongside the quay and sent over a thick hose that we lowered into the hold. The hose sucked our herring into the tank truck without anyone touching them further. It remained to wash the scales and gurry from the hold with pressured seawater, and wait for the next evening with attention to the weather.

Fishing follows a routine. But nature can interrupt it with a wind; men can interrupt it with a mistake. On July 23, 1988, the *Peter & Linda* started from Gloucester Harbor at 2:00 A.M. as usual, in company with others of the wooden-hulled Italian fleet. It passed the breakwater around 2:30 and headed along the Cape Ann coast toward its whiting grounds. An hour later, while the men aboard followed their usual routine with the skipper asleep after being relieved at the wheel,

Heading back to Gloucester after a day that began at 2 A.M., Frank Catania and Bobby Gross, with catch iced and nets secured, play cards in the small belowdecks galley of the *Peter and Linda*.

After delivering their catches from a day trip that began at midnight, Gloucester fishermen grab some late afternoon bar time before going home to dinner. Joey Testaverde is second from left while Bill McCloskey, author of *Fish Decks*, grins in at far right beside Ricky Beal.

A herring seiner working out of Gloucester brings its net and floats aboard. The boat fishes at night because that is the time when herring rise to the surface to feed.

Broken debris is all that remains from an overturned fishing boat that hit a heavy trough, rolled excessively, and capsized as horrified fishermen in nearby boats watched helplessly.

there was a series of bumps at the stern and suddenly, about a mile off Rockport, chaos erupted on a shoal known as Dry Salvages.

Joey Testaverde jumped awake at the first bump. The plotter and radar showed them on the wrong side of a marker buoy. As the boat started to roll and he grappled with the wheel, he threw on deck lights and booted open the pilothouse door. There, about twenty feet away, rose the tops of Salvages rocks, glistening under the lights, a surge breaking over them.

"Oh my Gawd," said Joey to himself, remembering later. "I felt, I knew we were going to have a lot of trouble." The boat started banging as it rolled, a terrible noise like the strike of sledgehammers. The worst pounding noise came from the stern, from the engine-room area just beneath the pilothouse. "I knew the stern wouldn't take that kind of beating. I mean, no boat could take that kind of beating in the stern."

The engine stalled and the engine alarm sounded with a piercing din. Joey found his way around from the pilothouse door on the side to the engine-room hatch facing aft, a rail-gripping walk of about ten paces. Despite water sloshing around the machinery below, he managed to restart the engine, and though the boat remained stuck to the rocks at least this kept the batteries charged. "But when I went in the engine room again, the water was over the alternator, half the engine under water. I was going to try put another pump on, but I don't think it would have helped, because just too much coming in at one time. So I got out of the engine room."

The men struggled into survival suits, buoyant foam-rubber coveralls sealed from head to foot but loose enough to pull quickly over boots and oilskins. The swells began to roll the boat forty-five degrees, slanting the deck downward like a chute. Their footing vanished. Surrounded by darkness they stared into black water. And the stern kept pounding. "You had to hold on so you wouldn't fall overboard," said Joey. "I didn't blame anybody being scared. Nobody wants to go in the water."

The *Sea Fox*, skippered by Joe's brother Tommy, had been traveling with the *Peter & Linda*. The two boats often fished together, especially now that they were experimenting with the new pair trawl gear. By now Tommy had radioed a Mayday to the Coast Guard in Gloucester, as Joey struggled around the boat checking the damage. "The Coast Guard told Tommy, leave him where he is till we come," Joey continued. (A boat stove on the rocks may be less likely to flood and sink if it stays there.) "I told Tommy on our own frequency, hell with the Coast Guard, pull me off. Nobody believed how bad we were rolling. And the stern pounding like that. We wouldn't have lasted."

The *Sea Fox* was hovering dangerously close to the rocks. Fortunately, the long ropes of the pair trawl project lay on the bow along with heaving lines made up and ready for passing the net between the boats. The *Sea Fox* caught the line, and managed to pull the *Peter & Linda* free. Away from the rocks and swells, the terrible rolling eased. But the boat floated ominously low in the water.

Joey evacuated his crewmen as first priority. When the boat appeared momentarily stable, he himself went back to save what he could of his fragile, expensive electronics equipment. With the others helping, he passed what he could grab across the gunnel to the *Sea Fox*. First the color plotter. The survival suit, with its necessarily clumsy construction and three-fingered hands, was impossible to work in. "Three fingered things, you can't do nothing," Joey declared. "I took my arms out, zipped it up halfway, kept moving. And then I heard Joe Squirril that was up in the bow of the *Sea Fox*, he yelled 'Joey, the stern's awash.' And I seen the water coming up. I was just working to get my telephone off, and I looked, the water was up to the pilothouse where I was working, so I said that's it, enough, and got off."

The *Peter & Linda* sank within another couple of minutes. The men crowding aboard the *Sea Fox* watched it go down. Its deck lights were still shining as the port and starboard running lights submerged. Then the water shorted the batteries and they exploded. Quietly, the rest of the darkened boat slipped beneath the water. It had hit the rock only fifteen to twenty minutes before.

They waited, with the Coast Guard nearby, numb with the shock of it, until dawn. It was a circumstance where no one thinks less of a man for weeping. Nothing remained visible of the *Peter & Linda* except its highest antenna. The boat had settled into fifty feet of water.

Ironically, the fault was a small human error on the sophisticated electronic plotter. Each course change from the harbor to the ground was programmed by code letters, and Bobby had inadvertently skipped one of the letters.

What happens to a man after his boat sinks? The *Peter & Linda* had a wooden hull, and so was uninsured. A month later, Joey was able to say, "It was hard. It was hard that morning. But now . . . been trying to cut my losses, just start again. Start practically from scratch. I've done it before, so I'll do it again." He laughed a little. Somebody could have drowned, things could have been worse.

For starters, Joe had a diver friend. By the next day, he had received back from the sea floor his glasses and key ring, and his charts and logbook marked with the irreplaceable observations of many years' experience, as well as the compass, the running lights, and a multitude of other objects that could be loosened. Later the diver salvaged all the detachable gear, including the new pair trawl nets and rigging.

The remains underwater proved how hard the stern had been pounded. Only a few months before, Joe had put on a new rudder and rudder post with heavy steel plate. "All that was torn off, just torn off." Most of the wooden hull was in good shape, but the deck had split open, apparently from the pressure of trapped air as the boat sank, and the pilothouse had fallen through the deck.

The plans to pair trawl with Tommy on the *Sea Fox* did not die. With the gear salvaged, they rigged it up on the *Linda* B for further trials. ("Can't I come along to watch?" asked John, whose boat was being usurped. "Maybe later," said his brothers. There is much to be said for fishermen who belong to large families that stay together.) Joey, a respected highline skipper, had just finished paying all his debts on the *Peter & Linda*, and credit waited for him at the bank for another boat.

Meanwhile he began to work on deck for Tommy aboard the *Sea Fox*. Shoveling fish lost him a few pounds, and a few weeks after the sinking he declared, "I feel good, feel great." It suited him fine, for a while, to bring fish aboard while somebody else worried about where to drop the net. As for Munza and Bobby, Joe Testaverde's crewmen were known quantities, welcome to fill in when other boats need a man. Munza made week-long runs to Georges Bank on a trip boat, but he hated the long absences from home. "Hurry up and get a boat," he told Joey whenever he saw him. "I'm dyin' out there."

The *Peter & Linda* has joined the ghostly community of sunken hulls and dreams carried to the bottom, decaying slowly, an X on the computerized plotters. The same issue of *Commercial Fisheries News* that wrote about this accident reported three other sinkings in New England fishing waters from July 20 to August 8, as well as a deck fire that forced a crew to abandon ship. Even fishing in calmer summer waters carries no automatic security.

Joey now has another boat, and the pair trawling venture with his brother continues. The new boat has a wooden hull like the late *Peter & Linda* and the other boats in the fleet of his community. "To tell the truth, I like wood; I like the feel of wood." And he has started making boat payments again from scratch. This is how fragile life can be on a fish deck. Salve Testaverde's sons never doubted it.

5

The Newfoundland
Grand Banks

I ronically, it was a British writer, Rudyard Kipling, who implanted
the image of Yankee cod fisherman most deeply in our minds with
his novel *Captains Courageous*. (Or was it Lionel Barrymore as the
lovable snarling skipper Disco in that memorable old movie version
that was true to the book only when convenient?) Kipling's fishermen
hailed from Gloucester, and "bankers" they called themselves like the
Labrador schoonermen, with whom they shared grounds on the
legendary Grand Banks off Newfoundland, Canada. Their eighty-
seven-foot schooner *We're Here* spent from May to December on the
Grand Banks—"a triangle two hundred and fifty miles on each side—
a waste or wallowing sea, cloaked with dank fog, vexed with gales,
harried with drifting ice, scored by the tracks of the reckless liners,
and dotted with the sails of the fishing fleet."

Covering 139,000 square miles, the Grand Banks are much larger
than Georges Bank off New England and Hamilton Bank off Labrador
combined. The vast submerged plateau of the banks comprises four
separate areas divided by deeper ocean gullies—Whale Bank, South-
east Shoal, Saint-Pierre Bank, and Green Bank. Depths range from
seventeen to fifty fathoms, compared to some ninety fathoms in the
gullies. A downward slope beyond the hundred fathom line quickly
plunges two thousand fathoms in a virtual wall to the deep ocean.

Each bank has its own surface and bottom characteristics that fishermen working them have mastered. The main body of fishermen—whether aboard sailing schooners that dropped two-man dories over the side or on today's large steel trawlers—have always concentrated their efforts around a central shoal area called the Virgin Rocks. Here lie the shallowest waters where fish congregate in the greatest numbers, and here the boats come to take their chances despite the dangers.

The waters around the Virgin Rocks are the most perilous on the Banks, since some of the area's submerged pinnacles lie only two or three fathoms beneath the surface. Its name reflects the early dominance of the Portuguese and Spaniards on the Banks: Mediterranean Catholics who invoked their most protective deity in naming the area. The Virgin Rocks area is shallow enough to reveal an awesome thrust of gleaming wet stone in the foaming water during heavy North Atlantic storms, pinnacles that even in mere choppy weather can rip the bottom from a ship. If ocean water preserved human bones, the Grand Banks seafloor would be littered with them, especially around Virgin Rocks, from men gone under when wind kicked up killer seas over the ocean shallows, or when water of the frigid Labrador current hit the warm Gulf Stream to create fogs that separated dorymen from their ships.

Until Canada declared two-hundred-mile jurisdiction of its resources in 1977 and claimed the Grand Banks its own, they were a gathering place for some of the Atlantic community's hardiest men. Fishermen are not the sort to keep diaries, so we can only speculate about the Basque fishermen who may have wandered there to fill their boats with cod long before Columbus rediscovered the New World (following the Leif Eriksson voyages and temporary Norse colonization circa A.D. 1000). The Englishman John Cabot returned from his 1497 expedition to report such an abundance of codfish off Newfoundland that his men scooped them up in baskets. It is certain that Cabot's report uncorked the bottle. With Catholic Europe providing a stable market for dried and salted fish on Fridays, the Lenten weeks, and abstinence days, a large and adventuresome fishing fleet was already in existence and had established itself as far west as Iceland. Following Cabot's news, hundreds of these boats from England, Portugal, Spain, and France converged on the Newfoundland banks.

[68]

Apparently the polyglot fleets liked what they found, because nets and lines have been dropped on the Grand Banks ever since. The men of different nations may have competed and quarreled with each other, but they all brought home fish. In the decade before 1977, big Soviet, German, and Polish factory trawlers dominated the area. Now medium-sized Canadian trawlers own the grounds.

The Portuguese became particularly identified with this area over the centuries. These men left a sunny homeland each year by the thousands to pass the prime years of their lives working in wet and cold under gray skies. Fishing on the Banks supported entire villages. Until 1952, the Portuguese clung to their traditional method, routine in the old days but long since abandoned by other fishermen who found it too dangerous, of working the Virgins from open dories. Their ships, collectively called the White Fleet, were a common presence along the quay of the closest port, St. John's in Newfoundland. However, when Canada's two-hundred-mile declaration in 1977 ended most foreign fishing on the Banks, the Portuguese were unable to negotiate any treaty that allowed them back. They had to leave the grounds where their countrymen's bones lay in profusion and where, if the ghosts of the drowned float restlessly, their unheard conversations are conducted primarily in Portuguese.

The Yankees were the new kids on the block when they arrived on the Grand Banks in the early seventeenth century. But by Kipling's time Gloucester schooners had for at least two centuries made their professional home both on Georges Bank, within a few dozen miles of port, and on the distant Grand Banks a thousand miles from home.

The prosaic account survives of a Gloucester man's trip to the Grand Banks in 1816 aboard the *Mary Elizabeth*, a topsail schooner of 113 tons that even then was referred to as "one of the old-time Bankers." The crew of twelve men left Gloucester on the first of April, and were gone ninety days. They fished with hand lines, on board the vessel (the practice of dory fishing had not yet been adopted by the fleet) "and caught 17,000 codfish in number. . . . The *Mary Elizabeth* had the high quarter deck peculiar to the Bankers, divided below into three compartments, the forward part used for the storage of fishing gear etc, the middle compartment as a pantry and kitchen, in which they cooked and ate, and the after part called the steerage where they lived and slept."

When the schooner arrived on the Bank,

they made everything as snug as possible, taking down the topsail and topgallant yards and lashing them across the stern. . . . Made 2,500 quintals [a hundred-pound weight] dry fish, the crew realizing as their share $24 for each thousand fish caught. . . . Her outfits were principally ship-bread, beans, rice, a little flour, some beef and pork, molasses, tea, and coffee, and some rum. Fish and beans and beef, with ship-bread, were the principal articles of diet, but on Sunday morning they would have fried pancakes—about half a bushel being required to go the rounds—as a sort of holiday treat, as they invariably refrained from fishing on Sunday. [Taken from *The Fishermen's Own Book* published 1882 in Gloucester.]

Kipling wrote a livelier description of the 1880s' scene on the Grand Banks (which, incidentally, he never saw himself):

There must have been nearly a hundred [anchored schooners] of every possible make and build, with, far away, a square-rigged Frenchman, all bowing and courtesying one to the other. From every boat dories were dropping away like bees from a crowded hive, and the clamour of voices, the rattling of ropes and blocks, and the splash of the oars carried for miles across the heaving water. The sails turned all colours, black, pearly-gray, and white, as the sun mounted; and more boats swung up through the mists to southward. The dories gathered in clusters, separated, reformed, and broke again, all heading one way; while men hailed and whistled and cat-called and sang, and the water was speckled with rubbish thrown overboard.

St. John's may be the closest city to the Grand Banks, but the fleets of Canadian draggers that now harvest most of the stocks have their homes in smaller places of good harbor where they can deliver to a local fish plant. Such places, fishing villages called "outports," are the home of most Grand Banks fishermen these days as well as fishermen who work closer to shore. Outports dot the rocky coast. They are the heart and soul of Newfoundland, the large Canadian island that provides North America's easternmost landfall in the Atlantic Ocean.

Before heading for the Grand Banks, I visited outport with fishermen on the small island of Fogo off the east Newfoundland coast. No place on earth is more oriented to fishing. In the village of Fogo—others of the six villages include Joe Batts Arm and Seldom Come By—I roomed at Mrs. Emma Payne's boardinghouse on a hill overlooking the harbor. I fished with Lloyd Payne and his two brothers (no relation to Emma) who lived in houses just down the rocks. Each morning before light, we putt-putted out several miles in their small "longliner" (the generic name Newfoundlanders give a fishing boat large enough to have a cabin), and by daybreak had lines in the water to jig for cod.

The September weather was raw and chilly without being rough. In a cabin the size of a large box, Tom, the youngest brother, boiled water on a single-burner propane stove as we bounced over choppy seas to the fishing ground. Wrapping our hands around the hot mugs, we managed to keep them warm, but the cold still numbed my feet and then penetrated everywhere else. We anchored at a spot that Lloyd triangulated by eye from the points of some low outer islands, dropped hooks thirty feet to the bottom, and waited for the single sharp tug that announced a fish.

There was no action. Everett and Tom pulled the anchor and Lloyd moved a few hundred feet for another sounding. On the fourth try the limp lines suddenly jerked to life. Up came one gray-green cod, then another, gasping briefly before becoming still. Soon the fish piled around our ankles and then our legs; the effort of pulling them aboard started the blood pumping agreeably.

At the end of the day, we headed in, with quiet jokes while gutting the catch. (We were up to our thighs in cod and happy to be, even though the chill of the fish penetrated our boots, oilskin pants, wool trousers, and thermals.) The gray sky turned to orange streaks against the low rocky land. It was dark by the time we reached the co-op fish plant, tossed the fish to the pier, lined up at a table to finish the gutting and heading, and returned home across the harbor.

While cleaning, everyone sliced himself a mess of "tongues", the meaty flesh from the cod throats. When I brought mine to Mrs. Payne, she fried them specially, and explained to the other guests around the table in her kitchen that the dish was only for Mr. McCloskey who had caught them himself. Cod tongues, each the size of a mouthful, have the richness of sweetbreads and the chewy consistency of clams. Like clams, they only look appetizing if you know the pleasure that awaits their consumption. None of the guests seemed to feel deprived in light of Mrs. Payne's caribou stew.

A generation ago, Fogo Islanders were considered by Ottawa bureaucrats to be a vanishing race. When Newfoundland became a province of Canada in 1949, the new government, trying for practical reasons to simplify the administrative and welfare structure within its new charge, pressured the inhabitants of the remotest outports to abandon and relocate. Closing local schools and subsidized fish plants became one of the most persuasive means of emptying a community that depended solely on its fishing. They did it in Fogo. The Fogo Islanders resisted, and the resistance so banded them together that they formed their own fishery cooperative. Contrary to bureaucratic predictions, the co-op succeeded. It is still going strong, now a model for similar enterprises, with a central fish plant at Seldom and some smaller ones around the island for local deliveries.

Fogo Island has little that could be called fancy even by the standards of remote Newfoundland. Emma and John Payne might have running water for the boardinghouse, but many in the village fetch their water in buckets attached to a woolen yoke held across the shoulders. There is electricity, however, and television too, thanks to satellite technology, which has permitted truly remote communities everywhere to make a single leap into the twentieth century despite the otherwise primitive conditions.

Every night at the boardinghouse, the living room, filled with stuffed chairs, velveteen decorations, and shelves of knickknacks, became a gathering place for guests who came to watch the TV. Discussions flowed above the noise of series sitcoms that had aired years earlier in the United States, or BBC educational programs conducted with scholarly interviews. On Sunday nights and prayer meeting nights, Mrs. Payne herself was scarce, but John Payne always occupied his particular lounge chair and led the conversation. When it grew late—say around 9:00—the guests retired after politely waiting a turn to use the bathroom. In the small house, in a village with no other accommodations, only on rare nights could a guest expect a room to himself; sometimes even beds had to be shared.

Mrs. Payne once ordered a drunken guest to pack and move out as the rest of us looked discreetly at our plates, but most fared better. One rainy evening, in from the boat, I piled my oilskins, a soggy wool shirt, and other fishy garments on the floor of the enclosed boot porch. Next day, with the sun shining (though it was too rough to go fishing in a small longliner), I could not find them. Thieves, on Fogo? I asked Mrs. Payne and she said seriously, "Yer oilers? De gools |gulls| must 'a took 'em." Everything had been washed and hung flapping in the wind, back of the shed out of sight, a fact that she left me to discover for myself.

On the night before leaving Fogo to board a Grand Banks trawler in another outport, the wind howled as it slammed rain against the windows. The rain continued in gray sheets during breakfast. The ferry at Seldom Come By was several miles away and I had no car. Fortunately, a salesman with whom I had shared a room was also leaving. He was a regular visitor to Mrs. Payne's when he came over every few months to service the small dry-goods stores of the island communities. We might have saved ourselves the rush across the rocky, marshy heart of the island. With wind blowing heavy over the channel, the ferry did not leave for four hours—and we were lucky that it left at all, since as autumn deepened there were many days when the ferry could make no trips at all because of ice. In winter, the ferry could run only in the wake of an icebreaker.

The ferry reached the mainland and my salesman friend took me as far as he went. I spent the rest of the day hitchhiking. Rain poured down occasionally, but most of the time the grey sky produced only a drizzle too piddling to bother a fisherman. The scenery was typical of Newfoundland's austere beauty a few miles from the coast, where rock remains the dominant material but greenery has succeeded in taking hold. Stands of aspen and small spruce grew in mossy beds settled in the gray rock, and their branches reflected in ponds of dark water trapped in rock hollows.

At dusk, two weary men, with the odor of the boats about them, gave me a few miles' lift in their clanking truck. They had been jigging for squid in an open punt since 2:00 A.M., this being the season when the little multitentacled creatures crowded into the bays. Until the late 1970s, all the squid went for bait, but now, they said, the Japanese were willing to pay a shocking price for split and cured squid. So the Newfoundland men harvested squid day after day, and the women hung them out to dry like draped laundry over lines, fences, and racks. Squid had become a cottage industry, thanks to the Japanese. The men who picked me up were headed home for a rest before going out to their punt again at 2:00 A.M.

It was to the village of Catalina that I headed to join the trawler Zamora for a trip to the Banks as a passenger. Catalina is located on the tip of the Bonavista Peninsula, one of several hundred-mile arms of rocky land that, jutting from the nucleus of the main island, extend the Newfoundland coastline to catch the seas and winds from all directions.

Fifty miles from Catalina it grew dark and began to rain in earnest. Hitchhiking holds little promise anywhere after nightfall. I waited two hours by the roadside until a bus passed going my way. In the dark bus, a thick-muscled young man made room on his seat, found a rack for my knapsack, and assured me my wetness wasn't going to melt him. Newfoundlanders are easy with conversation. I soon learned that he worked on a dragger of the sort I was headed to board, and that he had just passed a few days in St. John's between trips.

Before he got off to walk the mile home from the road, we talked about change. "And they *have* been changes for we, b'y," he declared. (Everyone around the Newfoundland boats calls each other "boy" familiarly, or "skipper" with more reserve.) "T'was bad conditions and worse money until just a few years ago in me own time." Then in 1971 fishermen throughout Newfoundland formed a union. "Now look at me fadder. Dragger-man same as me, hurt his hand on deck in March-month and here its September, drawing three hundred dollars a month sick pay. Nothing of that before the union, b'y, guarantee." Of course, it was still a hardship for the old man, since he could have expected to be making three to five times that much fishing.

The bad weather continued next morning, blowing enough that the Catalina office of Fishery Products International delayed the *Zamora's* projected 10:00 A.M. departure until at least midafternoon. The fish plant next to the office was one of the largest in the world despite its remote location, a testament to the rich harvest on the Grand Banks. To enter, one was required to walk through a trough containing several inches of a sterilizing liquid (everyone wore boots) and to wash hands in disinfectant. The long, brightly lit factory room contained an odor of fish tempered by the diligently clean smell of ammonia. Any fish boat deck, however hosed down and cleansed by the wash of the sea, was a dirty place compared to this.

Workers in white caps and plastic aprons stood on gratings above the general flow of water characteristic of seafood plants, occupying rows beside conveyor belts that carried fish and fillets. Most factory operations require that participants be stationary by the machines that contribute to their work, and this gives them a look of surreal impersonality, However, each individual in this organized army stood at his own table. On the initial lines, men cut pink-white fillets from recognizable fat cod, and on others men and women trimmed rough edges and discolorations. Hands with sharp knives sliced as diligently as machines, and the faces had the concentrated, empty look of people doing the same job over and over. But when the light flashed from my camera, the place suddenly exploded with laughs and catcalls as the subject of the picture grinned and blushed. The workers, in fact, all produced as individuals, putting their finished product in a named basket that was weighed and credited to them. The foreman wrote the quality of the product beside the weight tabulation. Paychecks reflected this judgment as well as the quantity produced.

The operation extended into rooms beyond, where others breaded the fillets or laid them together in the long hand-size boxes that would end up with bright fish labels in grocery store freezers. At the other end of the cycle flopping, glistening fish thumped in a spray of ice onto the belts from white plastic bins loaded in the holds of boats moored at the piers outside. As in all factories, time clocks recorded everyone's comings and goings, and a whistle announced rest periods, lunch break, and quitting time.

Catalina had little but the fish plant and a few houses. When lunch break sounded, the workers hung up their aprons and streamed out to their cars and trucks. One of the filleters—a quiet man who had plainly enjoyed my earlier picture taking as his knife continued to fly over the fish—gave me a ride across the peninsula to Bonavista, the largest town in the area. Five little ones he had, yes b'y, he said when questioned, and no going to sea on a stinkin' fish boat for he.

Back upstairs in the Fishery Products office, Pat Antle, captain of the trawler *Zamora*, lumbered in at about 5:00 P.M., growled hello, shouldered my knapsack before I could take it, and gestured for me to follow. He strode through the office area bantering and settling final business, then continued down a back stair, past loading docks saturated with the smell of fish. Several crewmen converged from other directions, talking little. Their normal two-day layover had been extended by the storm. It was not the kind of day when going to sea was a pleasure.

Aboard the *Zamora*, the men stowed new lines and chafing gear, battened for sea, and headed out. Squall spray soon put a haze over the low buildings of Catalina. By the time we passed a white lighthouse on the rocky coast, the water was whitecapping and the ship had settled into a steady roll that was to last most of the trip.

In the wheelhouse, Captain Antle set his course, then braced himself in a raised swivel chair and started a series of sideband calls to sister ships on the grounds. With the distortion of seagoing radio, the thick Newfie brogue—the product of an amalgam of dialects originally from Ireland, Cornwall, and Devon—could have been a foreign tongue to my American ears.

Leonard Pardy, the mate, a solid, vigorous, friendly man in his mid-thirties, jumped between the wheelhouse and deck, setting things straight for the night. Below on the mess deck, the cook, a lean bald man with a grin that seldom left him, served up a heavy chow of salt meat, potatoes, and boiled greens—the sort of meal with which to meet seasickness head-on, win or lose.

I bunked with Pardy, taking the curtained upper berth in his small, neat cabin. The Norwegian yard that had built the *Zamora* had inexplicably set her bunks beam to beam rather than fore and aft, so that every roll brought blood to the head. It was a restless night.

On the grounds next morning at the eastern edge of the Grand Banks, the motion eased. Pardy had held the mid-to-six watch on the bridge, but when the siren sounded to make the set he left his bunk automatically. On the wide enclosed deck aft of the cabins and galley, the men of the watch "rubbered up" in their foul weather clothing, then climbed to the open deck above. The rain slanted in as they started the cod end of the net down the stern ramp along with its multicolored chafing gear. There was a brief halt when they discovered a hole in the thick green web. Pardy and the bosun mended it with needles that worked furiously fast. Soon the noise of chain and metal balls scraping steel rattled through the ship as the rest of the net went over with its attendant hardware. Pardy returned to bed, and the watch settled around a mess table to read, doze, or play cards.

The ship carried thirteen men. A deck watch consisted of five or six, with the schedules staggered so that each man worked eight hours on, four off. The officers—captain, mate, chief engineer, and second engineer—followed a six-on, six-off pattern. Only the captain was immune from turning-to on deck.

Below on the mess deck, the men told me they received fifty-one dollars a day (Canadian) whether there were fish or not, but that with a good captain like Antle no one ever needed to call the company on a guaranteed minimum. Their pay averaged thirty-two thousand dollars a year. Echoing the man on the bus, they said that no such security had ever existed for Newfoundland fisherman before the formation of the provincewide fisherman's union.

At length, the siren gave a rasping whir, and everyone dressed for deck. The warps were already paying in, activated by Captain Pat in the wheelhouse. When the bag emerged up the stern ramp, it was medium-fat, with fish heads poking from the green mesh. An okay haul, said the captain: about four thousand pounds. The mass was emptied directly below through a chute opened on deck. We shot the trawl again, and then everyone went to the sheltered deck below to dress fish, and ice them.

The next haul was six thousand pounds. Along with cod and flounder were big flat skate fish, which we returned to sea through the scuppers at our feet along with the offal. The hauls increased as the weather calmed. One weighed twelve thousand pounds. The biggest arrived in the middle of the second day—fifteen thousand pounds. All hands from both watches turned-to, gutting fish, except the captain holding the bridge. I stood next to Pardy the mate, who again had lost his sleep. We joked and talked a bit, but the engine noise was too loud for any steady conversation.

The work was endless. Each time we gutted through a pile, another tumbled into place from the mountain of fish stuffed down the trapdoor from the deck. Cold seawater from hoses and scuppers sloshed over our boots. My hands began to cramp so that it became hard to grasp the fish by their heads while taking care that the quick sharp knife didn't lop off a finger. It was far more monotonous than the heavy but varied work on smaller fishing boats.

Toward the end, Bill the cook left the line to start chow. It was time for fancy stuff—thick pork chops. We hosed ourselves down and stuffed on the run, with the siren already sounding for the next set coming aboard.

After three days of mild seas (it was never calm) and rewarding hauls, a new storm blew over us. Then it left, taking the fish with it for a time—at least the big hauls. Added to the renewed heavy roll was a sour smell of fish offal that had gradually permeated all the work areas no matter how thoroughly they had been washed down. Un doubtedly, I noticed it more than the others. The hectic push had ended, everyone caught his full sleep, and monotony set in.

[77]

All fishermen experience stretches of boredom, when the work halts due to a storm, quota restrictions, or empty waters. However, a large ship that stays at sea for long periods, with regular watches, has a built-in monotony that is not as evident on smaller fishing boats where the whole crew works together on a more varied schedule. It might be called the assembly-line syndrome. It would be false to pretend that men who fish for a living do so for other than economic reasons. Yet, on small inshore boats, from Norway to North America to Japan, I have felt included in a difficult but decent way of life whose participants are content. The large deep-sea fishing ships of several nationalities that I have visited are different: their men seem to turn listless and restless after a while.

Aboard the *Zamora*, no crew could have been more friendly. But several men sought me out for conversation with more than hospitality on their minds. They regarded me wistfully, as if I held the key to better things. "Not much of a life, is it, skipper?" said one of the senior deck men matter-of-factly on a dark wet morning as we steadied our cups to keep the coffee from sloshing out. He had started his career aboard a Grand Banks schooner under sail, fishing from a dory. No, he wouldn't want to go back to those hard poverty days without guaranteed pay and warm modern ships. But . . .

Another of the men, born in a fishing outport and now equally committed to deepwater ships rather than inshore boats, asked, "Do you like the sea, b'y, eh?" It was a rolling day, with salt beef and potatoes heavy on my stomach, and I was far from certain, but I replied, "Sure, don't you?" His face, rough and weathered, had a guarded, sensitive, apologetic smile. "No, boy. Not anymore."

One night we had just shot the net, following a near-empty haul, and with no fish to clean everyone on watch had gone below to doze on the mess deck during the one- to two-hour tow. In the wheelhouse, the radio crackled with voices from other ships fishing the area. Suddenly, the captain jumped to attention and hurried to find locations on his chart. The thick brogues, along with the sputtering and distortion of the radio, made it difficult for me to understand the details, but clearly a fire had started in another ship's engine room. Pat sounded the siren and shouted to the men who appeared on deck to haul in the net, then took his microphone and announced to the ship in trouble that that he was forty miles away and headed over. Pardy, who had gone to bed, appeared on the bridge zipping his pants. He immediately began plotting fixes on the chart and laying course.

Fire is akin to sinking for a seafarer, because it leaves no place to go. The ship in trouble was the *Zelia*, a sister trawler. Everyone turned alert and tense. The *Zelia* men were the *Zamora* men's neighbors. By the time the cod end of the net reached the ramp, we were nosing into the seas at full speed. The men lashed down the net and other deck gear for a rough passage, then gathered on the bridge to listen to the radio. The bow pitched and dark seas slammed against the windows.

A half hour later, the captain of the *Zelia* announced that he had gained control over the fire. Most of the crewmen laughed off their relief and disappeared below. We retraced our course and, having lost a few hours, started fishing again.

Two days later, as we neared port, a sudden new alertness passed through the ship. The work was finished, the hold was full of iced fish, and the gear lay on deck in a limp, orderly heap of orange nets and big grey bobbins. Everyone drifted to the wheelhouse to watch the landfall at Cape Race and then the coastline leading home. Men with a nine-day stubble and a look of perpetual tiredness, who had worn the same rough clothes all trip, suddenly emerged from below clean shaven, wearing pressed pants, and looking ten years younger. The mate's cabin smelled of detergent from a complete scrubbing he gave the bulkheads. Shortly thereafter, the sweet odor of aftershave filled the small room.

It was as if spring had arrived after a long winter. The sun shone overhead, and the water sparkled blue, although by midnight the weather had turned foggy. The cook served a final meal, scrubbed down, and locked away the food. As we entered the harbor and tied to the pier of the Fishery Products plant, wives and children waved. Pat moored the ship smoothly, snapped off the electronic equipment, left the bridge, and before long walked across the gangway and disappeared into the dark of the plant complex. The men locked their cabin doors on oilskins and greasy coveralls, and came ashore with little more than handbags. Within minutes, a company watchman had sole charge of the ship.

6

Smokey on the Labrador

The northern Labrador coast consists of islands and inlets built of rock, great boulders of it that disappear into black water. Harsh, cold winds prevail for most of the year from the ice fields and glaciers further north. Most vegetation stays close to the rocks—marshy mosses, tart orange berries, and small, exquisite, vulnerable flowers. Wiry bushes bear leaves the size of thumbtacks in a climate that supports no effulgence, and tight, short-limbed spruce trees labor for generations to reach a height of a dozen feet. Harbors freeze solid in the winter, and winter lasts from mid-October through mid-May or later.

It was this coast that the Viking Leif Eriksson bypassed in A.D. 1000 for an easier one to the south, dismissing it with the accurate name "Land of Stones," and which the Frenchman Jacques Cartier in 1534 called "the land God gave to Cain" as he, too, went exploring more hospitable places. By Cartier's time, however, the Labrador waters had become cod and whale grounds for fishermen from England, Portugal, and the Basque regions of Spain and France. It was the stony land itself that Europeans left to the nomadic Indians and Eskimos.

Europeans began to settle permanently only two centuries ago, when the Hudson's Bay Company established trading posts in some of the coastal inlets. The rock shore and long winters have never supported large numbers of people. The northern Labrador coast still has a mere five year-round communities, and the southern coast only a few more, none with more than a few hundred permanent residents. The total year-round population is only ten thousand. This population traditionally swells with Newfoundlander fishermen from the south during the few weeks of summer after the ice melts, as first the salmon swim home to their spawning rivers and then the cod appear in world-class abundance from the long continental shelf called Hamilton Bank, which parallels the coast a few miles to sea.

It was mid-August, a stormy day too rough for a ship to maneuver comfortably among the multitude of islands that guarded the coast like big rock bunkers. The 215-foot coastal steamer *Bonavista* bellowed its whistle several times, stopped engines, and waited. No buildings were visible among the empty waterways to warrant stopping. Wind chopped the water and rain gusted slantwise, as white petrels with black underbodies planed easily a few feet from the surface and a whale spouted seaward. A few individuals lined the rail with bags and boxes, ready to depart, but most of the hundred-plus passengers continued eating big ham-and-egg breakfasts in the dining room. The majority were Labrador regulars riding their summer bus line, and this was only Smokey, a routine stop on the three-day trip south from Nain to the principal Labrador town of Goose Bay.

Presently, a skiff powered by an outboard motor appeared from among the rocks, leaving a wake as it bounced over the choppy waves. Two men stood the whole trip, balancing with the ease of those born to boats as spray and rain streamed glistening down their oilskins. A woman sat on the center thwart—the only one clear of boxes and plastic buckets—with limp, gutted cod swishing around her boots.

Other skiffs began to emerge from a cut in the rocks. On ship, two crewmen hand-lowered a gangway attached to the side. As the first skiff surged level with the platform at the base of the gangway, one of the men jumped to it casually. He had not shaved recently, and from the look of his grease-rimmed woolen collar he might not have changed or bathed either. His face had the leanness of a man who ate only as necessary, but he appeared healthy and good-humored.

The woman, about thirty, handed over a scuffed suitcase and several heavy-seeming plastic buckets. Her face was scrubbed and round—not fat—with hair tied in a neat bun except for a strand or two, and a black straw hat pinned on top. A simple, clean dress

[82]

showed beneath her parka. A young steward came down the suspended gangway to help. As they all walked up the clanging rungs, the couple began chatting with friends at the rails—as if they had last seen them five minutes before rather than probable months—about the state of the fishing and the ripeness of the local berries called bakeapples.

Soon, a community of skiffs had clustered gunnel to gunnel around the platform. Meanwhile, the man who remained in the first skiff drifted alongside the ship to its cargo deck. He tossed up a bowline, which one of the passengers caught handily and secured, then loaded his boxes into a cargo net that a crewman lowered, and received down several long boards.

At the platform, which dipped in and out of the water with the ship's motion, people waited turns with their boats, or passed packages hand to hand and then followed themselves. One boat maneuvered as close as it could, others giving way, and an older man aboard negotiated the bobbing gunnels to the gangway. He moved with authority, even across the shifting boats, his eminence clear from the necktie beneath his rain jacket and from the briefcase in his hand. He proceeded straight to the wheelhouse (restricted to passengers), and soon after appeared on the bridge wing chatting with the captain.

"Don't mess with that fellow, now," muttered one passenger appreciatively, with a knowledgeable, sidewise jerk of his head. "Hard ticket he is and no joke, guarantee."

The woman from the first skiff went below to buy a ticket from the purser, who, wearing a braided cap and puffing on a pipe, opened his little caged window for the purpose. No beds were available for the remaining night of the trip, unfortunately. She did not appear upset. Last seen she had found a place on a bench in the small lounge and was knitting as she chatted about good bucketfuls of the tart orange bakeapples, but until the boats left she stayed on deck. Her husband went to the open door of the galley, took off his wool cap, and peered in without entering. Soon the cook, his muscular arms bare despite the chill, emerged to negotiate for the fish in the skiff. They made a deal, and the man hauled up the fish by bucket and rope.

After visiting the captain, the man with the briefcase returned to the gangway where people took turns approaching him. He stood with legs apart, sturdy but with the appearance of a slight stoop

[83]

under floppy scuffed oilskins, his tie squeezed against a neck beginning to gather folds. The Labrador weather plays enough on faces
that his age could have been anywhere between fifty-five and eighty.
His face had the knobbiness of a wood carving in which the knife
cannot cut fine details. It seemed a face used to authority, not
accustomed to smiling, one with an expression that might be called a
scowl, yet not unpleasant. " 'Ow you gettin on with the fish?" he
asked one man from the skiffs; "Okay, my love" he said to a woman
with a long-winded tale. He paid a fish settlement to the man in the
first skiff—who handed part of the money to his wife—commenting
in a wiry voice that gathered a chuckle from those listening: "What
the hell, it's 'alf for livin and 'alf for the other 'alf, eh?"

"That's Baxter Parsons, of course," explained the captain. "In
Smokey here, he's the man, been around most of the two decades I've
sailed the coast." Parsons managed the fish buying station of the J. W.
Hiscock Company that included the only store, saltery, telephone,
and post office within fifty sea miles. "A few years ago, now, when the
Russians were scraping the cod clean, out on Hamilton Bank, there'd
been no Smokey for the few boats wanted to try a living but for Baxter
and Hiscock's. Now it's all changed a bit, although Baxter still runs
his share. The share's just no longer a hundred percent, you see."

Within twenty minutes, the host of skiffs had exchanged passengers and cargo. The *Bonavista*'s engine started throbbing again, the
whistle bellowed, people waved and called between the rail and the
skiffs, and off the ship went. Her black smoke rose above the rock
islands for a while, but quickly the slanting rain wiped all traces. Her
next stop would be Indian Harbor, an alternative bay for fishermen on
the same island as Smokey.

The skiffs from Smokey rounded a cape and some of the life behind
the seaward rocks revealed itself. They passed a black-hulled ship
larger than the coastal steamer, the Portuguese processor *Sao Goncalinho*, waiting to buy fish. Most proceeded further through sheltered
waterways, to the pier and cluster of buildings at Baxter Parsons' fish
station, or to the enclave beyond this where a government barge
floated at anchor. The barge had been placed there to provide
services to fishermen and a mooring for tenders from fish plants in
other locations along the coast. There were no fishing boats to be
seen, however, since they had all put to sea several hours earlier to
reach the grounds by first light.

Fogo Island, Newfoundland. Everett Payne, left, guides a brailerful of cod aboard the longliner he owns with his brothers.

The ship rolls aboard a Grand Banks trawler. All hands grab lines to steady the raised net and its shaggy chafing gear.

A bag of flounder and cod comes aboard the *Zamora*.

Newfoundlander crewmen of the trawler *Zamora*.

Although most permanent residents of coastal Labrador live by fishing, Smokey is a traditional enclave of fishermen from the island of Newfoundland to the south. Administratively, both entities are part of Canada's Newfoundland Province, but the 42,000-square-mile island bears the name and holds legislative control over the 112,000 square miles of Labrador. In the summer, whole colonies of fishermen bring their boats north—"down to the Labrador"—from such Newfoundland outports as Shoe Cove, Fogo, Twillingate, Griquet, and Cook's Harbor. Smokey/Indian Harbor has for generations been one of their major gathering places. The Newfoundlanders come in fishing boats of a seagoing size, between forty and sixty-five feet long, which they generically call "longliners." They also come aboard the coastal steamers, their skiffs transported on deck, often as whole families, to occupy shacks ashore like those around the Hiscock station in Smokey.

I left my bags at the government barge while I waited for the longliners to return. A small coastal ship was unloading some machinery and drums of oil. The skiff people, such a lively presence out at the steamer, seemed to have disappeared. A couple had beached in front of some shacks on a ridge a half mile across the water, and their distant figures could be seen picking seaweed from a long net and mending it. It remained quiet until early afternoon. Then one by one the fishing boats began to return. Several tied to the barge and the men aboard began pitching their fish, already gutted, from bins on the open deck into the hold of a waiting tender. The limp carcasses flew through the air and landed with a steady flop as the men joked in their staccato outport brogues.

I joined the sixty-three-foot wooden longliner *Sealer* when it arrived. It was skippered by Cyril Oxford of Green Bay in Newfoundland. Cyril owned the boat equally with his dad, sixty-year-old Maxwell Oxford, who had fished out of Smokey and Indian Harbor for forty years. Claude Weir, a neighbor's boy, completed the crew. They came in late, having first delivered to the *Sao Goncalinho*. As soon as they moored, Claude jumped into the skiff attached to their buoy and, with barely a flip of the bailing can to remove the worst of the rainy bilge around his legs, started the outboard motor and sputtered off toward the Hiscock station a mile down the water.

"Poor boy, sweet toot's near to explode," said Cyril, as he handed his dad the engine's power-takeoff attachment from a trapdoor beneath the wheel. He was a muscular man in his forties, body close to the ground, face sunny and thick-featured as a Toby jug. They were anchored together with others from their outport, and soon a heavy thump on the deck boards outside announced some neighbors come to visit.

An oil leak in the engine became the evening's project, with everybody's hands greasy and no lack of advice or opinion. New-foundlanders have their own way of speaking: The words flow fast with unnecessary syllables often skipped and the easiest pronunciation used. A literal transcription on paper appears more exotic than the actual flow, but then, to an ear unaccustomed, the rapid flow can become a foreign language. Cyril spoke while puzzling out the reassembly of the power-takeoff: "Now, I 'tinks dis'll change the rotation, see? 'E's on the motor, 'e's dere like dat now, so, he's gotta turn this way, so watch your finger. Dere, see what you t'inks 'at dere."

One of the visitors (who still wore his bib slicker pants in the warm cabin) after examining the mechanism replied, "Dat's not th'reason why 'e's leakin, because 'at spring's not dere. . . . No, no . . . I wouldn' say, I wouldn' say unless 'at pressure. . . ."

Claude returned empty-handed. The store at the fish station had closed fifteen minutes before he arrived, and it went without saying that Baxter Parsons would not reopen. Guarantee not, to fellows who sold their fish to the Portuguese rather than to Hiscock Company. The dinner Claude prepared, his hands clean, was a solid one of boiled beef and boiled potatoes. By 10:00 P.M., with the gray sky still grudgingly light in the long northern day, the engine had been reassembled, each skiff was tied back at its own mooring, and the inhabitants of the boats were beginning to snore in their bunks. The only sound came from the lowered fire in the stove, a modest, distant roar.

At 4:00 A.M., Oxford started the tea pot and put thick slabs of bacon in the pan. Quickly, Cyril grunted and slipped into the boots beside his bunk. Young Claude clung to his covers until the last possible moment, but by 4:30 breakfast had ended, the reassembled engine was making a noise that shook the cabin, Claude had gone out in the rain to unfasten the mooring, and we were off through black waterways with half a dozen other longliners. Rain and spray dashed over the wheelhouse window while we stayed dry inside. We passed the Portuguese ship, dark except for deck lights, and wove among islands with rock profiles silhouetted in the first light. Before long the open sea had picked up the boat and given the deck a lively pitch.

What did we talk about? The engine, of course, every cough and sputter. And a joke or two about Claude, who lay curled back under his covers. The weather rated a word, since the wind had increased in a direction "down nor'dy [northeast], nor'dy way" that could bring a blow. On this shore, any easterly wind blows up a heavy sea, but northeast seas are especially cold and rough. In addition, Maxwell wanted to know what President Reagan had in mind on several topics, and he assumed that a fellow fresh from the States would have the answers readily. Cyril listened, too. The conversation went on at a shout above the furiously noisy engine.

A white object loomed ahead, too irregular for a ship. As we approached, it took the form of a smooth arch with a jagged wing. All over the place this year, icebergs like that, Cyril observed. The current that carried them must have been running closer to shore. We passed an occasional growler—smaller pieces still larger than the boat—and many chunks that just barely broke the water, both types dangerous if the boat hit them. Maxwell pointed to another big one just becoming visible. "Not often you sees oice this generous in August-month."

The iceberg slowly modified its shape as we approached and our relative position altered, to reveal an immense opening through the center. It resembled a donut for giants. The whiteness in profile intensified against the gray sky and water, but the closer we came the deeper grew a green-blue color within the ice itself that gave the interior flash of a precious stone. Some ice facets glowed with such an unusual turquoise, a color so much more pure and bright than any other around, that they seemed arbitrarily splashed by of an artist's brush.

In cities, there is seldom the chance to approach an object of such size in an unobstructed line. The iceberg seemed to grow, lacking reference to any nearby object of comparable size. Cyril stopped the engine and we floated within thirty feet. Ice in a refrigerator cube might be called inanimate, but not that in iceberg form. The berg creaked and groaned. Its height obstructed the sky. Close to the boat a long ice shelf rose and fell just at the surface as the ocean sucked over it and rushed back in green waterfalls.

We watched with the admiration men give to objects biggger than they can handle, knowing that beneath the structure, with its shelf

[87]

the size of a fish plant floor, rode a mass nine times as great. Sometimes icebergs split and calve with a crash like a fallen redwood; occasionally they overturn as their balance alters through melting. "Don't want to get caught under he," said Max respectfully. We moved away.

Cyril had a small radar, and he knew the approximate position of the buoys holding the ends of his net, but we still spent a half hour searching. There was always the possibility that a growler had dragged over the buoy and moved it—or that an iceberg had simply absorbed it to carry nets with all their fish on a far journey south over the Grand Banks toward Bermuda.

Claude, the junior man, now wore his boots and oilers as he stood on deck peering for buoys through the rain, then checking the painted numbers on any he sighted. When at last he found one belonging to the *Sealer*, both Max and Cyril dressed for the weather—they had stayed comfortably free of their wet gear since the evening before—and the day began.

The deck, which occupied the two-thirds of the boat aft of the wheelhouse, had a simple layout that could be altered from open space to bins by rearranging boards. Cyril took his station amidships at the starboard rail beside the roller and gurdy. The gurdy, a revolving drum or wheel, is the basic piece of fish-deck gear for pulling in heavy lines, nets, or pots. It used to be a device hand-cranked like an oldtime hurdy-gurdy from which the name derived, back in the days when fishermen would pop their muscles turning it hour after hour. An engine-powered gurdy was one of the great gifts of the mechanical age to fishermen (along with engines themselves, which spared them the oars). The gurdy aboard the *Sealer*, like most in the Smokey fleet, had been assembled from old automobile parts. It operated through the power-takeoff, an auxiliary drive attached to the main engine.

Cyril threw out a grapple, hooked the buoy, and pulled it in with the end of the net attached. He passed the net between the leads to pass over a self-rotating roller, and then pulled further to wrap it around the horizontally rotating gurdy which consisted of a rim and a worn tire. Nets may be light stuff skein by skein, but like most objects they accumulate a surprising weight in quantity. The fishermen in Smokey set their nets in "fleets" of several tied together, usually a string of ten fifty-fathom lengths that totaled more than half a mile.

[88]

When such a quantity of net came up fifty fathoms from the bottom with multitudes of fish trapped in its meshes, it needed pulling by more than the strongest set of backs.

Claude took his station by the gurdy where the youngest muscles were needed, since this kind of gurdy could move the only net with friction applied. Maxwell and I continued drawing the net aft, then stacking it evenly from side to side across the stern so that it would pay without snags during the next set. All three of us picked fish entangled in the meshes. Cyril held the most demanding job as roller man. Close beside his hands were mounted the levers for remote steering and engine control as well as those for the gurdy. He alone could watch the net emerging from the water, to gaff aboard any fish that might be too heavy or loosely snagged to make it over the rail, or to back the engine for quick slack if the net strained taut to indicate a hang-up on the bottom that might snap it.

Picking gill nets: That was the work of the day. Fishing nets come in different types and mesh sizes for catching different fish. Gill nets, of relatively wide mesh, snag fish by the gills as they attempt to swim through. Then there are nets of tighter mesh for trawls and seines that simply entrap the fish. A net's use determines the way it is "hung" or sewed into shape. Gill nets—used by all the Smokey fishermen—unfold underwater into a straight up-and-down wall weighted to the seafloor on the lower edge and buoyed with small floats on the upper. These are passive nets, set in position and left to "soak" for hours or days, spider webs awaiting their victims.

Trawls and seines are the active nets. A trawl is bag-shaped with long flared ends, and a trawler, or dragger, pulls it through the water either along the bottom (bottom trawl) or midwater (pelagic trawl) depending on the schooling/feeding habits of the target fish. Seines stretch in a long horizontal line as do gill nets, but they catch fish on the surface rather than on the bottom.

The mesh of trawls and seines, which must be strong enough to hold thousand-weights, can be thick as cord because the fish is trapped by the time he becomes alarmed. Gill nets do not need to take the same strain, but their presence must be more discreet because a fish still swimming free has the option of bounding away if a threatening wall of mesh spooks him. Thus, the material of gill nets, these days, is a thin but tough, wiry synthetic fiber like nylon, translucent enough to blend with the water. It is not stiff. This means that the net can be as springy as rubber bands, treacherously apt to bunch into a mess.

Removing fish from a gill net requires special dexterity that fishermen acquire with experience. The cod have a devilish ability to entangle themselves like Br'er Rabbit in the Tar Baby. The net not only holds them by the gills so that they cannot pull out, but also snags them by the tail as they thrash. Sometimes the net wraps them in layers, or twists them in a bag of mesh. Net strands can cut the fingers like taut piano wire as you yank and maneuver the fish free. Some fish are dead, but those snagged recently continue to flip and gasp. How brutal can you bring yourself to be in grabbing a still-living creature by the mouth or eye socket, and yanking its slippery body through a mesh too tight for it to go by itself? Fairly brutal, after the several-hundredth fish with hundreds to go before you can start thinking of rest. Brutal without a thought except to avoid tearing the meat, when you're handling the twenty-thousandth cod of one season in a lifetime of seasons.

Cod is a dull-eyed, passive fish, easy to overlook as a fellow creature with rights. On a hook, it jerks once and then gives up, unlike a salmon that fights for minutes or a halibut that fights for hours. Unlike salmon or mackerel or herring, whose silver bodies flash, almost coruscate, cod have the color of brackish water, a spotted muddy green on top, a brown greenish-white on the underbelly. Their eyes are expressionless even by fish standards. When alive and swimming, their distinguishing character trait is gluttony. They will gobble anything smaller than themselves, the young of any species. Carnivorous humans need not judge this trait too harshly—after all, we hire somebody else to kill the calves and lambs we enjoy eating—but crab fishermen have little enthusiasm for the sight of two dozen tiny crabs in a single cod belly.

Many would argue, with sincere conviction, that the Lord put cod in the earth's seas for the great purpose of man's livelihood and appetite. Indeed, the cod serves this purpose well. It is a fish of many edible parts that reproduces in enough abundance that many can catch it and more than the rich can afford it. A staple served fresh on tables along the entire North Atlantic coast from New England to Norway, cod also lends itself to preservation by salting and drying. In these forms, its sturdily flavored meat has nourished the masses far from any cod grounds. The common village dish of Portugal is bacalao made from salt cod. Napoleon's troops conquered Europe on a diet of Newfoundland dried cod, for good or bad. Cod revenues have funded whole communities of fine houses with silver and mahogany furnishings (like those of Newfoundland merchants during the Napoleonic Wars), have sustained entire national economies, have led to competitive wars that sometimes reach international proportions, and have been the means over centuries for millions of fishermen in cold waters to raise their families. For the New-foundlander and Labradorian, the creature is basic. They may call flounder "flounder" and turbot "turbot," but when they use the word "fish" they mean specifically the passive, homely, blue-collar cod.

As the morning continued, the *Sealer's* nets came aboard fathom by lengthening fathom, sometimes bare (the sight of this occasionally meant relief, a time to straighten the back for a moment), more often with fish hanging like apples on a branch. Each fish we liberated from the meshes went flying into bins on the portside deck. The wind blew waves enough to keep the deck rolling and to slop cold water around our feet most of the time. After pulling each fleet, Cyril maneuvered the boat, guided by bottom contours on a fathometer and by his memory bearings on distant rocks. At a shout, Claude in the stern threw out the lead marker buoy to set the net again. The boat's forward motion pulled the meshes over the rail with a soft zip as they payed out smoothly.

The *Sealer* had nine fleets of nets soaked. Each took a bit less than an hour to finish. Fish piled in the bins, while the cold of the air and frigid water penetrated our thermals and numbed our feet. By the fourth or fifth fleet, I had begun to crave food and warmth, expecting after each set that the others would declare a break. At length, some seven hours beyond breakfast, I mentioned it. Lunch? Rest? With the work not halfway done? They urged me to go below and make myself at home, boil the kettle, open any can, crawl in. But no, thanks all the same, they just ate a while back. I did indeed hustle a cup of tea and a sandwich of bacon left in the pan but, peer ethos (not pressure) being contagious, I was back on deck in ten minutes, bracing a chilly fish against my side to pull him from the net.

The work had an easy rhythm, but it proceeded nonstop. There were jokes, and spurts of serious conversation—the Reagan ques-tions continued—and long periods of just a word or a grunt as needed. Young Clyde was bashful and spoke little, but his bounce reflected a man glad in his work. He was eighteen, Maxwell noted as we picked fish together, one of a large family on hard times since the father died the year before. The Oxfords had taken him aboard that spring.

The water bore more than cod. Ice of varying sizes moved slowly south, flashing that interior tropical blue. From beneath the surface came other fish—flat-bodied flounders that went back overboard, and three sparkling silver salmon that Maxwell carefully placed to one side (for dinner, I thought with pleasure). There were twiglike and leafy pieces of kelp, and stubby white branch coral coated with bright purple lichens that faded within a few hours of exposure to the air. The nets also inundated us with dwarf crabs—unfortunately best picked, given the pressure to make a living, by first smashing them with a boot heel. The worst of the by-catch were sea urchins, their brown shells bristling with needlelike quills that spiked the fingers straight through cotton gloves. "Whore's eggs," the Labrador fishermen called them, and "mess a' 'or's" Cyril would warn from the rail if he saw them coming.

Maxwell's hands picked fish as fast as the net brought them aboard—the meanest tangle opened for him in seconds—but his eyes remained on constant scan. "Whale dere," he said once, but by the time we focused over the gray choppy water the breeze had dissolved the spout into vapor. Later, a whale spouted close enough that we heard its vapory snort, and then enjoyed the sight as the glistening black body curved above the surface and sounded with a shake of its flukes.

There had been a period of relative calm, but the breeze gradually increased. "Makin' nor'dy dere, Cyril," barked Maxwell above the deck and engine noises. Newfoundlanders tend to speak in a staccato, high-pitched voice. "Heavy by tonight, what you 'tinks, eh?" The two discussed whether to leave the nets soaking. If the blow halted fishing for several days, they would have a mess to pick. They decided to take their chances, since nets out of the water worked for nobody.

At length, we finished picking and resetting the nine fleets of gill net. Cyril headed the boat back through the growlers and icebergs, past flat islands of bare gray rock toward the invisible shore. Afternoon had barely started by the clock, although the hours of a nine-to-five workday had long been fulfilled. Would we have a lunch break at last? As spray flew aft from the slap of the bow on waves, Maxwell and Claude snapped tight the necks of their oilskins and, positioning heavy boards into brackets, constructed a congeries of bins. Then they erected a wooden table and started honing knives.

"Anybody hungry?" I ventured.

"No sir," said Cyril. "But you go down and make yourself at home. Anything you find."

I did make tea—the strong kind to local taste in which a nail might stand upright—and whether from politeness or inclination they drank it with thanks.

The trip back over roughening water took longer than the one out, perhaps two hours. We spent the time dressing the catch, then throwing it into heavy-meshed cargo nets that occupied a bin each. Some two thousand cod needed to be sliced across the belly and eviscerated. As with picking nets, the fingers could not work efficiently encased in thick, warm, slick waterproof gloves. Rough-woven cotton ones provided a far tighter grip, but they also transmitted directly the chill of fish intestines.

The handiest way to grip a fish for cleaning is with a finger poked deep into a gill or an eye socket, since the body itself is as slippery as wet soap. Blood, guts, and gurry covered everything, although spray kept washing the top part of us. Dissecting a single cod on a clean kitchen table might be a squeamish problem, as the creature's stomach flops out accompanied by lines of intestine, followed (in a female) by the grainy roe in two rose-colored sacks, and then the smooth gray-white liver. The sensibilities dull, however, to any job repeated over and over. The hours at the gutting table became the bright, messy, good-humored highlight of the day, with the abundance of a harvest washing around our legs.

As noted, the fishermen in Smokey had three markets for their catch. Baxter Parsons' fish station bought cod that had been gutted, headed, and split—the latter a process requiring dexterity with a sharp knife that removes the backbone and spread-eagles the meat. This is the preparation for salting, a traditional process that, by preserving fish without refrigeration, has made far-seas fishing practical for centuries. The Portuguese ship also salted, but it did this with its own crew, and bought fish that had been merely "head-on gutted" as we had just done—a far less laborious process—for which they paid less. The government barge offered the third option, to sell gutted fish to a tender that took them to a freezer plant in Cartwright a hundred miles south.

Other boats had already gathered beside the Portuguese ship *Sao Goncalinho* to wait their turns. A cargo net stuffed with fish rose from a boat alongside and disappeared into the ship's housing, then returned as a dripping, empty rag. Wind and seas were increasing steadily so that boats rose and fell on surges against the black hull of the processor ship. We waited inside the warm wheelhouse—eating, finally: sandwiches made with cold tinned meat washed down with mugs of tea—as Cyril and Maxwell speculated on the weather.

This time of year, at least, a bad blow might last only a day or two. No more staying in Smokey anymore after August-month or the first week of September, the way they did once into October when it blew for seventeen days. They'd had no choice with all their nets in the water and it too rough to pull them, of course. "Caught in breeze saten'teen days, here on the collar, never got out," declared Maxwell. "Ar's one breeze come, and 'e blow out, de odder one come, jus' around and around. Saten'teen days . . . we was some bored, eh?"

"An' when we got out," Cyril continued, "I tell you we had some stayin'. Kellup, rocks, dead fish, loive fish, flounder, sculpins, every'ting doon 'ere, we 'ad it in the nets. Oh but really a stink!"

There came an opening and Cyril gunned us in before anyone else could take our place. Claude threw a painter from the bow which a Portuguese kid of the same age caught and secured. They grinned at each other, cocks of the walk, as water surged between the hulls and drenched them. Despite the lee produced by the ship, the boat thrashed against the steel side and the wind, after the warmth of the wheelhouse, became chatteringly cold. We had to shout to be heard. A large swarthy-faced man in yellow oilskins stood on deck directing the cargo operation. He greeted Max heartily in Portuguese, the gist of it being "Did you break the asses of those two puppies on your boat, you old fart?" (The two were contemporaries.)

"Not so rough, skipper, considerin' de wedder," Max called back with equal gusto, and tossed up a burlap bag with the salmon he had saved. The Portuguese caught it, raised a finger as if he had just remembered something, and produced from stowage nearby a big sack of bread which he threw down. Other boats engaged in barters that earned them made-aboard "brandy".

We slipped the four ends of a netful of fish over the cargo hook they lowered, bracing our knees into the soft fish to keep from being bounced overboard as hook and net loops swung wildly. The load—about two thousand pounds, dripping slime—steadied as soon as it rose free of our pitching deck.

On ship, the bag paused suspended over a high open housing, beside a shack covered against the wind with flapping sheets of plastic, while a man recorded the weight from a scale attached to the hoist. Claude jumped the surging rails from boat to ship and hurried up a ladder to check the weight master's reading. (Fishermen do this everywhere, usually with no insult to the buyer in a business that respects common sense and survival instincts.) When the bag reached the floor of the housing below the main deck, workers in boots and aprons shook out the fish while others delivered them in wheelbarrows to various stations.

Below decks, an entire crew of young Portuguese men sang loudly and rhythmically in unison as they split the cod at long tables. Their voices rose in waves over the noises on deck. Two further decks below, another crew spread the split fillets row by row between layers of salt. Except for the scrape of shovels, this second place was a curiously quiet world where the salt which whitened clothes and faces seemed to absorb all sound. I saw this all on a subsequent visit, when I also ate bacalao, a standard Portuguese dish served nearly every meal on the ship, concocted with several variations of salt cod, olive oil, and tomato-based sauces. Today, with weather rising, we shoved free as soon as they weighed the last netful and Claude had leaped precipitously back aboard.

Further into the rocky lees, the water lay calmer. We moored to our anchor in the boat community by the barge and Claude, without a thought to the weather, took off in the skiff bailing as he went. An hour later, he returned chewing a candy bar, dripping and grinning, with two bags of groceries. Like prizes, one by one, he slammed on the table cans of milk, Spam, stew, and soup, as well as a big sack of sugar and several jars of jam. Within a minute, one of the jams was being spread on a thick slice of the Portuguese bread.

An earlier encounter with cod in Norway had convinced me that the livers are as good eating as the meat. (As are the "tongues," or throats, mentioned earlier.) I had saved some livers from the gutting table and announced my intention to fix them for dinner. Maxwell looked startled for a minute, then announced sturdily that that would be fine with him. Cyril chuckled uncertainly. Claude stopped eating jam and edged up the ladder to the wheelhouse.

I duly chopped the liver into finger-sized chunks and boiled them for a few minutes, explaining how fresh cod liver has a rich, nonfishy flavor that bears no resemblance to cod liver oil. Max and Cyril nodded, glancing at each other. Meanwhile, Max had prepared a standard meal of fried cod and boiled potatoes. He set the frying pan and the pot on the table slowly as I ladled my concoction into a dish. Suddenly, he remembered that he needed to fetch something from a friend's boat before it grew completely dark.

"But you can save me some of that liver, skipper."

Cyril smiled, and poured some of the liver and its oily juice over his potatoes as I instructed. He ate it, and declared politely that it was very tasty. However: "No seconds, no sir, thank you."

Claude had long since put on his oilers and found something that needed doing on deck.

Claude Weir (his is the jelly sandwich), and Maxwell Oxford, grab a quick snack in the galley-foc's'le of the *Sealer* after ten hours of work on deck. This is home during the entire summer cod season. Oxford has made the seasonal fishing trip "down" to Labrador for nearly five decades.

Cyril Oxford and his father Maxwell (far lower left and right) discuss an engine problem with visitors from a boat anchored alongside in Smokey, Labrador. The men are neighbors back home in Green Bay, a small Newfoundland outport.

Open skiffs and a longliner deliver to the Hiscock Company pier on the remote summer station at Smokey, Labrador. The next-closest store, telephone, and buying station is fifty sea miles away in Rigolet.

Baxter Parsons, for many years manager of the Hiscock facility in Smokey, built a reputation for operating with the autonomy that in olden days would have earned him the title "Station king."

7

A Paradise, My Friend

It did indeed blow. Throughout the night, the wind slammed rain against the wheelhouse with such vigor that we could hear it from the bunks below, hear it clearly over the low roar of the stove and the slap of waves against the hull just inches from our heads. Next morning, there was no question of going to sea. Each of the long-liners strained in the same direction on their taut anchor chains as whitecaps rolled past. Fishermen on all the boats settled into a diminished life of eat, sleep, mend, and repair that, in fact, lasted for three days.

Aboard the *Sealer*, the power-takeoff and the engine itself gained a total overhaul. The wheelhouse, usually shipshape, became an obstacle course of flywheels and blackened rags, a place heavy with the smell of oil, dim in gray light that filtered through windows streaming with rain. There were also rips in the nets to be mended—wet and chilly deck work that had the compensation of fresh air and the pleasant knowledge that, given no pressure to bring in fish, there could be as many mug-ups in the warmth below as one cared to take.

Over on shore, the weather had also confined the families living in shacks who fished from open skiffs, but at the J. W. Hiscock Company station some of the men found a few hours' pay salting fish that had been delivered in hopper-load quantities the night before. The weathered old saltery on the pier had a comfortable smell of leather-like fish. Banks of layered cod splits lined the walls, dripping brine from the salt on them that liquefied as it drew out the moisture in the meat. Two lean-faced brothers grinned as they hustled, so happy did they appear to be for the opportunity to be drawing easy pay on a day when the skiffs lay beached. They bounced hundred-pound bags of salt on their shoulders across a slippery plank from a new warehouse to a wheelbarrow, then wheeled them at a clip to the saltery. Inside, they worked nonstop as if on a single breath, spreading the split cod like shingles in a long row and layering them with salt.

At this time, in 1982, the station at Smokey was dominated by the loading pier and the adjacent saltery shed. Surrounding it was an assortment of lesser buildings, all of them weathered by decades of wet blows and patched with varying degrees of skill. From afternoon to night on a fishing day, boats and skiffs tied to the pilings to deliver. A simple crane brought up the catches, and the fish proceeded to the saltery in wheelbarrows. Further up the hill, in a small frame house that combined living quarters with the store and post office, the station master himself sat at table buttering a hot biscuit that his housekeeper had just brought from the oven. Driving rain beat against the roof. Outside on the porch, somebody rapped, then pounded, the door to the store two rooms away, but neither of those inside acknowledged.

"This fishery nowadays is a sort of a citified thing," declared Baxter Parsons with the conviction of experience, one eye a-squint and his face ticked in a scowl. "If my father happened to step in 'ere now, he'd be in a different world entirely. The breed of men is gone. They would take a set of oars and row the whole day, and we can't scull across the tickle. [A tickle, in Labrador parlance, is a narrow stretch of water.] The fellow now, he gets out of bed at five-six o'clock, the sun already shining. Out to his nets, he stands dry in a wheelhouse, and down in the galley there's a stove roarin' night and day. He don't even have to put on his oilskins until he gets on the fishing ground. And them oilskins that was, my friend! It's a *paradise* now."

The oldtime Newfoundland oilskins—a retired teacher in St. John's told me once about those. The smell and feel of them, he claimed, when as a boy he worked in open boats with his father, had decided him to seek any life but that of a fisherman. His mother made their oilskins fresh every spring, saturating coarse cloth over and over with linseed oil. "Oh, how they stank," the teacher remembered. "They

[98]

crackled on you like an old tent, especially in the cold, and the oil never stopped seeping into the rest of your clothes."

Parsons passed the biscuits, still steaming, but kept the butter until he had taken his fill. He lived in Newfoundland of course, he said, but, summers for the past fourteen years, he had come down from home in Bay Roberts to manage the station at Smokey. "But now, when I first come down, that was half a century ago, in 1937 as a lad to fish with my father and brothers." They fished with hand lines from an open boat, although others fished with traps. A bit different then, I ventured, and his snort indicated the extent of the understatement. "You'd leave in the morning at 2:30 roughly." They were mechanized, he admitted, but "the motor boats at that time, if you had h'eight 'orsepower in the boat you was overpowered. You'd steam for four hours to where the fish was, maybe thirty miles away, taking spray, sun, wind, rain all that time in the open boat. Then you'd jig your load, get back six, seven, in the afternoon with eighteen or twenty barrel of fish, have to split that and put it under salt before ever a thought of rest." A cod-oil "torch"—a wick dipped in cod oil— provided the light to split and salt late into the night. The torch burned with a black smoke that coated the nostrils and stung the eyes. "Next morning, we was gone again with probably one hour's sleep, for six nights of the week."

I first encountered Baxter Parsons by hearing the other end of a phone conversation he was conducting from Smokey with his boss, Dave Hiscock, at the home office of the J. W. Hiscock Company in Brigus, Newfoundland. Brigus, an hour's drive around Conception Bay from the city of St. John's, is as picturesque a town as Smokey is bare, a lovely Newfoundland outport built on hills that overlook a secure natural harbor opening to the sea. Hiscock's grandfather established the company in 1894, and it has now survived to be the oldest salt fish company in Newfoundland. A dark briny odor permeated the small office; it was separated only by doors and paneling from a warehouse where forklift trucks carried boxes of cardboardlike salt fillets to a shipping dock for destinations in Africa and the Mediterranean.

Dave Hiscock's long-distance conversation with Baxter Parsons concerned a fisherman in Smokey who questioned the way Parsons graded his fish. Number One grade brings nearly twice as much as Number Two, while in the salt-fish business large cod are worth more than small ones. It is customary to take samples of the fleet's delivery and fix a percentage of small to large that are currently coming from the grounds. The difference represented several cents a pound, an amount that could accumulate to make or break a season for fisherman and buyer both. Parsons had determined that the boats were bringing twenty percent smalls, and the man claimed fifteen percent. The man was a newcomer, Parsons declared. The old-time regulars accepted his judgment.

In the old days only a decade before, when Hiscock had been the sole buyer in the area, the problem would not have merited an expensive telephone discussion. But now a foreign processor ship waited around the corner, and the government barge provided a platform for buyer boats from other places. Tenders from a fish plant in Cartwright, fifty miles south of Smokey, were (they said) figuring only a five-percent penalty for smalls.

"If you're satisfied that what you're doin' is right," declared Hiscock in a rich Newfie brogue, "then no problem there. Tell buddy to go straight you-know-where, and the faster he goes the better. If we can't buy it properly, I don't want it!" In a scarce season for cod in most places but Smokey, this was bold talk. However, a fish buyer who misjudged the quality he bought courted ruin in a narrow-profit business.

When the phone conversation ended, Hiscock explained, "What it is, it's a crowd of fellows that have never been down the Labrador before, don't know but what they're goin' into St. John's somewhere. They can't go into a shop and get their breaded chicken and their french fries. And they bitch. They didn't come supplied, like the old-timers always do. They can't expect to go in for a gallon of gas—one of Baxter's men in Smokey starts pumping out a single gallon from an oil drum, he'll never do nothin' else that hour."

In most places, the past casts some shadow over the present. Cities with ancient ruins or venerable architecture live with the past in sight. In Labrador, where many near-feudal conditions changed barely a generation ago, an occasional building survives the years but the past lives particularly in current memory. Baxter Parsons had his own recollection of supplies the old schoonermen would bring for the summer to augment a diet of fresh cod. "There was no vegetables at all, not a potato or cabbage. You took salt beef, salt pork, a sack of beans, a sack of peas round or split whatever your fancy was, and two bags of 'ard bread. Then you'd get your butter, sugar, tea, and molasses, and that was your diet."

At the station in Smokey, teatime ended and the hour arrived for the store to open. On the minute, Parsons unlocked the door. Several people were waiting, most in foul-weather clothing as the rain swirled around the open porch. A line had also formed to use the only phone on the island, which Baxter passed out the window on an extension from a small room between kitchen and store that served as his office. Beyond that porch, the rain splashed little geysers on puddles in the rocks, and further beyond that grayed the longliners that pulled at anchor in the wind.

"Yes, my dear, what'll you 'ave?" he asked a rawboned woman with a plastic kerchief pulled around her head. She asked for a can of beans and one of lard, which he picked from clusters of individual items on the shelves. And three apples. The apples, small and wiry with a touch of pale red on their green exterior, lay in an open carton alongside a box of dry-looking oranges. "That's all then, is it?" And one taffy bar, please. He joked about her sweet tooth, but she appeared too reserved to reply as he wrote the purchases in a book.

Parsons proceeded to the next customer. The men in line were equally rawboned, their faces darkened from an outdoor life. They answered Parsons' banter with bashful good humor. The conviviality seemed unique to the buying ceremony. Later, wearing a cowboy hat and surrounded by a coterie of employees, he stalked without speaking through a group of the same fishermen on the path to the shacks. Soon, he was berating one of his employees loudly, in front of the others.

"In Smokey 'ere, now, I'm king," Parsons liked to declare affably. This sounded like a voice from the nineteenth century, from the days of men whom the Norwegians used to call "station czars." People sometimes admitted to trepidation when they brought him their fish for sale, since he alone had the power to judge and grade. The Hiscock station that Parsons managed comprised the only store, saltery, telephone, and post office within fifty sea miles. A small domain, perhaps, but let someone try buying jam elsewhere, given the wilderness of rock, tundra, and water that lies between Smokey and Rigolet or Cartwright to the south, or Makkovik to the north.

|101|

Nobody lives permanently at Smokey/Indian Harbor, where nothing but ice and wind prevail from autumn to spring. (The place earned its name, they say, from the way that wind can churn spray into smokelike vapor as it howls across the water.) By October, according to Bart Higgins, the young, bearded new manager of the Hiscock station, the cold can blow into a house so bitterly that water freezes a few feet from a roaring stove. Smokey is one of numerous Labrador summer stations, established by fishermen for seasonal quarters located as close as possible to the fishing grounds, accessible only by boat or (these days) by pontoon plane.

What happened here a century ago occurs yet at least in part, and within the same social framework. Fishermen still work long hours in an environment of few comforts, although they can thank for an easier life their boats driven by engines rather than oar and sail, hydraulic pumps that pull the heaviest nets from the water, and the cushions against disaster that modern communications and aircraft provide. The structure of the Labrador fisheries remains that of three distinct groups: land-based visiting Newfoundlanders, called "stationers"; sea-based visiting Newfoundlanders, called "floaters"; and land-based permanent Labradorians, called "settlers," who also become stationers when they move to summer quarters nearer the fish.

The stationers, both Labradorians and Newfoundlanders, fish from open skiffs close to shore as they did in the past, some still rowing although most now travel to their sites pushed by capable outboard motors. For the season that runs from June to September, most Labrador settler families (also in the old days called "liv'yeres," for "live here") move from their winter homes in sheltered bays to summer stations a few miles closer to the fish, on the exposed rocks of the outer coast. Newfoundland "outsiders" (a term used by both groups) also come as families to stations and to isolated sites they have often held traditionally. The outsiders' stations are usually separate from those the Labradorians occupy, although no rule is absolute. Indian Harbor was a Newfoundlander station, as so now is Smokey just across the hill.

The sea-based Newfoundlanders—the floaters—fish in Labrador aboard boats on which they live. Some call them also "bankers," from the old days when many of the larger boats also fished the Grand Banks at other times of the year. (Some would call them carpetbaggers, since they take fish but contribute nothing to the local economy.) Long-liners now constitute the floater fleet, but during the heyday of Indian Harbor—in fact, until World War II and a bit beyond—the floater fishermen came in large sailing schooners.

As noted before, Labrador is part of Canada's Newfoundland Province, a 112,000-square-mile northern extension of the 42,000-square-mile island of Newfoundland proper. Its apparent satellite status increasingly chafes Labradorians. Most administrators who deal with Labrador, both in government and in business, merely fly from the Newfoundland capital in St. John's for visits into Goose Bay/Happy Valley, the Labrador capital, or they do time there on temporary duty. The irony is that while Newfoundlanders often regard Labradorians as underdeveloped dependents, historically the "Newfs" themselves have occupied the same position as the poorest of relations in British and Canadian eyes. Labradorians of this generation are beginning to feel a collective identity and to push for greater autonomy. They fly a flag of their own.

Historians and semanticists have no certain origin for the name "Labrador." Some claim it a contraction of the French "Le Bras d'Or," although even the wealth of cod would seem no justification for fantasizing this austere coast as a Golden Arm. Another speculation seems more fitting for a land that requires such heavy work to survive—that the Portuguese explorer Corte Real named Labrador in 1501 after the "lavrador," or laborer, in his expedition who first sighted the land. The first Europeans to settle were deserters from the early fishing and exploring voyages, during which thousands of fishermen from England, Portugal, and the Basque regions came looking for cod and whales.

The coast lives by itself and always has. The twenty-six permanent communities are located in the closest safe harbor to the fish and seals, a condition which, given the rocky wilderness terrain, allows for no roads to connect them with each other or with the interior. As with coastal Norway and Alaska, which also have series of fishing towns located in remote bays, Labrador depends on its boat connections. The itineraries of the two ferry systems that operate along the Labrador coast provide an atlas of this isolated world. Traveling south from far northern Nain (population 950), the stops include Davis Inlet (pop. 335), Hopedale (pop. 480), Postville (pop. 190), Makkovik (pop.

335), Rigolet (pop. 275) and finally Goose Bay/Happy Valley (pop. 7,000). Most of these towns are predominantly or partially native, reflecting generations of accepted intermarriage.

The second ferry system, which starts in Goose Bay, connects southern Labrador with the island of Newfoundland. The communities to the south that front the North Atlantic are all settler, with an ancestry principally British-Scottish. They include Cartwright (population 685), Black Tickle (pop. 215), Charlottetown (pop. 270), Port Hope Simpson (pop. 582), Fox Harbor/St Lewis (pop. 300) and Mary's Harbor (pop. 420), as well as such summer stations as Batteau, Bolster's Rock, Triangle, Square Island, and Battle Harbor. There are also several communities west of the coastal ferry system on the "French Shore" close to Quebec Province, actually connected by road and facing the northern shore of Newfoundland proper across the Strait of Belle Isle, that bear such names of their French origin as Forteau and L'Anse-au-Loup.

The ferry or "steamer" trip to the Labrador is an ingrained part of the Newfoundland-Labrador fishing tradition. Whole families traveled north by steerage each summer, to pursue the primitive life of catching and salting cod that constituted one of their few means of income. Even today the ferries schedule trips in early summer that are open only to licensed fishermen and their families, to take them north with their skiffs and paraphernalia.

The most famous of the coastal steamers, a self-contained legend, was the SS *Kyle*, commissioned in 1913 and not replaced until 1959. Besides furnishing transportation, she carried supplies, mail, a doctor and dentist of sorts (usually medical students or new graduates)—and she carried an aura. The *Kyle* was a luxury ship for those who could afford it. Some dozen staterooms provided comfort amid elegant public rooms for the station managers, teachers, inspectors, and other titled people as well as tourists who traveled the coast. Ruth Peters of St. John's, writing in *Them Days Magazine*, a Goose Bay quarterly devoted to preserving the heritage of Labradorians through their own words, remembered of trips between 1925 and 1943 "the beauty of the ship with its mahogany paneling, crimson velvet curtains, shining brasswork, and especially the dining salon with spotless white linen tablecloths, silver cutlery, and silver sugar bowls."

Steerage was a different experience. The stationer going down to Battle Harbor, Indian Harbor, Cape Harrison, and other summer locations made the entire trip for about two dollars on what was called a fisherman's ticket. The ticket provided passage and nothing more. He brought his own food, his skiff, and his entire household including children as well as the family sheep, goats, hens, dogs, and cats.

Baxter Parsons, riding the Kyle in the late 1930s on a fisherman's passage, remembered "five hundred souls—wives, children, the whole families with their cats and dogs. Now for meals, you brought your own. All day long, you couldn't get into the galley because the crew and first-class passengers had to be fed. At six o'clock, they would declare it open, and five hundred people came to boil their kettle in that one galley, or if they had a pot of beans. . . . At those times you couldn't get a bed, the men couldn't, because of course the women got first choice. Us fellows would sleep up in the jolly boats, the lifeboats."

There was also the "field bunk" for sleeping, where hay was kept for the animals aboard: "The first four what got in, they'd have three, four, hours' sleep; then they'd have to bail out and let others go in. As far as lice was concerned, you could nearly rake 'em." Parsons paused, wary of a city man's easy judgment. "You know—all those people in one boat, everybody sleeping in each other's bed, and the times wasn't that good. But people always looked out for each other, them days."

A more recent reminiscence for *Them Days* by Jack Holwell of Spotted Islands, circa 1957, indicates how slowly things changed on the Labrador: "We were back in steerage with the two little ones. My God, oh boy, oh boy, 'twas fierce! Only one washroom for men and one for women and you had to go upstairs to get to that. . . . By God, there was people everywhere, down in the hole, in every crook and corner of her."

According to other accounts, the steerage families piled aboard in noisy good cheer (although it surely must have been a determined race among the women to stake out bunks). "The passage was fun," wrote J.D.A. Widdowson of Brigus, recalling trips as a child circa 1920. "I remember the troops of young fishermen who gathered around someone with an accordion or fiddle, and seeing them stepping it out on the steerage floor. Some crews brought single girls as their cooks for the summer and it was usual for them to secure berths in secluded areas for amorous reasons. These were forbidden areas for children. . . ."

The trip promised companionship and change, and many looked forward to a Labrador summer despite the hardship involved. The same zest for the rigors ahead characterizes Norwegian fishermen embarking in February for the frigid Lofotens, Newfoundland sealers headed to the ice, Japanese readying for muscle-popping fights with three-hundred-pound tuna, crews aboard Kodiak seiners and Bristol Bay gill-netters gearing for the explosions of Alaskan salmon that will lead to haggard eyes and bleeding hands. The steerage passengers were accustomed to heavy work, short rations with little variety, limited options. The towns where the steamers stopped to pack them aboard—Harbor Grace, Carbonear, Catalina, Bonavista, Fogo, Twillingate—were places only a little less primitive and isolated than those on the Labrador coast. Making do was the pattern of their lives.

The scene at Smokey has changed a bit since my first visit in 1982. Baxter Parsons, the station king, died of cancer in 1986. The Portuguese processor ship, which began its career taking its countrymen to fish on the Grand Banks, and then moved to Smokey to buy what Portuguese could no longer catch when two-hundred-mile jurisdictions closed the traditional grounds to them, has sailed elsewhere with its chanting splitters and salters who would rather have been pulling nets.

Without this guaranteed market for head-on gutted cod, fewer longliners assembled in Smokey, since the Newfoundland floater crews could now fish within delivery distance of new freezer plants around Cartwright, Black Tickle, and Punchbowl. (Baxter Parsons had it right about the present breed: Men did not want to work all night splitting their fish if they could sell it otherwise and then sleep a bit.) Meanwhile, ironically, the provincial government has made conditions more attractive to floater fishermen by expanding the barge facilities to include a pier, and permanent buildings—guy-wired on an adjacent rock against high tides and wind—that offer showers and laundry machines.

Baxter Parsons' successor, Bart Higgins; at thirty-eight brings a background that symbolizes much of a new generation on the Lab-

[106]

rador. Toronto born, college educated, he taught history and human-
ities at York University, then in the late 1970s changed life-styles. He
and his wife Charlene (a former systems analyst who, in the Toronto
spirit of the new life-style, retains her maiden name Liska) fished
salmon and cod for several seasons at a single-shack station a few
miles across the water from Smokey. Charlene had her first pregnancy
there, helping pull nets in the open boat until her eighth month. The
family, committed to Labrador, lives winters in the home they built
themselves in Paradise River, a Labrador coastal community so iced
in that they must stock their entire winter's supply before the freeze.
"Smokey's the big city for us now," Higgins declares from his desk
scattered with invoices in the little office beside the store.

At Smokey, modernization begun under Parsons has resulted in a
large new saltery of warehouse proportions with a concrete floor, and
an adjacent area under the same roof for storing thousands of salt
bags required in a season. The saltery has its own loading pier. "You
won't recognize the place," Dave Hiscock assured me in Brigus. There
was also indeed a new bunkhouse and a cook shack. However, the
place seemed little changed overall. There is too much stone and too
much water for a few new buildings to make a difference.

Out along the reach, the path still leads over soft pockets of moss
and ridges of bare rock to shacks where stovepipes puff the sweet
odor of wood smoke. Down from the station and across the water
from the barge stands a growing community of such one-room
structures, which everybody calls Aspenite Village after the composi-
tion board used in most of their construction. Each houses a skiff
"crew"—husband-wife, brothers, father-son, buddies, uncle-nephew
—with little more inside than cots and a stove.

At the Hiscock station, there is now an actual phone booth on the
old pier. Baxter under pressure had made the change after occasional
tugs-of-war for custody between office and porch. He first provided a
converted outhouse with styrofoam patches over the seat holes.
Wind would gust through the patches, while the old boards never lost
the aroma of their former use. One day, a visiting company official
happened to use this phone instead of the one in the office, and a
new booth followed shortly thereafter.

Other changes are coming, slowly. The salt manufacturers now put
up seventy-five pound bags instead of hundred-pound ones. Ask the
man who must shoulder them routinely if he knows the difference.

Bart Higgins runs the station with banter of a lighter variety than Baxter's. Like Baxter, he remains fisherman enough to work a few nets of his own. There is nothing lax about the place under his reign, but laughter does come easier. Higgins hopes to lure back the long-liners. He keeps fewer permanent hands, and makes it known that "when the fish come in, we hire everybody can walk." This encourages fishermen to bring their families, since wives and older children can expect to make an income of their own. Women, who kept their place in Baxter's time, can work at what they prove capable. Meanwhile, as the crews wait restlessly for the cod to appear, Higgins hires men as he can "to help out" with new roofs and other maintenance jobs.

Peace to Baxter Parsons. He was a hard man in a place that gave little quarter, a man who came along the hard way and saw no reason to augment the relative ease of the new life for a younger generation. Paradise itself is relative.

As with the beach seiners of Madras, so with the cod fishermen of the Labrador when it comes to the sea's promises. Consult all the oceanographers, marine biologists, and weathermen you like, but be prepared nevertheless to take your chances. Smokey's recent history pegged the cod to appear in mid-July. The stationers had come north on the coastal boats a full six weeks earlier with their skiffs, to net the salmon and then hustle a change of gear in time for Fish. The salmon ran their course, but the water stayed "slubby", a condition of slime in the water that repelled cod.

July passed at Smokey. Bart Higgins hired as he could to keep the stationers in bread, but the days stretched on and on. A few long-liners tried their nets thirty miles from shore but with the cost of fuel and the work of cleaning slubby nets there was little incentive to do more than test occasionally so long as the water condition remained unchanged. And then, Saturday, August 16th, the gill nets began to fill with backbreaking weights of fish, and the run began. There was not a day off at this Hiscock station from then until October 11th. The stationers with their open boats were forced to wait another two weeks before the cod moved inshore, but every man, woman, and older child of them had work for wages at the saltery.

Runs that appear in mid-July usually end in August, but this year the late run continued late. The weather turned cold. Ice began to form a skin on puddles in the rock, and a line of white appeared each

[108]

morning along the waterline. Geese flew south overhead, in a hurry, but the weather remained calm. As days grew shorter, the northern lights played across the sky each night and reflected in the water. By early September, the stationers with children reluctantly packed and took the steamer home in time for school. Those who stayed fished and fished.

The appearance of fish, in itself, did not necessarily mean good luck. Just as the times turned for the best, both of the Hurley family's outboard motors broke the same day, broke beyond repair. They managed to borrow a motor to augment a little twenty-horsepower they had left, but these proved only enough to take them out for jigging. With their assorted children, they took the steamer home to prepare for a hard-luck winter.

The enforced wait had allowed time for the arrival by boat of equipment shipped earlier. Higgins could modernize the Hiscock station to compete with new plants down the line, all of them hungry for fish. The summer of 1987, in fact, saw the entrance of Smokey into the mid- (not the late-) twentieth century. Imagine a splitting machine, and a forklift truck! Remember that in the general Labrador experience things were done by hand. While motors and engines now propelled the boats, and hydraulics drove the longliner winches, this was not a society that had ever been able to rely on machines for the heavy work. Washers, cogs, gears, cams, belts, and snapping blades had played no part in most daily patterns.

The splitting machines from Baader in Germany had only the relative sophistication of technology twenty-five years earlier, unwieldy contraptions of chains, sprockets, and levers all in the open. This was good. It enabled everyone to follow simple lines of mechanical cause and effect when something went wrong, without fretting over microchip drives and hidden refinements. Higgins, wriggling from under the new contraption with grease and gurry drippings slapped across his face and coveralls, could find the perspective to say, "Well, the only teacher on machinery's a breakdown."

Bart Higgins became a man accustomed to daily four-hour sleeps. Sometimes, even this rest fell short. There was the night when one of the fellows accidentally wedged a seven-inch spike into the splitting machine, and the unholy din of clanks and sputters stopped abruptly. Fish lay all over the floor ready to be processed, while boats waited by the pier outside to unload more fish. "I mean," said Bart, "I just, I

. . . screeched right out." The spike had broken one of the chain drives. They had to "make up some parts" to fix it. Everybody gathered to share ideas and decipher the problem.

As for the fellow with the loose spike: "I had to report it to the head office in Brigus and their instructions were to fire him. But I didn't, because it was an accident; he just wasn't used to being around machinery. After we got the drive chain fixed, I gathered everybody together and gave them a lecture on the stupidity factor. Pointed out that it could be somebody's thumb in there; they've got to be careful working on these machines."

A second splitting machine arrived by boat on Sunday, the day the forklift truck froze with fish stacked on it three pallets high. The hydraulic oil had leaked out. With new oil in place, the machine struggled to lift the pallets and broke both chains. That small crisis took two hours to fix.

The splitting machines have proven to be a curious experience for people whom the Industrial Revolution never really touched. "H'it never stops to take a blow, that's the thing," said one fisherman turned factory hand, frowning. No matter how hard people worked to feed it headed-gutted fish or to gather out the splits at the other end, the machine demanded more. "The thing's inexorable," according to Higgins. "It's Victorian. Imagine the English Midlands in the 1840s with people harnessed to these machines; that's what it's like." He rotated people on the machines so that they remained careful, efficient, and in good spirits. Workmen in a Detroit auto plant would scoff, wistfully, at such concern for boredom. But Labradorians who build their own houses and their own boats, and trek the freezing wilderness to hunt their own meat, have not yet been hammered into the mold of assembly-line pressures, no matter how hard the labor they accept as their lot.

By the second week of October, the bonanza had run its course. The weather stayed mercifully calm; injuries were all minor. (A doctor flew in about once a month.) One fright occurred when an open boat failed to return from the nets one evening and everyone spent the night searching. The man had indeed suffered an engine breakdown, but he managed to anchor on one of the "knobs," a shallow spot in midwater, and so avoided being carried across the North Atlantic by prevailing winds and currents. He was cold enough when they found him, to be sure, but otherwise unharmed and soon back to his nets.

A young Newfoundland fisherman watches the calculation of his payment as a fish buyer on the Labrador coast writes a ticket for the fish just delivered.

Bart Higgins, station manager, chats with fishermen and helps his wife Charlene tend the Hiscock Company store in Smokey. The stock is basic, ranging from canned groceries to gloves and boots.

A single foundation is all that remains of the famous Grenfell Mission hospital at Indian Harbor, Labrador. Dr. Wilfred Grenfell established the hospital to care for fishermen during the summer fishing season.

Bob Bowers and Morris Noble of the Newfoundland-based *Cape Nipper* warm up with a bit of horseplay before starting a several hour stint gutting their day's catch off the Labrador coast.

On October 11th, the remaining crews on Smokey celebrated Canadian Thanksgiving day with a huge meal in the cookhouse. They said prayers for the good season, and shoveled in with gusto the feast Joyce Bradbury, the station's cook, had prepared ingeniously from near-depleted stocks of cans and barrels. Then they cut loose in a celebration.

8

Indian Harbor:
Ghostly Images

W hen the Parsons boys and other Newfoundlanders fished the
Labrador in 1937, they came not to Smokey but to Indian
Harbor, four miles away on the same island over swamp and scrubby
hills or a skiff's bounce around the headlands by water. For more than
a century, Indian Harbor was one of the busiest places on the coast
during summers and the site of the only Grenfell Mission hospital in
Labrador outside of the central one (at the time) in Battle Harbor—a
place now of legend. A nineteenth-century Newfoundland fisherman's song begins, "Jack was every inch a sailor, Five and twenty
years a whaler":

> When Jack grew up to be a man
> He went to Lab'ador.
> He fished in Indian 'arbor.
> Where his fadder fished before.

Indian Harbor now has only a few "crews" in scattered shacks to
serve all this memory, and the action centers around Smokey. What
happened to Indian Harbor? According to Baxter Parsons: "The families that run the fish companies there for generations, they stopped
havin' sons to look after their interests, that's what 'appened." There

were other reasons besides to account for the disappearing merchant families of Jerrett and Pomeroy from their Indian Harbor fiefdoms and for the dwindling of boats, reasons that had to do with men's changing alternatives and a lessened abundance of fish.

Shortly after World War II, in 1949, Canada absorbed Newfoundland and contiguous Labrador as a province. Most of its people lived at the marginal edge of poverty, tied to feudal ways by their dependence on humble fish and seals for a living. At about the same time, a new force entered the world fishery scene—factory trawlers and factory processor ships. Foreign nations designed large ships that could fish for months on end in distant waters. They moved quickly to the great seafood grounds of North America, where no Canadian or U.S. law prevented their fishing beyond three miles from land—to the Gulf of Alaska and the Bering Sea in the Pacific, and to Georges Bank, the Grand Banks, and Hamilton Bank in the Atlantic. By 1968, the foreign fishing pressure on Hamilton Bank, the spawning ground for Labrador cod, had become so intense that there were few fish left each summer to migrate to the coast. The Labrador inshore fishery, already dwindling, now all but disappeared.

Then, in 1977, Canada (following the lead of the United States) declared and enforced jurisdiction over the marine resources within two hundred miles of its coasts (see appendix). The action halted at last the heavy, often irresponsible, overfishing by the foreign fleets. By the early 1980s, cod began to reappear along the Labrador coast. Logically, the stationers and floater crews should have returned to Indian Harbor, which has sheltered moorings against the winds that even in summer can scream in at fifty and seventy knots. But Smokey had facilities intact when the need for them arose again because the J. W. Hiscock Company had remained all those years to service the few remaining fishermen. With the government barge and field station now located there, the eclipse of Indian Harbor is probably permanent.

I visited Indian Harbor in July 1987. The skiff left Smokey, a place busy with boats and the sounds ashore of hammering on new roofs and men joking as they mended a net, to pass around the cape into a waterway between long rock islands where wind made the only sound. As the skiff traveled through a maze of natural harbors, a building would suddenly appear. Often we were almost abreast before we noticed it. But for boxy corners, it was nearly invisible, its

[114]

weathered boards blending into the gray-black stone and its rusty paints camouflaged by scrub. Stone and water dominated in all directions.

One skiff passed us headed toward the sea. The men hunched in dark oilskins had their hoods up and backs turned. We followed the sight of smoke and the sound of chopping to a collection of buildings better kept than the others. Beside a clapboard house, where the smoke puffed from a stovepipe, stood sheds painted a dark red, even the frame of a building under construction. Smooth long rocks that resembled beached whales surrounded the point. We jumped ashore and tied the skiff to a stake driven into a crevice. An older man with receding white hair and a bristly mustache, sunburned and bare-headed despite the chilly July breeze, looked up from his chopping, welcomed us—total strangers—in a loud voice, and led the way to the house.

The house, pleasantly warm inside, consisted of a large kitchen and two side rooms. Jim Roberts settled into a straight-backed chair and declared jovially, "Welcome to the Roberts plantation, sir. I first come here as an infant baby." Mrs. Roberts added wood to the stove and brought the tea kettle to a boil, then spread an array of home-baked bread, pie, and cakes. "See that beam up there?" Roberts continued. "Schooner spar, set in place before my time." Because the Labrador winter freezes deep without intermittent thaws, it does not deteriorate wood quickly. The house still has timbers a century old as well as the original sawdust insulation.

The Jim Roberts plantation remains intact on Roberts' Bight within sight and earshot of the open sea. Roberts at sixty-four now sets only a few nets, but he and his wife, Gladys, return each summer from home in Brigus "for love of the place." He can clock off four Roberts generations before his own that have fished this site for salmon in early summer and then cod—most from the same house—as well as a son and grandchildren who have at least pulled some nets.

"In my early memory here to Indian Harbor, there was in vicinity of fifty fishing crews." This was in addition to the schooner fleet. "In the middle of summer with all the crews established, that was some five hundred, six hundred people. They all come down aboard the Newfoundland Railway steamers—the *Kyle*, the *Ungava*. . . . Something they'd look forward to every spring, even if they come and starved which was just about, at that time. Money and an ivory buckle was

[115]

much alike, equal scarce. Not but that fish was plentiful. When I was a boy you could almost dip the fish up on the beaches, when the capelin come in."

Roberts leaned forward for emphasis. "There's a nasty part to the fishery on the Labrador shore. The fishermen, those what was catching the fish, they were gypped right and left. You see, you bought your goods on credit from the store; they'd supply you. If you owned a large account, then you signed an agreement you'd ship all your fish to them. The merchants—that was Jerrett and Pomeroy and Hiscock in my time—if you were a good fish killer they only loved for you to stretch your account out, so that you'd have no balance end of season. They kept the books. End of year, you'd ask, 'How much I got comin'?' and the answer would be 'Nothin', boy, you owe me.' One year I shipped 1600 quintals of fish [at the old quintal-weight of 113 pounds that was over 180,000 pounds of cod that had been split, salted, and dried], and in spring ready to come down the next year I didn't have enough of money to buy a pair of trousers."

Confederation with Canada brought changes to the Newfoundland/Labrador coast, and not the least of it was a change in what the fishermen would accept. Newfoundlanders started a militant fishermen's union in 1969 (more of this later), and Roberts himself helped instigate the Salt Fish Corporation. SFC is a government-run monopoly that now purchases and markets all the salt cod produced in Newfoundland and Nova Scotia, and in the spring, following sales, distributes any profits' back to the fishermen. With the Salt Fish Corporation in control, the price of Robert's fish rose from three and four cents a pound to thirty-five and forty cents within two years.

The SFC quickly altered one of the oldest of the merchants' exploitative devices by redefining the weight of a quintal (pronounced "kan'-tal," still a standard measure). For generations, the merchants paid only 100 pounds' price for a weight of 113 pounds of salt fish, claiming the extra baker's dozen as a spoilage margin. Now a quintal-weight is an even hundred pounds.

Roberts strolled his domain of rock with a Chesapeake Bay (not Labrador!) retriever who eagerly chased sticks through puddles and ponds, even into the frigid harbor water itself. The stone of the terrain rose in billows, terraces, rounded bluffs, the shapes as varied as ocean waves and often resembling them. It would seem a barren country, even sinister, but while certainly austere it had a beauty that even an outsider could feel. Time and water had removed the sharp edges from this rock, a gabrose. (Gabrose resembles granite but differs in that it contains no free quartz.) The earth's forces expelled it as molten magma, then deformed it into its present shapes one and a half billion years ago. In more immediate time, the smooth rock close to the house served as the Roberts' drying stage, when the split fish used to be removed from the salt and washed, then dried in the air, before the merchant bought them. These days, companies like Hiscock buy directly from the salt pile and do the drying themselves, saving the fisherman one further round of labor for his pay in quintal-weights.

As we walked, Roberts pointed out level green patches that each indicated the site once of a house. Not a stick remained, but Jim could name the family and its individuals who had occupied the space. Once the eye picked them out, the patches repeated and repeated. Jim was in a mood to remember. He mentioned people long gone from the scene, some whose subsequent histories he knew well, some who might still be living, or dead.

As he looked over the water, he spoke also of the schooners, "the white fleet coming across the bay here, a beautiful sight." A classic movie device shows someone musing on a scene of former activity while ghostly images pass in double exposure. Such ghosts seemed in heavy attendance.

The sailing legacy remains strong in memory—some came by sail as late as the early 1950s, so that fishermen still active, like Maxwell Oxford, fished many summers past aboard schooners. Prevailing winds made the trip north a downwind sail, and no one even now—not the greenest lad—ever speaks of the northward trip from New-foundland as anything but going "down" to Labrador—usually to "the" Labrador at that, as if it were an edifice rather than a place.

The schooners, some hundred feet and longer, carried a crew of six to ten "and a boy," with hold space for 90,000 to 300,000 pounds of salt fish. At the turn of the century, an estimated 1,500 to 1,800 of them, carrying 15,000 to 20,000 fishermen, worked the Labrador coast each summer. The men fished from dories carried on board, working traps and sometimes hand lines. The schooners were big enough to fish further to sea than could the open skiffs of the stationers, and this enabled them to find larger fish, in greater abundance, for longer in the season. Since even now few Labradorians own enclosed boats—the fishing season is too short between thaw and freeze for large craft to earn their keep—the same pattern remains. According to one old-time Labrador stationer, John Edmonds of Postville: "There was no competition between the Newfoundlanders and the Labrador people them times. If they 'Newfoundlanders' was gettin' more than they could handle and you was around, they would give you a load of fish from their trap. Or probably sometimes you'd work aboard of a schooner for a day and they'd help you out on fish from the trap that way."

Harold Paul, still a floater fisherman aboard a longliner when I met him in Makkovik, shipped as a schooner's boy at age thirteen in 1945. "That year I was down, we started in the spring of the year, got ready for it, went to St. John's to pick up our load of salt. On the grounds, out in the dory, you'd 'aul your cod traps and come in, throw your fish aboard the schooner, then gut it and head it and salt it. Work about four in the morning until next morning." Paul's quarter share as a boy amounted to 150 dollars, with a full shareman bringing home some 600 dollars for his work from May through October. Someone else remembered, "The schooners used to come down from Newfoundland with their cod traps, and they'd be rushin' for these good berths. Whoever got the berths first twas he's, that's the way it was with the schooners."

Elizabeth Goudie, a Labradorian who in old age wrote so expressively of the hard early Labrador years that the main government building in Goose Bay now bears her name, recalled the scene at Indian Harbor in 1917 when she worked at the hospital: "The ships came in until the harbor was almost filled up, that would be on Saturday. They'd all be dropping their anchors. The boats would be swinging with the tide. Sunday morning you'd get up and the whole harbor was full of white sails, everybody hoisting their sails to dry them out again for Monday. They'd be there all day Sunday; nobody worked on Sunday them days. You'd see them strolling around the hillside and walking around looking at the town."

One of the merchant princes also left his mark on Mrs. Goudie's memory: "Old Mr. Jerrett was always on the side of the hill with his beer bottle, or rum bottle, spyin' at the crowd to see that they were all on the job."

Bessie Flynn spoke of life in a community similar to Indian Harbor, with its combination of shore-based and sea-based fishermen: "Years ago, when I was a child, every man and boy was in the fishing boat early and late. They used to go in boat about three or four o'clock in the morning and at six the women would start their day. . . . Many nights I spent on the wharf splitting the fish or sitting up keeping the kettle boiled for when my husband returned from the sea. . . . Nobody paid any mind to hard work then because they knew nothing, only work. . . .

"When the bankers came—that was the Newfoundland schooners—every Saturday they'd come into the settlement for a dance and they would be sure to stay for prayers the next day. Nobody worked on a Sunday then. You'd look at the spars of the schooners in the harbor and they'd look like a dense forest against the deep blue sky."

Elizabeth Goudie recalled Sundays at Indian Harbor: "Dr. Paddon [head of the hospital] always prepared services—morning and evening with all his other work—and all the fishermen would come ashore and fill the church for the service. T'was really nice watchin' them comin' ashore in their little punts, crowded you know. The Salvation Army people would be in their uniforms, there'd be Catholics and Protestants."

At Indian Harbor there was the famous Grenfell Mission Hospital, which was known well beyond the borders of Newfoundland and Labrador. During my visit, after a search along the shore, we spotted a low concrete wall halfway up a hill of naturally terraced rock, all that remains of the hospital and its outbuildings. We beached the skiff against a smooth boulder, and came ashore rock over rock until our boots sank into spongy mosses. The climb was relatively steep, since the hospital had a location that commanded the harbor.

To schoolboys of my generation—at least those with an appreciation for the romantic in sources beyond the swashbuckle of Zorro—the name of Labrador was synonymous with that of an Englishman, Sir Wilfred T. Grenfell (1865–1940). He was a man with a frosted mustache and windburned face hooded in Eskimo furs, who mushed his dog team through the frozen north and sailed its stormy capes bringing medical care to a forgotten society that had never before seen a doctor. Older Labradorians still remember Dr. Grenfell personally, and speak with pride of having known him.

In 1892, young Dr. Grenfell went to Labrador as the first area medical missionary for the Royal National Mission for Deep Sea Fishermen. An athletic, religious man, Grenfell was appalled at once by the crippling effects he saw from poor sanitation and medical ignorance on people with even simple ailments. Tuberculosis was rampant. Fishermen contracted terrible infections from fish bacteria that entered through cuts caused by fish hooks and fish-cleaning knives, from salt sores (which remain the bane of sea fishermen), or from the chafing of oilskins on wrists at the gutting tables. The infections left untreated often progressed from swelling to blood poisoning, to agonizing pain, to amputations, even to death, all for lack of basic care.

The charismatic Grenfell presented accounts of what he had seen to the businessmen of St. John's, much of whose prosperity derived from the Labrador cod fishery, and persuaded them (more likely browbeat and shamed them) into providing the money for two hospitals. He built the first at Battle Harbor in 1893 for year-round service, and the second at Indian Harbor in 1894 for service during the fishing season. In 1900, he was able to add a hospital boat.

In 1913, Grenfell established the International Grenfell Association, which he supported through contributions and lecture fees. The IGA remains intact, supported since 1964 by the government of Newfoundland. It maintains nursing stations at several communities along the coast, as well as a central hospital at North West River near Goose Bay in Labrador (just closed in 1985 because facilities in Goose Bay have become adequate for the area), and a larger main hospital at St. Anthony in northern Newfoundland. The St. Anthony facility can take advantage of better supply lines than any available in Labrador proper, while planes (depending on weather, of course) can now render a quick emergency airlift.

In the course of raising funds, Dr. Grenfell, like his near-contemporary Albert Schweitzer in Africa, made himself into an institution and a walking legend. Some remember him in later years more as a man grown impatient, undoubtedly enjoying his fame (which included a knighthood) but also chafing over the need to give the press more attention than the mission in order to maintain a flow of contributions.

Two descriptions of Grenfell's appearances at Indian Harbor characterize the man: "Dr. Grenfell is about to descend on us, as a welcome cyclone," wrote Dr. Harry Paddon in 1915. And a nurse, Kate Austen, recalled from 1928: "Sir Wilfred's bronze face and white hair were everywhere at once, and everybody who talked with him felt useful and happy. He scoured the island, he crawled under the hospital and looked at the props, he chatted with the patients and held long consultations. . . . Then before you knew it he was out back of the hospital on a little flat patch of ground setting up a deck tennis court, and had a game in full swing."

Grenfell's chief deputy, Dr. Harry L. Paddon, (1874–1939), lives with equal warmth in the memories of older Labradorians—some say greater. It was he who ran the Indian Harbor Hospital, holding the line and doing the scut work while Grenfell gathered the funds and the glory. A photograph from 1930 shows a lean man with graying hair and a full mustache, his eyes, set in a nest of crow's-feet, glancing sharply and keenly out of the frame. He wears a proper tweed jacket, but an askew and rumpled tie. His appearance is dynamic, probably kind (perhaps also impatient), and every inch a gentleman.

Dr. Paddon's duty included opening the Indian Harbor Hospital each year. He would arrive with a small work force in late May to repair the damages of winter before the fishermen started to arrive on the steamers, pushing his boat through the last of the ice. As Nurse Kate Austen reported in 1928: "The men were stowing freight, carrying it up the long boardwalk on hand barrows. They took the shutters off and patched the roof. Doctor [Paddon] . . . worked all day on the pipeline which came down from a rock reservoir up near the back of the Indian's neck. Though the pipes had been disconnected and drained, water had seeped into some, frozen, and split the iron." Leaking roofs were a frequent problem, as was the stability of the buildings themselves. "I went to bed, and the bed swayed in the whistling wind," wrote Austen.

Paddon needed to be handy with a pipe wrench as well as a stethoscope, and to be a man of the stature and conviction to lead prayers on Sundays. He had to be a boatman in tricky waters as well. Paddon skippered a sailboat up and down the Labrador coast, bringing horse-and-buggy medical care to the outports. The forty-five-foot ketch *Yale* had been built for Grenfell with contributions from Yale University. She had a double oak hull, bronze fastenings, a short stubby mast, and massive canvas. Her "hot head" diesel engine, unmuffled, could be heard approaching from at least three miles to sea. According to Paddon's son, Dr. Anthony ("Tony") Paddon: "Father loved that boat with all his heart, could take her anywhere." By 1928, the Yale was too small—she had no room for a dispensary. The seventy-five-foot sail/diesel schooner Maraval that replaced her remained in service until 1962, when airplanes made the service less necessary.

Dr. Grenfell, too, was an enthusiastic sailor who skippered the Yale from port to port. He and Paddon had different styles, said Dr. Tony, an experienced sailor who inherited the bridge of the Maraval in later years: "Father was a better navigator than Grenfell. Grenfell knew all the rocks from having hit them; father knew where they were before he hit them. Grenfell was a bit reckless, very daring. Father was conservative."

Following his World War II naval service young Dr. Tony Paddon ran what became the main Labradorian Grenfell hospital, in Northwest River near Goose Bay. He trekked the Labrador coast winters by snowshoe and dogsled, and sailed it summers by hospital boat, to keep medical attention available. After retiring, he served four years as lieutenant governor of Newfoundland Province, returning from St. John's at the end of this in 1986 to his home in Northwest River. When I visited him in mid-1987, he had just acquired a small house in Indian Harbor directly below the old hospital site. For those who knew Indian Harbor, it remains special.

Them Days contains a beguiling reminiscence of life at the Indian Harbor Hospital in 1930 by the author Elliott Merrick. Merrick, who wrote Northern Nurse based on the memoirs of the Grenfell hospital nurse Kate Austen (who later became his wife), served a season in his early twenties as a station volunteer along with another youth. The volunteers, a fraternity that remembers its service with justifiable pride, were called "wops" (derived from "without pay"). Writes Merrick:

> We had been hospital orderlies when the Doctor [Dr. Paddon] was operating before the nurses came. Every rainy day somebody got out the binoculars and spied the wireless man's old trousers a-flap on the distant Marconi station pole at Smokey, which meant we had a mile to row and four miles of swamp to run through after a message. It sounds bad, but we liked it. . . . I went down to supper in the square high-

[122]

ceilinged dining room, where the floor creaked when the Doctor carved even codfish . . . the eternal codfish in one of its many disguises. . . . Rain was beating against the window, and the fire roared in the stovepipe. . . .

I stumbled through the rain to the Doctor's shack, where my bed was. It was a prefabricated cottage guyed with steel cables to ringbolts leaded into rock ledge. Doctor came in soon, and together we put up the wooden two-by-four props from wall to wall, an invention of his own design to prevent the wind from crushing the building flat. I got into bed, leaving my trousers tucked in my boots close beside the chair with sweater and oilskins and mitts.

Doctor set the kerosene lamp on a chair beside his head and commenced to read. After an unusual gust, he laid the book on his knees and remarked, "By Jupiter, I've never in my life seen a place like this for wind. . . . But you must get some sleep. It's your watch from twelve to two." |The watch was a wet lookout on a high rock behind the hospital, waiting for the whistle that announced the arrival of the coastal ship Kyle: there was a patient at the hospital who needed to be shipped aboard her.|

|"Steamer' comin'," announced the other lookout at ten of twelve.| Doctor was dressed before I was. He was buttoning his sou'wester under his chin when he heard her blow in the harbor. We groped in the rain. Lights were springing up in the hospital. When Tom and I rolled old Captain Willet onto the stretcher, it hurt him badly. The motorboat was at the wharf and Joe and the intern helped us lay the stretcher crosswise on the gunwales. He seemed to feel better with the boat rocking under him. Tom lifted a corner of the protective canvas. "How's that, Captain?" "All shipshape, son," the sick man smiled.

The young Merrick continues with a memory of the Kyle, a ship which achieved its legendary status at least in part through the contrast it offered those living in the Land of Stones:

Now in the darkness round about we could hear the irregular, intermingled pung-pung-pung pung-pung of fishermen's exhausts, come from all the coves and bights and tickles within a mile or two to see the floating palace, the herald of the other world, the news-bearer, the steamer. . . . Inside the first-class quarters . . . Tom and I go down the carpeted, branching stairs, feeling the smooth mahogany bannisters with pagan joy. Ostensibly it is to talk with Sam, the steward, in the spic-and-span dining saloon and get him to sell us a couple of

|123|

oranges. But really it is to contrast the white, speckless woodwork and the shining brass, this strong interior elegance, with the black, ruthless night outside.

Many years later, in 1988, Elliott Merrick wrote from Asheville, North Carolina, where he and Mrs. Merrick, the former Northern Nurse, now live: "What people can't comprehend about those summers was the esprit-de-corps we had, working ourselves to skin and bones, every one of us, and proud to be doing it."

Above the hospital site towers a lumpy formation of black rock that resembles an Indian's head in profile. It was here—on the forehead— that Merrick and his fellow wop stood lookout in the rain. Nurse Austen wrote that the coastal steamer could sometimes be spotted thirty miles away. "Way down below it was the hospital, flat-roofed, its clapboards the gray of storm-scoured whitewash. Around it were buildings known as the Mission Room, Laundry, Doctor's Cottage. A long board walk led up from the shore. The place was quite established, complete even to a graveyard."

Inside the hospital were "oil lamps, a bathroom, linoleum on the corridor floor, woodstoves, porches on the back or south side with netting. . . . The ground floor consisted of a dispensary, doctor's office, a bath, and ten-bed men's ward. . . . Upstairs was a ten-bed women's ward, operating room with skylight, a couple of single rooms, another bath, an oilstove, a kerosene sterilizer."

Nothing but a square foundation of one building remains—no boards, surgical instruments, bed frames, pots, or even rusty nails. I found a cast-iron shard half buried, and someone identified it later as part of a stove leg. A single thick ring bolt driven into one of the surrounding rocks looked firm enough still to hold a guy wire against the wind.

Surrounding the foundation, slowly reclaiming it, were mosses, lichens, and other wild plants. Nothing grew large during the short season between freezes. In level places, cavities in the rock held permanent caches of clean, brown water. Tadpole-like creatures lived in the puddles without ever appearing to become frogs. Subdued grasses and lacy white fists of deer moss an inch high grew where half-inch bands of soil accumulated. Wildflowers were the wonder of the terrain. I had seen their like before only on the treeless mountains of the Aleutian Islands in Alaska, buried in the rain-blown scrub.

Here, in the spongy moss, their tiny petals showed as dots of white, yellow, and purple. There were daisies, tulips, hollyhocks, daffodils— or cousins of these—all exquisitely wrought in dollhouse size. Some were lovelier and stranger yet. A careless foot obliterated them. Picked, they withered as you watched. Other sturdier small plants had each a single orange-red ball growing from the center of a white blossom. By late summer, these would ripen into bakeapples, the tart berry (downright sour to many outside tastes) that Labradorians consider a delicacy.

On top the Indian Head, with wind chilling the eardrums, I could see the rock stretching into long fingers. Tickles of water divided the farthest rocks into islands that opened a labyrinth into the sea. Beyond the last island, the surf and ocean waves began. White specks of icebergs floated southward along the far horizon. The few remaining structures of the former fishermen's metropolis only reinforced the solitude.

By any reckoning, it is an old landscape, the huge shapes worn by time. Across the water rose a mountain of crushed and weathered stone, the main lines of it slanting on a diagonal in colors ranging from gray to lavender with black intrusions. Geologists date the rock back one and a half billion years, some of the oldest on earth.

Ghosts? If I were directing a movie I would surely, at this point, superimpose an old photograph of schooner masts and skiffs in the water, weathered rooftops fringing the shore, and a gentlemanly doctor on his knees in worn denims patching rusty pipes. And I would provide a soundtrack of murmured voices bouncing from the walls of a tiny operating room, the clunk of wheelbarrow rims on loose boards, steamer whistles, the roar of an unmuffled engine reverberating in the distance, sails flapping, and the creak of oars being sculled in their pegs.

That was the Labrador past. In 1982, I was fishing out of Smokey with Brooklyn Bowers aboard his Newfoundland longliner *Cape Nipper*, along with his older brother Bob. There was no scooping fish from shore as in the old days, but out from shore some thirty miles we landed a few thousand pounds of fish each day, then worked late into the night to split and deliver them to the Hiscock station.

One afternoon after good fishing since dawn, as the boat bounced toward harbor over rough water, Bob sliced his hand to the bone at the gutting table. It was a frightening, ugly cut that quickly saturated a towel with blood. The day of medical care at Indian Harbor or anywhere else in the vicinity had long passed.

Steve Chubbs, manager of the government barge, started for his radio to request an emergency flight from Goose Bay. Just then, a small float plane landed beside the barge to discharge a fishery mechanic. The weather was clear—lucky, since two evenings later such a blow rose that no plane could land or take off for several days.

Bob protested that his hand would be fine in the morning, and what about that load of fish to dress? (Dr. Paddon had had the same problem at the Indian Harbor Hospital: Fishermen would let their injuries wait when the fish were running—or because they could not afford to quit—until the injury became dangerously infected.) We bundled a mournful and apprehensive Bob into the plane. Then we set up tables on the deck of the barge to start, shorthanded, for a long night's work delayed by the emergency.

Josh Burdett, a young Labradorian fishery officer, walked away in his uniform and returned in oilskins. He sharpened a knife and set to work at the splitting table. Others helped with the less skilled work of pitching and gutting. The mosquitos—nippers they called them in Labrador—descended, to be slapped by hands full of gurry and then finally ignored. Around midnight, Ina Chubbs, up in the barge's kitchen, fried a big skilletfull of cod tongues and britches (roe) for the volunteers. Someone with a guitar began strumming chords, and after we had all sung a bit Josh took over. He was handy with songs, as someone said. They were Labrador rhymes picked up from uncles and friends, then added to here and there and sung to one repeated tune. One song, about a hunting trip, ran some thirty versus, just the thing for passing time as hands pulled automatically at chilly cod. It ran in part:

> And now we're up and breakin' camp
> We must be on our way
> Cause all the geese and black ducks
> Are further down the bay.
>
> Our next stop took 'er Round 'ook
> A rich prize there will be
> We'll ask 'em how the hunting is
> And 'ave a cup of tea.

Indian Harbor: Ghostly Images

Our next stop's Pumphrey's Island
That is a likely spot
But we stayed there for one whole day
And never got a shot.

Now we-have' some be-er stowed away
To wetten our dry throats,
And we just think we'll drink some
To lighten up our boat.

And we all started drinkin' then
When we 'ad three or four,
Arch stood up to stretch his legs
And he fell clear through the door.

Down on 'is knees just sits there
A-laughin at the fun
I'm not sure but I'll split my sides
Before this trip is done.

And now we're on our way again
The weather it is right
Our final destination
Is down in Rattler's Bight. . . .

Next afternoon, the plane returned to pick up the mechanic. Bob Bowers stepped out, grinning at sight of the *Cape Nipper* moored and waiting. He waved a stitched hand, grandly wrapped in waterproof tape (Labrador doctors are realists), and announced his readiness to get on with the fish. With the crew complete again, off went the *Cape Nipper* to sea for a late pull at the nets.

9

Stationers

It is difficult to stop describing rock when writing about the Labrador coast. Rock absolutely dominates any space not covered by water. Even though the water is fluid and the rock unyielding, the rock has equal vitality. Its shapes are as varied as those the sea assumes through calm and storm. On the coast by Emily Harbor near Smokey, the rock towered in ancient cracked pillars and descended in vertical slashes. It plunged so straight that a boat could maneuver within touching distance and never scrape its keel. When the sun shone on it full through the clouds, it had the gray whiteness of spent embers, but when rain and spray made the surfaces glisten it darkened to the tones of the sea.

The Hurleys' station at Emily Harbor consisted of three houses, each with only one or two small windows, and a pier with a large adjacent work shed that Newfoundlanders call a "stage". There were piles of firewood, and clothes flapping on lines. A washing machine stood exposed on the rocks. Down away from the pier was a two-seater outhouse secured directly over boulders washed by the tide, and beside it a little smokehouse. Wes Hurley, whose windburned face shone the color of his faded red oilskins, was one of three brothers. When he had joined the others, Jim and Terry, seven years before, he built his own quarters with lumber, nails, and tools shipped on the coastal boat.

[129]

Wes's door opened with a string-pulled wooden latch, needed only "to shut out the nippers." The main room was a neatly kept kitchen with linoleum on the floor, separate propane and wood stoves, benches, and tables. Two small bedrooms led off from this. Leah Hurley, a woman with a direct smile to match her husband's rosy good humor and the bright curiosity of their young son Tom, filled a basin with hot water from the kettle so that we could wash the salt from our faces. She dipped the water from a barrel. Quite potable, it had a brown color from its source in a bog up among the rocks.

"Slubby, b'y," declared Jim with no pleasure, standing in the boat as Wes maneuvered alongside the first net. "Wonnerful little fish'll come, she stays dirty like this." We were looking into water so clear that the rock twenty feet below appeared to be within touching distance. Later, Bart Higgins explained a Labrador anomaly that fishermen knew by experience, that the water gave an illusion of clarity (and quite tangible visibility) by reflecting light off myriad algae that choked other life and repelled the cod. When the water turned "clean," the eye saw it as dark and opaque.

Each three-hundred-foot string of salmon gill net was secured to the rocks by a long leader, kept afloat by plastic bleach bottles, weighted open by quarter pieces of brick. The net was nine feet deep, but a strong tide this evening pulled it half horizontal. As the boat moved in parallel, any salmon enmeshed in the web glowed green-white in the clear water and Jim or Terry pulled up the net to pick it. Flapping underfoot, their scales caught the light alternately as silver or an obverse black. The net itself had meshes coated with slime, and in some places big stems and leaves of seaweed weighted it further. "Some slubby, and look at the kelp!"

We picked seven strings, the work of an hour. By now, the sun, its rays alternately hiding in the clouds and shining full, had settled between the cloud cover and the horizon to cast a clear orange light on the corrugated faces of rock. Around our feet lay a nice haul of salmon, some of them large. It seemed an easy afternoon's work, with the chill of late day setting in and the warmth of the kitchen waiting back at the station.

"Now, that was the fun part, eh?" said Wes cheerfully. He passed out wire loops attached to handles that resembled carpet beaters. "These whip sticks ought to hold." We spent the next four hours passing each net over the gunnels, beating off the slime and picking

The three-family summer fishing station of Emily Harbor in Labrador. The families come north from Newfoundland by coastal steamer in late spring with their skiffs, nets, and all supplies. Note community outhouse far right, located atop rocks washed by the tide.

The Hurley brothers of Seal Cove, Newfoundland, working salmon gillnets near Emily Harbor. Left to right, Jim, Terry, and Wes.

An open boat bounces in choppy water toward the cod nets off Square Islands. The fishermen wear hooded oilskins since the spray is cold even in July.

The summer station of Square Islands, located only a ridge of rock away from the open sea, as close as possible to the cod. Those who fish here are resident Labradorians who live in Charlottetown on the sheltered mainland two hours away by motorboat. They consider Square Islands an extension of home.

out the fronds and tubes of kelp. It grew cold. The last of the sun glowed against the striations of rock, then dimmed and darkened. It began to rain. Flecks of slime—slub indeed described it—collected in mounds thrown overboard by the handful. Slub clung to the sides of the boat and trickled down our oilskins. The nets were not struck gently. One by one, the wire in the homemade whip handles pulled loose and had to be retaped.

When we returned home five hours after leaving, a final streak of orange in the dark sky silhouetted the houses. Oil lanterns flickered in the windows. Wes scrubbed the boat, dashing off the slub with hard splashes from a cut-off plastic bottle dipped in the water. Jim and Terry climbed the ladder of wide boards, gathered the salmon that Wes tossed up, and cleaned them in the stage.

Up at the houses, one of the men started the generator and each small window brightened. Leah and the other wives were waiting with hot water in a basin and supper. The children had long been put to bed. There was a good fry of salmon at the Wes Hurley house, a few jokes ("Watch that nipper at you now!" followed by the pursuit and slapping of individual mosquitoes), a trip by flashlight to the out-house on the rocks, and then quickly to bed.

Life is not always so congenial for Newfoundlanders come to the Labrador. At one single-family station on another part of the coast, while a taciturn fisherman and his two beefy, unsmiling sons split and salted their day's catch down at the stage, the wife in the house on the rocks boiled water to do her laundry. "Countin' the days till we gits out of this, home to Carbonear," she confided glumly. "I hates it here."

At the end of the Labrador season, the Hurleys, like the other itinerant stationers, pack all their gear—bedding, nets, skiff, genera-tor, washing machine—and carry it home to Newfoundland aboard one of the coastal ferries. Wind and snow take over their little houses. By November, no ship can navigate through the ice, and soon the ice can hold the few who might want to travel the coast by snowmobile or dogsled. The outer stations of the visiting Newfoundlanders lie deserted.

The stations of those who live in Labrador, on the other hand, are located only a few miles from their winter homes up the bays. If they fancy a blustering ride over the ice in the middle of January—following the usual November–December trips inland after snow

covers the ground, to cut and haul out trees enough for winter fuel—
they can visit their station casually. And in summer they stay in touch
with both homes by boat. The proximity makes the stations of
Labradorians a permanent extension of their lives.

I first came to the Labradorian station of Square Islands, near Charlottetown (pop. 270) as a hitchhiker aboard a helicopter. The circling
aircraft showed a much more centralized community than the one at
Smokey, certainly than those stations of two or three weathered
shacks. The harbor was shaped like a horseshoe, with structures
concentrated at the bend and thinning at the ends where rocks rose
to end in promontories. Storage buildings and a pier dominated the
center. A slanting boardwalk led up to a small general store. Bridges
and paths along the rocky terrain connected some twenty houses.
There was even a small church.

The day was sunny, and with enough buildings painted, the community had a look of brightness and cohesion. Even the people
below moved purposefully—men in shirts predominantly red rolled
oildrums, pushed wheelbarrows full of salt bags, and climbed around
their boats. A network of piers lined the waterside. The harbor
reflected blue sky, accentuating the white of triangular wakes that
opened behind skiffs on the move. Square Islands looked like a nice
place, one going about its business content with itself.

The helicopter dropped me by an outcropping of rocks near one of
the promontories not far from the church, and promptly left. Mosquitoes moved in immediately. So did a few curious children. It turned
out that Frank Clarke, whose name I carried from a mutual friend,
lived directly across the bay at the far end of the opposite promon-
tory. I could see the house with its porch high on the rocks, lines of
flapping laundry, the outbuildings nested around two piers—a plantation quite its own separated by boulders from any other. Close as it
was in a straight line, it lay a good two miles' trek around the
horseshoe.

I left my knapsack on a boulder—some of the children remained to
stare at it, part of the package that had dropped from the sky—and
walked through marshy grass to the closest house. Inside the dark
main room, three men in boots and oilskin pants were gulping
supper. They'd skiff me across, yes indeed, going back to the nets

anyhow in a minute, just let them finish. They offered a chair and a forkful of meat from a tin. A few minutes later on the other side of the harbor, I climbed a ladder of wide boards to the Clarke stage. As we headed across, a man had started down from the house. By the time we arrived, he stood on the pier to take the knapsack—without question—and to pass a few words with the others about the fishing.

Frank Clarke shook hands and regarded me with polite curiosity. He was a man my own age, midfifties, sturdy, not tall, with a small brushy mustache and a slight squint. I explained apologetically that John McGrath in Goose Bay had given his name and suggested I might go fishing with him, but with no phone in Square Islands and no time to write . . . Needing no further introduction, he picked up the knapsack and led the way to the house. To his wife, Mary, alert, wiry, graying, he said, "This man's going to stay a while." And that was it. In a house of four small bedrooms occupied by children and grandchildren, someone quietly emptied a room for my use while we had a cup of tea in the kitchen. (I did not realize for two days that Franki, the youngest son, had moved onto the floor of another room.) Within the hour, I was out in an open boat in choppy waters, helping to pull a net, assimilated.

Clarke had come as a youth to the site of present-day Charlotte-town to fish in summer and go logging in the winter. He helped Ben Powell found the town, and is now a man respected enough to serve on the Newfoundland Shrimp Licensing Board. He and Mary raised their family of three boys and five girls in a house he built himself.

At Square Islands, where thirty years ago he bought his lofty site from "Old Captain Pike" who could trace back ownership for nearly a century, Clarke had also constructed most of the present buildings, as well as the solid, watertight wooden skiff in which he went to his gill nets, not to mention the wider, heavier skiff for working the traps. How did he learn to build houses and boats? "I figured it out. You just make up your mind to do it, eh." All in all, he had constructed twenty-five open boats. The next was going to be a longliner like the Newfoundlanders had, something with cabin and galley that could take him far to sea when the inshore fish grew scarce.

He stood on his porch overlooking the stage, the pier, and the boats rocking on the tide, the net locker with its separate pier, and the smaller storage buildings and smokehouse connected by boardwalks along the rocks, all of it bearing his hand, and declared, "This place is me 'art and soul."

During my first visit in 1982, second son Lester, then eighteen, occupied one of the bedrooms at Square Islands, with his wife Sheila and their infant daughter. By my most recent visit in 1987, Lester, now father also of a son, had completed his own quarters at the Square Islands station, as well as a winter home in Charlottetown with porch, basement, and well-crafted trim. He had also built the skiff he rode. The lumber for all the houses and boats came from wood the family logged themselves among stands of timber a few miles inland and then cut into boards at their own small sawmill. By 1987, the senior Frank was also completing a large new home in Charlottetown that had a sunken living room and a spacious view of the harbor. Had he helped Lester build his first boat? "No, I was too busy on my own house, I told him how to do some things and he was quick, he done it."

At Square Islands, as elsewhere on the Labrador coast, the Clarkes and their neighbors fished first for salmon, then sank gill nets for the bottom-dwelling cod. When the cod finally arrived in abundance, they set traps, elaborate arrangements of net that corralled the fish. They also jigged with hand lines when cod were too scarce to fill nets and traps.

Jigging is a method of catching fish that was probably preceded in man's history only by spearing them with a sharp stick. Some of the Gloucester fishermen who went to the Grand Banks in the 1890s, as depicted by Kipling in *Captains Courageous*, jigged for cod in dories launched from their schooners, as did Portuguese fishermen on Grand Banks from the 1600s through the 1950s. It remains a remarkably inexpensive way for a man to collect his share of fish, since the total investment—boat and strong arms excluded—is a hook and a few hundred feet of line.

The hook, unbaited, must sink some thirty to fifty fathoms to reach fish in Square Islands waters. The basic technique is this: Feel the touch of the bottom and raise the hook about six inches, then jerk the line every few seconds with a full sweep of the arm, always keeping the line taut. If cod are there, feeding as they do slightly off the seafloor, they bite at the hook since the voracious creatures seem to regard as prey anything smaller than themselves. Quick tugs signal a strike, and up the line must come at once without losing slack which might be caused by a bouncing boat. The cod, unlike salmon and halibut that struggle angrily when hooked, gives up almost at once except for an occasional twitch during the upward haul.

Lester, Franki, and I became the cod jiggers, since three filled the skiff and Frank had many fathoms of net ashore to mend. We joined other skiffs around an entrance of rocks where the fish seemed to congregate. Crews called to each other across the windy water, usually with the short in-joke phrases of people who see each other every day, but also with amused comments about the newcomer. There seemed only a patch of cod, so that it was easy to drift off them. When one crew started holding dead lines, they looked for action among the others, pulled up hooks, and moved. During slack, boats eased together to visit as the men talked about fishing and discretely counted each others' catch.

Whenever a Clarke crew headed in, from whatever direction, Mary would appear on the porch, descend the rocks with birdlike energy, and be waiting on the pier. The house commanded a castle's view, and it would have required subterfuge to sneak into the landing. Mary, and Frank when he was home, harbor-watched by second nature. It was their cinema, TV, party line, and other entertainment combined. The windows of the warm kitchen faced on a vista that was indeed worth watching. It encompassed houses and stages on the opposite leg of the horseshoe, the open sea and floating icebergs beyond, and all the low rock islands around which boats might enter.

Boats that appeared identical to a stranger each had its identity. "Look, Don's comin' in from trap," Mary would declare, watching a skiff with three silhouetted figures. "Riding low he is, moving slow. Fish, I thinks, eh?" Frank would take down his binoculars and focus. "I'd say three kant'l he's got. Little less, maybe two and a half kant'l. Comin' from west, must be that second trap he set last week."

Every week or so, one of the coastal steamers would pass in the distance on its way in to Charlottetown, and then on the way out stop at Square Islands. Even though no ship on the Labrador coast—given the weather—traveled a schedule more exact than the approximate day of arrival, everyone at the nets knew at once when the *Taverner*, *Bonavista*, or *Northern Ranger* was handy. One rainy night, a few of the stages still showed flickering lights, although we were just settling to a final lunch before bed after salting the catch, when the *Taverner* blew its whistle. The ship, sparkling with lights, had hove to so close that we could hear the thrum of its idled engines.

The dark, quiet water suddenly filled with moving lanterns and gleams of phosphorus stirred by engine wakes. Skiffs soon were clustered around the steamer's gangway, sides scraping, and people hopped gunnel to gunnel to clamor up the metal steps. Passengers lined the rail and called to people in the skiffs. Some boys from one skiff ran up the gangway with a sackful of fish to sell to the cook, while the manager of the community store maneuvered his skiff alongside the main deck to receive a cargo-netful of supplies from the hold. It was like a village fair.

In fifteen minutes, all business had been transacted. The whistle sounded, people clamored back into the skiffs, up went the gangway, and the ship was gone. Five minutes later, the harbor of Square Islands stretched below us utterly dark again, the only sign of life a glow against the rain clouds as the sparkling *Taverner*—whose passenger/crew complement exceeded the entire population of Square Islands—continued its way north to Goose Bay or south to Newfoundland.

Fishing might have dominated life at the Clarkes' station, but mealtimes framed the activity. Like hard-firing furnaces that needed stoking, the men settled at table every three or four hours unless they happened to be pulling nets. On one day, for example, an early breakfast of hot dogs and fried brews (soaked biscuit that had been served with salt cod the night before), was followed by a 10:00 A.M. lunch of cod tongues. Dinner just past noon included home-canned hare and seal, peas pudding, salt beef, turnips, and berry pie. The 4:00 P.M. lunch was trout smoked on the premises. Supper at 7:00 P.M. (after hauling traps) consisted of leftover brews, hare, and seal. Another lunch at 10:00 P.M. (after splitting and salting the fish) centered around pie and cold salmon.

Cooking kept Mary busy, but in a milieu where everybody worked all the time she would not have known what to do with idleness. There always seemed to be a row of heavy work clothes flapping on a long line that stretched by pully from the house to a pole on the other side of a small ravine. (Monday was wash day, but the sun did not always shine Mondays.) She loved to talk. When working alone— there was always something cooking or baking—she sang snatches of hymns in a high church voice with such cheerful enthusiasm that they might have been the latest hits.

Anybody up from the stage washed in a basin replenished from a hot kettle, but on Saturday nights Mary boiled pots of water to fill the bathroom tub, and everyone took his turn. The Charlottetown community is one of the few on the coast that still keeps the Sabbath. No matter how abundant the fish runs, the Clarkes' nets stayed idle in the water on Sundays. Some at the station rode their skiffs to town (an hour's ride in smooth weather), but a traveling minister held evening services at Square Islands in a small church.

Frank and Mary dressed in sober clothes (Mary with a hat) and took the skiff across the harbor to attend. The Pentecostal service was emotional and cathartic, heavy with the images of blood and the agony of the cross. Fishermen who were stalwart as redwoods when pulling two-hundred-pound nets from the sea groveled and cried out their sins. The sermon had a fervor that most city people have forgotten, but after the two-hour service neighbors visited outside the church as refreshed and chatty as any parishioners having done their duty.

Whenever we returned with fish in the boat we raised them by the bucketload with the help of a small wooden crane on the pier. Then we moved them by wheelbarrow to a bin by the gutting table in the dockside work shed, the "stage." The Clarke's dark, cool stage smelled of salt and cured fish, mellow old odors sunk deep into the wood. They were the sort of smells that triggered Proustian images of an entire society. Nothing so identifies an outport as the stage within sight of every fisherman's house, a roofed utility shed "handy" to the object most the extension of himself: his boat. Fishermen visit each other in the stage, not the kitchen or living room. A stage is to a fisherman from Labrador or Newfoundland what a barn would be to an Iowa or Saskatchewan farmer. It holds his gear, it shelters his harvest.

The Clarke stage was longer than many, reflecting the ableness of a man who could build what he fancied. Without windows, it had the comfortable solidness of the boulders from which it protruded on pilings. Considering the gales that scream around the island each winter, it was indeed a structure that could hold its own. The siding had weathered as gray as the rocks, except for the front. This faced the sea and the harshest winds and was painted a faded turquoise.

The stage had a typical layout. The rectangular shed opened onto the pier by the boats, with a wide enough entrance to accommodate cargo of any size. A smaller opening on the side led up to the house. Against the wall by the pier stood the heavy, knife-scarred gutting table with a few cracks in the floor for fish offal to drop onto the rocks and sea below. At the other end lay the split fish, placed row on row like shingles between layers of salt. The rows grew as the season progressed, a wall oozing brine, with an occasional maverick tail protruding from lines of pink-white fillets laid as neatly as bricks. Between the sheltered back wall and the table were stacks of salt bags, hooks for oilskins, and the paraphernalia of the work: nets, floats, sinkers, twine, tubs, shovels, wheelbarrows.

Frank started a generator, so that a bare bulb shone over the table. Everyone set to work. Lester laid out the fish on the table in rows, I sliced open their bellies, Franki gutted and headed them, and Frank senior, alone on the other side of the table, split them. Lester washed the splits and took them in a wheelbarrow to the back of the stage for salting. The mosquitos descended greedily. Labradorian hides must toughen to the nippers, because I was the only one slapping with hands that soon coated my face with streams of gurry.

The splitter's job required a fair amount of skill. Holding the slippery flap, Frank sliced a sharp knife along the spine to separate the meat in a strip. If the knife hit bone, it made a ragged fillet, and if it cut too far away it wasted the most saleable part of the meat. Frank's smooth knife could have been slicing butter. The first cut left the backbone exposed on one side. The knife then eased beneath the backbone and cut it free with another buttery stroke, to leave a spread-eagle of pure boneless meat. He performed the job so dexterously that it appeared easy. We had our laughs whenever I tried it, to admonitions not to slice off a finger (a present danger). The split would come out so ragged that we either cooked it for dinner or threw it away, but certainly did not incorporate it in the pile for salting.

The salted splits are the treasure of the stage. There is no need to keep a season's score in any other way since the height of the stack tells it all. Day by day, the splits accumulated with enough rock salt between each layer to cover the fish lightly. Salt cures the fish by drawing out the moisture. The liquefied brine trickles down the stack and through the wide floorboards to the sea beneath, but enough

The Clarke family in their "stage" at Square Islands. Frank, left, performs the skilled job of splitting the morning's catch of cod, while sons Franki and Lester prepare the fish by gutting and heading them.

Lester Clarke lays split cod in rows like cordwood, covering each layer with salt. The salt draws out the moisture and cures the fish so that they can be kept unrefrigerated for very long periods.

A gillnet weighted with large fish from several fathoms's depth, can be monstrously heavy. Rick Wills and a friend pull, while Lester Clarke waits to spell them.

A neighbor visits with Frank Clarke and his son Franki between pulling nets. Labradorians live in their boats as much as their houses.

Boots dry in the oven while Mary Clarke prepares a meal. The family comes in for "lunch" two or three times a day between working nets and cleaning fish.

salt crystals remain for a dusty coating to hands and oilskins when in fall the stiff splits have cured enough to be shipped. Cod was preserved the same way to feed the crews of Columbus and the troops of Napoleon.

"Six kant'l, maybe seven," Frank declared following a good midseason haul. Our oilskins were streaming with gurry. It began to rain and blow on the way home, and salty spray broke over the bow. The fish-laden skiff rode low in the water, its engine pushing slowly, as Frank steered in a lee close to the boulders around which surf had begun to break. The sweat that had accumulated under our oilskins turned chilly, and even with hoods up to deflect wind and spray we huddled cold and wet, with the chill of the fish creeping through thin boot rubber and soggy "waterproof" gloves. Miserable? Hell, we laughed and shouted and sang. Franki chucked a fish at his older brother and received it back slammed full against him. Even Frank, a generally sober man, smiled as he held the tiller and squinted through the rain.

Mary waited on the pier. It was already growing dark. We went up to the kitchen for tea and a supper of fried salmon, pickles, and home-baked pie (except Lester, who hated fish and opened a can of Spam instead). When Mary told her husband to eat seconds and insisted after he shook his head, he tickled her and she told him to behave himself. A little later, the work table was being readied on the stage and, given the load, Mary exchanged her apron for oilskins and a kerchief to help with the gutting. Into the night we split and salted, pausing only three hours later for another supper. The salt pile rose a satisfying three layers.

When the last of the offal and gurry had been washed into the sea beneath the stage (water came down under gravity pressure from a pond above the house), we hosed each other clean and climbed the rocks. From the porch, we could look over the black water to a single lantern flickering inside another stage, and with binoculars we could see shapes inside still at work with the splitting.

We piled wet boots and socks and gloves around the kitchen stove, even inside the open oven. Lester, still in boots, relaxed with his guitar, singing little songs to infant Paula. Frank tested the outside world with his shortwave radio, and raised someone in California willing to exchange call names. (He himself is "Rippling Stream.") The kids gathered in the living room around a small black-and-white TV set that delivered a single channel via satellite.

When Mary had heated some jarred seal, she called everyone to table. We of course said grace, then speared the rich meat and sopped the gravy with biscuits she had baked. Quickly after, Franki went out to bring in stove wood for the morning and stop the generator. The house blackened except for an oil lamp in the bathroom. Soon, everybody was asleep, with a single snore coming from one of the rooms.

10

Back to the Inuit Grandfathers

Matilda Pardy, wearing a T-shirt imprinted with a smiling "Have a Good Day" face, sat by a tub in her tent scraping rolls of blood-laced white blubber from the skin of a seal that her husband had pulled from his fishing net. She used a traditional Inuit *ulu*, a crescent-shaped blade gripped by a handhold close to the cutting edge. As the curved blade sliced closer to the striated underside of the skin, each pass cut less until it produced only little curls of fat. "Back living in my nice house in Happy Valley, never thought I'd be doing this again," she said ruefully, and smiled in the fashion of Eskimos who put a cheerful face to adversity. It was stuffy in the tent, but sunlight on the brown canvas suffused the interior with an orange glow. Nearby some dough in a tin can waited to be fried into bread for supper. Out back a sealskin had been pegged taut to dry on a makeshift frame.

The camp had five tents, pitched on a flat space between the water and a hundred-foot slope that graduated upward through wiry brush to a four-thousand-foot mountain. Across Saglek Fjord—an arm of Saglek Bay in northern Labrador—other mountains rose straight from the water that reflected them in calm weather. Most were smooth, their tops squared by weather and time. Geologists date these among the oldest rock in the world. The remains of snow under the July sun streaked like vanilla ice cream down the ridges.

In front of an adjacent tent Ernestine Tuglavina sat on the big pebbles of the beach with a baby in her lap, scraping another seal pelt. Painfully shy, she smiled without looking up as her hands moved with quick assurance. "Don't cut into skin," she explained in a soft voice barely above a mumble. "But . . . don't leave fat, that's no good either, skin go bad." She had first scraped a skin when she was eighteen, and thought she had done a pretty good job. "But then my grandmother, she took off a lot more." To avoid further conversation she bent over the skin and scraped harder.

Unlike her bashful neighbor, Matilda Pardy yearned to talk and be cheerful. She and her husband John had lived 21 years in Goose Bay/ Happy Valley where he worked as a janitor at the Canadian-US air base. The base, built during World War II, had changed the economic expectations for hundreds of native Labradorians like the Pardys. Then in 1976 the Americans left and a large part of the base closed. Without work, John decided to return to Nain and the Eskimo, or Inuit, ways of his origin. Matilda, who thought the rest of her life would be passed among the comforts provided by stores with ready-made goods, found herself back in a summer fishing camp scraping seals as she had done when a girl.

Saglek Bay was a place far away and alone by any standards, even those of the Labrador. It was located 120 miles north of Nain, the northernmost town on the Atlantic coast of North America, or, to talk of the real world for Matilda Pardy, nearly 400 miles by air or about 700 miles by sea from Goose Bay/Happy Valley. However, no scheduled plane or coastal steamer traveled here, nor was it the place of any permanent habitation. The waters remained solidly iced from late September through June. Before the discovery of oil in the sea off Labrador, it was visited by none but the Inuit who, until a generation ago, came traditionally during the short summer when char filled the water and herds of caribou fattened on tundra grasses. When New-foundland became part of Canada in 1949, and the central government closed down the village of Hebron located one bay to the south, even the Inuit stopped coming.

"I fished here with my grandfather," said Abel Leo, the oldest man in camp. "That was a long time ago." Now, in 1982, a new organization run by coastal Labradorians, about eighty-five percent of them

Inuit, had found the means to return in order to catch and market the local arctic char, a splendid fish with a flavor resembling a mild salmon. For younger men it was their first look at the austere country of raw stone that had become for them a place of legend and heritage. There were even ancient Eskimo burial sites in one long alluvial valley, attesting to ancestors who trod the beaches before them.

As in the past, and again during the early 1980s, Inuit families traveled in open boats from the south, or portaged across a flat peninsula from Fort Chimo on Ungava Bay. The campsites of forty families dotted some thirty miles of shoreline. Each camp was its own settlement, linked only by a collector boat that took the catches back to a processor ship anchored in a central part of the bay.

The collector boat made daily rounds. It cruised the shoreline, where mountains rose from a curve of rocky beach or jutted straight from black-shadowed water. Falls plunged between crevices, carrying summer meltwater from peaks where snow would accumulate again within a month or two. As we traveled, the men aboard the boats— they were members after all of a hunting society that looked for dinner on land as well as in the sea–scanned for caribou and seal. They would point ashore, and chuckle at my inability to see any of a dozen graceful brown animals with mossy antlers camouflaged among the mats of green brush.

Tents stood in coves and on promontories, small buff shapes noticeable only by their angularity against gray rock and white snow. We tooted a whistle. Men emerged from the tents pulling up hip boots. They quickly loaded boxes into small open punts and rowed toward us. Usually one man climbed aboard to help, while the others handed up the plastic containers with big silver char. Each box, with its fish packed in snow, represented the catch of an individual. A crewman scribbled the fisherman's number on a piece of cardboard and placed it inside. Back on the processor ship the fish would be washed, and their weight credited to the number.

One boat, no longer than twenty feet, had a jury-rigged housing of plyboard and greasy canvas built over the stern. From the dark cubicle peered a woman and three children. Boxes and bags covered with plastic lay heaped on deck. The family was returning to Nain, a one- or two-night journey down the coast over open water, where nothing but bare wilderness waited ashore in the event of storm, fog, or breakdown.

The collector boat followed a businesslike but leisurely course among the camps, with extended palavers and occasional visits ashore. Some camps were neat, others junkyards. They all had racks for drying meat and fish. I represented mere supercargo in most places, separated at once by an inability to speak the Eskimo language, Inupik. In one tent, a wrinkled old woman served tea to everyone but me. When someone pointed out the omission, she handed me a cup of tepid water and a teabag, scowling. Others were more hospitable, but extremely reticent.

I recognized some of the faces, and this may have been part of the problem. During the previous summer I had spent several days in Nain, where a permanent population of less than one thousand left little chance for a stranger to remain anonymous. In the single hostelry, a barracks-like building of basic accommodation, I ate with the itinerant judge of the region. I then spent hours sitting on a hard folding chair as he conducted his court. The circuit of the judge, a man part Inuit himself, took him every second month the length of coastal Labrador accompanied by a defending lawyer and a prosecutor. In the Nain community hall where the flags of both Canada and Labrador flanked the desk he used for a bench, wearing the black scarlet-trimmed robe of Canadian justices, he presided in English with friendly gravity. An Inuit interpreter translated often. The crimes he considered were sad things perpetrated by glum, inarticulate, sometimes weeping native people—breaking into the fish plant to steal frozen fish, theft of three bottles of whiskey (which sold for $100 a bottle at the only bar in town), a drunken teenage girl's rampage that included threats with a knife and a rifle.

Ninety-eight percent of his cases in the northern native communities, the judge told me wearily, were rooted in booze. He found the problem especially acute among families who had drifted away from religion. Indeed, while the boxy green-roofed white steeple of Nain's dominant Moravian church remained the landfall visible from water or air before any other part of town, I had never seen people around it in any number even on Sundays. The Moravian fathers, who founded Nain for the Inuit in 1771, once ruled there absolutely.

Here at Saglek Bay I now encountered some of the same people who had been defendants, witnesses, and spectators, handling their skiffs and working their nets with sober efficiency. By directive and mutual agreement, everyone had outlawed alcohol in the camps. Individuals whose faces I remembered had become straighter and more alert. But, from their viewpoint, what was a white stranger up to, barging into their traditional life after keeping company with the judge and witnessing their shame? I visited camps all day before finding that of Abel Leo, the Tuglavina cousins, and the Pardys, where an atmosphere less than clannish prevailed. Abel Leo, a respected community leader, was a dignified, wrinkled, articulate man in his sixties. Since his wife had remained in Nain, he had a tent to himself. Might I bunk in with him for a few days and help with his nets? I asked. We were lounging on grass inside his tent, drinking tea, with boxes of supplies stacked neatly in the narrow corners. He considered, then declared pleasantly, with the slow deliberateness that characterized his speech: "If you wish."

I had come to Saglek Bay through a series of encounters that started in Goose Bay with Alex Saunders, a lean, driven young Labradorian fisherman of combined Inuit and European heritage, who headed the Torngat Fish Producers Cooperative. The co-op, named for a jagged mountain range to the north of Saglek to which the Inuit attributed mystic powers, had been established in 1980 with the help of the Newfoundland provincial government to allow northern Labradorians to control their own inshore fisheries.

The Labrador coastal economy has always been a fragile one. Coastal Labradorians, especially the Inuit and Indians who live farthest north, have only been able to support themselves marginally by non-native standards. However, an abundance of shrimp school in Canadian waters north of Labrador. The rough open sea necessitates oceangoing ships to harvest them so that they are not part of any local fishery, but the government, in order to preserve the stocks, has issued only a few shrimping licenses. They assigned the profits from one of these licenses to the Torngat Co-Op in order to furnish it annual operating funds. With such backing, Alex and the Torngat directors had reopened the traditional native fishery in Saglek Bay as a commercial enterprise.

In the old days the Inuit dried or salted fish for their own consumption, but to make Arctic char a viable commercial product it needed to be frozen and packaged attractively. This meant bringing an entire processing operation into the wilderness of Saglek Bay in order to support the fishermen and their families for the summer. The co-op leased a 165-foot ship, refitted with a blast freezer and a vacuum packing machine, and brought it north with a ship's crew of Newfoundlanders. They hired an Inuit processor crew in Nain.

The two groups ate in separate mess halls on opposite sides of the galley and, perhaps inevitably, some tensions developed. The "Newfs" were more experienced ship handlers than Labradorians and they regarded the Inuit with the disdain of superior achievement. (There has simply been no history of boats beyond about thirty-five feet among Labradorians, whose long periods of iced harbors have always made it impractical to keep boats that cannot be carried ashore.) The Inuit crewmen felt discriminated against. The cook kept the ship's stores locked because of them, they charged. And even though he served everyone the same food, didn't the cook give more kitchen privileges to his fellow Newfoundlanders? And who had the best cabins? (In practice, choice accommodations went to the first people aboard, who all happened to be Newfoundlanders since the ship started from St. John's.)

Alex Saunders had his hands full without the added burden of a labor dispute. He had brought north with him a marketing expert from Montreal, a fisheries planner from St. John's, and a packaging engineer from a major American chemical firm. Everything was happening at once. There were supplies to buy, machinery to shake down, and payrolls to meet before any income started coming in. A broken part had halted factory operations until weather permitted a charter plane to bring another at great expense. We ourselves had left Goose Bay in hot sunshine. Four hours into the six-hour flight fogs forced us to turn back, since we could not land in Nain to refuel from drums on the small airstrip. During this flight and the one next day we could barely move in the small plane because a bulky industrial scale, which supposedly had been shipped to Saglek Bay weeks earlier, was still waiting and we had to take it with us. Mess table talk among the leaders centered around shatter packs versus freeze packs, of the fillet market opposed to the headed-gutted market, of a label design for the product. There were decisions required everywhere.

Back at the camp where I was staying, the distant sea came in fast enough to hiss gently among the stones and lap at Ernestine Tuglavina's boots as she scraped the seal skin. It carried with it a rim of fish spines and heads—the residue after filleting for a jerky the

[146]

Eskimos call "pepsi"—along with cans, bottles, and pieces of old net that would eventually wash away with a strong tide. A skinned seal carcass bobbed in the water, rolling as little waves washed over it. Tidiness is a cultural priority of the white man. No one here was going to bother disposing of anything that nature would eventually take care of itself.

The other families in the camp had aspired less mightily than the Pardys with their former life in Goose Bay, and they regarded the summer expedition to traditional Inuit fishing grounds as a great picnic. In the tent of Elias "Jerry" Tuglavina his wife Juliana diced potatoes and fresh caribou meat for a stew while gossiping lightly with another wife. Outside, the men sat in conference on a spot of grass in the sun as they discussed the next day's fishing. The Tuglavina kids of assorted ages played a throw-ball game nearby. When the oldest son, about twelve, returned with his dad from the nets he joined the game without bothering to roll down his hip boots. His presence turned the play into a match of shouting and tumbling and wrestling. But when Jerry called over and told the boy to row to the anchored trap boat for something forgotten, he jumped from the ground cheerfully and ran to obey.

Juliana announced supper and the family crowded into the Tuglavina tent. The tent was constructed in a traditional pattern verified by the remains of other Inuit tent sites in the Saglek Bay area that archaeologists date back at least a century. (Heavy ice during most of the year and lack of extensive habitation tends to keep things stable in Saglek Bay.) The back half of the tent had a circular shape like a church apse. A board platform covered the ground in this section, and the bedding of the seven Tuglavinas lay folded back to allow space.

The front half of the tent, left with its natural flooring of beach gravel, encompassed the living section. Juliana cooked on a stove made from half an oildrum set on a hearth. It had an opening cut to feed it fuel and an exhaust pipe that rose through an insulated opening in the tent. The top of the drum had space enough for a teapot, a saucepan of simmering venison stew, and a skillet in which Juliana fried thick pancakes of bread. The bread was greasy on the outside, but chewy and good. The caribou—Jerry had just shot it two days before when a small herd passed nearby—had a fresh gamey flavor. Served in a stew with dumplings, the chunks had sinews but they were tender. Everyone found a place around a low table, sitting on the two or three chairs, the edge of the platform, or the gravel. The oldest girl helped her mother. The place had the aspect of a home.

After the meal some of the others in camp raised the tent flap, received an invitation, and entered through a layer of mosquito netting. The men settled back comfortably, picking their teeth and smoking, as Juliana served instant coffee and tea in an assortment of plastic and enameled cups. A can of Pet milk passed from hand to hand. The oldest boy, now wearing short boots for knockabout, found a comfortable corner against a wad of laundry and concentrated on aligning the bright colored squares of a Rubic cube.

Next morning Abel Leo and I rose in the dark. He lit a candle and heated water for tea on a small Coleman stove which also warmed the tent. Outside, slapping mosquitos, we each took handfuls of caribou jerky from an open rack where strips of meat had been drying. We reached Abel's trap boat in an open punt which we rowed among the rocks jutting up at low tide. The oars of the men from the other tents dipped quietly around us as we all headed to anchorages beyond the mossy, barnacled nearshore rocks. The trap boats were rough-built, and their upkeep would not have passed muster at a regatta, but they had small cabins and enough deck space for working nets and carrying fish.

Each man had his own set of gillnets. They were tied to shore at one end, generally to a stake driven into a crevice in the rocks. To pick nets they traversed them from shore to boat in their punts. These little craft, only a few feet long and narrow as canoes, seemed ready to up-end with the sole occupant in the boxy stern and the bow jutting upward, but Abel and the other fishermen all handled them alone. They sprang about inside with graceful shifts of balance, and none capsized.

A heavy tidal flow had tangled one of our nets, and large fronds of kelp choked another. Nevertheless, fat six-pound and eight-pound char began to flap their last around our boots. Dawn filled the sky long before the sun made it over the mountains. The early light played in pinks and then oranges over the gashes of snow on the high sloping ridges. A fresh salty smell filled the air. After harvesting, we rowed ashore to a patch of snow, and shoveled it into the plastic boxes. Water gushed in torrents around us. We stood in one of the

Inuit families camp for summer fishing at Saglek Bay, northern Labrador. Strips of fish and caribou dry in the sun. The tents, with curved backs, follow a traditional Inuit design confirmed by archaeologists from remains of ancient campsites still detectable in the area.

L-R Abel Leo, Jerry Tuglavina, and John Pardy confer outside their tents in Saglek Bay between trips to work their nets.

Balancing gingerly in his narrow punt, Jerry Tuglavina examines a net attached to the rocks ashore at one end and anchored in the water at the other.

Under a July sun in Saglek Bay, Inuit fishermen stop ashore to clean the char just picked from their nets and to ice them down from a nearby snowbank.

streams and gutted the fish, leaving the offal for the tide, then iced them down firmly.

The tangled net, its wiry nylon fibers a nightmare of twists and bunches, took more than an hour to straighten, then another hour to clean of seaweed and set in place again. We spoke little. Abel remained cheerful, but he revealed some of his values as he spoke of an official from Goose Bay who recently had made a promise and then failed to deliver. "That man, he's a liar," Abel declared calmly as a matter of fact. "He will not be invited into my house again."

As breakfast food to be eaten while handling nets, the caribou jerky was strong stuff. Some native Labradorians ate it all the time, but for a novice it had a strong, soapy, half-sickening taste. It did not help when we returned to camp to see the thin-sliced fresh meat on the racks covered with black flies, and to see the same flies swarmed over human excrement deposited casually not far in back of the tent.

We made two other trips to the nets each day, and later more as the numbers of char increased during the short season. On some evenings Joe Tuglavina, Jerry's cousin, sang songs in Inupik that he had composed himself, and his wife Ernestine joined in quietly. It was a slow-paced life by city standards, but it had unity.

After a while the catches fell off. Jerry Tuglavina, only half Inuit but the natural leader of the camp since he had the largest tent and the largest trap boat, decided to go exploring for better areas, declaring: "We'd better try somepin', I s'pose, go down furder, eh?" He left his young son to work the nets. Everyone waved him off for the overnight trip, his bright twin daughters with hair in side braids jumping and calling after until the boat disappeared among the fjords. However, the fish had migrated out of Saglek Bay and soon most of the camp groups as well as the processor ship followed the fish to the next bay south. When I left the camp, Juliana, Matilda, and then even shy Ernestine gave me a hug.

Unfortunately, the Torngat Co-op was not able to sustain the char fishery in the remote Saglek area. The fish were there, but the logistics were too complex and costly to make the venture pay. Later in retrospect, a high Labrador official commented that such a fragile new enterprise should have been developed first with the full resources of the provincial government behind it, rather than left to a fledgeling organization just finding its way. On the other hand observed another official: "Like in a poker game, you can't really learn to play until you play with your own money." The Torngat Co-op still exists, with its same source of funding. Its work now follows a more modest schedule of maintaining storage plants in some of the isolated northern communities, so that people have a place to sell their fish.

11

The Wicked Sealers

Item in the *Baltimore Sun* of August 8, 1987: SEAL RESCUED BY DUTCH IS SHOT TO SAVE FISH. A seal that was rescued from starvation in the Netherlands only two weeks ago and flown to the Arctic met its end yesterday at the hands of angry Icelandic fish farmers. The seal was one of six flown to northern Iceland by the Dutch Seal Protection Institute in a widely publicized operation that brought fierce criticism from the fishermen. Police gave an experienced rifleman permission to shoot the seal, which fish farmers said threatened expensive salmon fry being hatched in the harbor of the northern town of Husavik.

On the 31st of March, 1914, 120 men left their ship, the *Newfound-land*, to walk miles on the ice in search of seals, as they did routinely. A blizzard descended and trapped them away from both their ship and another one in the vicinity that had irresponsibly sent them "home." The men, dirt-poor outporters, wore thin clothing and carried virtually no food, nor was there shelter for them anywhere on the miles of ice. Those who survived did so by moving constantly, despite agonizing fatigue and frozen limbs. Any who gave in to lie down for a rest, died. When the weather cleared enough to rescue the men two days later, two-thirds had frozen to death. Seventy unthawed bodies (eight others were never recovered) made the trip back to St. John's stacked on deck like boards, to be greeted by shock and island-wide mourning.

Hugh Mouland was one of those who survived. At eighty-eight, Hughie was half blind and mostly toothless. But for a visitor who had come to hear the story that he undoubtedly had told hundreds of times, the old man energetically reenacted his two horrible nights on the ice. He stomped and clawed at his feet, as he had done all those years before to keep warm, while rolling his eyes and sucking his breath in remembered agony. "I bit meself to keep alive," he declared, "and me teeth cracked from the cold. Poor men around me was cryin': 'I'll never see me wife no more, I got children and how they goin' to live?' . . . One man, he were so crazy with pain he drove gaff into his eyes, then he died. . . . Me friend Tom, turned blind on the ice, I led him with a rope. . . . Hard life, sir!"

During the reminiscence, Mrs. Eva Mouland energetically plied me with cuts of a blueberry pie she had just baked. We sat in a big kitchen centered around a stove that radiated heat where, to judge from needles and half-knitted socks on a side table and a padded chair with a footstool lumpy from indentations, the Moulands spent most of their time throughout the winter. The bathroom was a clean, fresh-limed outhouse an easy walk from the back door.

Hughie no longer went sealing on the ships after the disaster, but having begun at age seven with his dad, he continued as a fisherman for the rest of his working life. At one point as we talked, he said, "Fetch it for me, lass," and Mrs. Mouland (thirteen years younger and brightly active) flitted upstairs to find the mufflerlike "cassock" that had covered his head and saved him. "Goin' to be buried in that," he declared. "It goes in the coffin along wit me." Now his day was bounded by a walk to the bar for an afternoon shot on days when it did not blow too hard. As I left, putting on hiking shoes with big treads that I had deposited in the pantry, Hughie called out, "I likes your boots, b'y. Tell you what—if you dies first you leave 'em to me, eh?"

"That I will, b'y," I promised. Meanwhile, I stopped at the bar and left enough with the owner to set up Hughie for a few afternoon rounds. "He likes 'em strong, reaches him better," the bartender noted. Hughie never inherited my boots. He died in 1984. Mrs. Mouland still makes thick blueberry pies, however, as she spends winters with her daughter and son-in-law in Gander and returns summers to her pink house in Bonavista. After a visit in 1987, she

[152]

wrote in a carefully rounded hand that wavered only occasionally, "Well my dear I was some glad you come to see me. I only wish that Hughie was alive so as he could have a nice chat with you. He use to speak of you quite often after we meet you here at home it seem as if we wasn't strangers at all, so any time you come this way be sure and drop in and get a cup of tea, don't forget."

The world now frowns upon sealing—at least those people of the world who live in cities, and slaughter nothing bigger than a fly although they eat and wear the products of other people's kills. Norwegian and Icelandic fishermen still prize the seal for its meat and fur, but none relied on it so deeply in the year's fishing cycle as did the Newfoundlanders.

In Newfoundland, sealing is as old as the earliest settlers from Europe. They chose the rocky, desolate sites of their villages for the proximity to seals and to cod, giving only secondary thoughts to a comforting climate or to soil that might foster an agriculture. The native Indians and Inuit (Eskimos) had harvested the attractive marine mammals long before this, as the explorer Jacques Cartier recorded in 1534. Seal meat has always been a protein staple of the area, available for the hunting in communities too remote or poor (still) to buy commercial meats, and relished for its rich flavor. Families can it in jars for the table year-round.

Especially abundant and valued for meat, and for their saleable fur and fat, are harp seals, so called for a pattern resembling an Irish harp on the back of the adults. A migratory marine mammal, harps welp (give birth) annually in March, on ice floes that pass along the eastern Newfoundland coast and also enter the Gulf of Saint Lawrence, which encircles the island's western coast. This availability makes them vulnerable to being hunted—or harvested, or slaughtered, depending on one's frame of reference. Few activities have aroused such emotional opposition in recent years as this hunt for the harp seals, primarily because sealers kill the majority as pups, many not yet weaned. The fact that they are clubbed only makes it worse.

In March 1982, the St. Lawrence ice off Quebec and Newfoundland was a gleaming flatland, broken by hummocks, booby-trapped under snow with concealed water holes that threatened anything from a wet leg to drowning. This was still relatively easy and safe compared to some ice I had traversed, where gaps of water and slush separated small "pans" that dipped or sank a few inches when you stepped on them.

"Can't stop to talk," snapped Dan McDermott of Greenpeace, a man in his late twenties with a wisp of beard and windburned cheeks beneath a cap pulled nearly to his eyes. "The point is to save these babies." We found a white-coated harp seal pup every few hundred feet on the ice, most alone, some still with their dams. "Ssst" went the spray can, followed by a lively squawk from the pup as a stream of cold green paint hit its skin. The dams flippered clumsily to a safe distance, or disappeared through a blowhole. "There, baby, you're safe now." And he was off to find the next.

The green paint presumably rendered the pups' white coats commercially unfit, and at any rate did nothing worse to the pup than startle it. The spraying had started that morning from the Greenpeace ship *Rainbow Warrior* which now stood with its bow into the ice a quarter mile away. It was conducted under the distant, ominous surveillance of the Canadian Coast Guard ship *Tupper*. This was the second round, following lunch. "Don't they see us spraying?" asked one of the four others, since I had just walked the mile on ice from the Canadian ship. "They *are* going to arrest us, aren't they?"

"Can't say." Anxious to remain a neutral observer, I had declared to both sides my unwillingness to carry either tales or information. Actually, the Canadian ship was a-bristle with Mounties (Royal Canadian Mounted Police). Following a conference decision, it was only a matter of time and organization before the arrests would occur. Canadian law declared it illegal for anyone without a sealing license to come close to the seals at whelping time.

The surface of the ice bore more than live seals. Here and there lay the dark-blooded carcasses of others killed and skinned several days before. It meant that the sealers had already passed through. In fact, this morning before joining the protesters I had visited one of the two sealing ships in the area. The crewmen of the *Techno-Venture*, dirty and tired, were shouting lusty jokes from the rail in French (it being a ship from Quebec Province). Having taken their quota, they were headed first to deliver their pelts and meat in Newfoundland, then home.

"I hear the *Techno-Venture* quit this morning and ran off after hearing how close we'd come to them," said one of the Greenpeace group with quiet satisfaction. Sssst.

At length, three orange helicopters alongside the *Tupper* rose to the distant thrum of rotor blades, and headed our way over the ice. McDermott grabbed his walkie-talkie and announced back to the *Rainbow Warrior*: "They're coming to get us!" General excitement gripped the sprayers. It was not unrealistic to compare the engulfing racket of the choppers to battle noise, given the amount of machinery that buzzed the group and then landed, or the number of Mounties who poured out to make three arrests from a group of only four.

Two of the sprayers, a girl from Boston and a boy from Newfoundland (inland sawmill town), stopped their work and went off placidly. The third, a Dutch boy sent from the Netherlands Greenpeace for the occasion, doggedly continued to spray until two Mounties, each bigger than he, escorted him by the arms to the helicopter. He grinned spontaneously as they buckled his seat belt, then became solemn at sight of my camera.

The Greenpeace ship (since sunk in a New Zealand harbor by French frogman-thugs to prevent it from protesting French nuclear testing in the South Pacific) flaunted a grass-green hull embossed with a multicolored chevron. It presented a brave sight against the white ice and blue sky. Both crewmen and reporters crowded to the rail when McDermott returned and climbed a Jacob's ladder from the ice. As leader and observer, he had refrained from spraying when the Mounties came, to avoid arrest and be able to report back. "Was it violent?" demanded a lean young journalist with a German accent. The reporters, recruited to ride for the spraying, were upset that the arrests had not occurred earlier, or later, since after a cold morning on the ice they had elected to wait aboard.

The chief greeter was Patrick Moore, expedition leader and head of Canadian Greenpeace. An unshaven, tired-eyed man in worn clothing, his mustache shaggy from lack of trim, Moore nevertheless had the level directness of a man who could take charge. "Good, good," he said of the Dutch sprayer's conduct, and to the handful of those crowded around with notebooks and pens, with emphasis, "Resisted arrest, but they arrested him."

Moore also had cause for greater elation. The word passed from the radio room to deck and mess hall: "The European Economic Community has just closed down the seal hunt!" (It was actually a preliminary vote on the shipment of seal products, but the final action a year later did have that result.) Moore claimed personal credit for much of it, based on his steady efforts to bring Common Market legislators to Canada for a firsthand look at the seal killing. If the antisealing activist Brian Davies had been aboard he would surely have claimed credit also. However, he was in Europe, serving as "technical adviser" to the environmental committee of the EEC Parliament which had generated the antisealing vote. Davies was in fact the sole source of the committee's information, according to a frustrated, resentful Canadian official whom I interviewed later. Countersources representing the Canadian viewpoint had been ignored.

The arrested sprayers spent a while warming up aboard the *Tupper*, then went by helicopter to a guarded motel room in the chief town of the Magdalen Islands, en route to arraignment on the Quebec mainland. Two years before this, the townspeople of Grindstone (whose sealing livelihood was indeed being threatened) had surrounded a group of those arrested to shout bitter epithets and, possibly— depending on which side tells it—had threatened violence. But tonight nothing happened.

A concerted effort to halt the Newfoundland harp seal hunt began in the mid-1960s. It finally succeeded in 1983, when the nations of the European Economic Community, barraged with passionate arguments and selective data, banned the import of products derived from young seals. (The EEC vote was actually taken on a "morality" provision in its charter written to curb the international flow of pornography.) The ban, by closing the principal market for seal fur, essentially ended commercial sealing, because in the popular mind the hunt for any seal species of any age became unacceptable.

Sealing has traditionally been part of the annual fishing cycle in the outports of northern Newfoundland and southeastern Quebec. The ice that blocks harbors for nearly six months and makes work impossible with trawls and gill nets providentially brings with it the ice-loving mammals. For nearly two hundred years—until 1983— men of the outports found their way to central harbors in "March-month" to obtain a berth on a sealing ship headed for the Atlantic ice pack off Newfoundland known as the Front. But for over four hundred years, from the time of European settlements in this part of the New World, the outport fishermen have also hunted gray, harp, and hooded seals closer to land on a less concentrated basis. To do it, they set nets, walked out on the ice when it was stable, or maneu-

[156]

vered their boats through openings in the ice when it broke into pans.

The pressures against the Canadian seal hunt began for good reasons. In the 1950s, outsiders became enticed by high prices for seal fur, easy pickings from a herd nearly twice the size of the present one due to a slack in sealing during the war years, and an absence of regulations. They overran the ice in helicopters as well as ships, killing indiscriminately and without skill. Often, undoubtedly, they showed no regard for humaneness in their zeal to grab what they could. Legitimate sealers found their unattended pans pirated by quick-landing helicopters. Animals were wasted. The adventurers would kill more than they could carry, then abandon whole pans of pelts. With all the random killing, the size of the herd suddenly started to plummet.

The Ontario Humane Society and the Canadian Audubon Society were the first to blow the whistle. The Canadian government began to listen. But government often moves sluggishly until a bonfire ignites it. In 1964, the Artek film company of Montreal went to the ice to make a routine nature movie about seals, and returned with a horror sequence that depicted a seal being skinned alive on the ice. The film stirred international revulsion, as did an emotional article that the movie inspired entitled "Murder Island." Long after the film had made its impact, the man who skinned the seal signed an affidavit that he had been paid to do it for the camera—he claimed he was drunk—while two other of the sealers shown in the action were identified as members of the film crew. Such retractions after the fact do not, however, affect the hammer blow of original impressions.

In the same year as the Artek movie, the Canadian government began passing laws that halted the random killing and regulated killing methods. Over a longer term, it started the machinery to study the herds and set quotas that would sustain both the seals and the hunt. The Canadians claimed that eventually they ran the most regulated outdoor abattoir in the world, and that through their diligent research to determine whether the stocks were being threatened with depletion more now is known about the habits and populations of harp seals than about any other marine mammal. Within a few years, the original objectors, including the Ontario Humane Society, declared themselves satisfied.

[157]

The hunt, however, had been discovered. By the 1970s, its "cruelty" and "immorality" had became rallying issues for most of the animal protection societies of the world, fanned by several groups formed specifically for protest. The organizations had varying focuses that distilled into two: the cruelty of the kill, and the depletion of the stocks. While Greenpeace was only one of several that included the Fund For Animals, the Friends of Animals, and The International Fund For Animal Welfare, all the protesters became known as "Greenpeacers." The organizations made the hunt a media event by recruiting celebrity protesters, and, in various years between 1975 and 1979, always in front of cameras, by having members confront sealers on the ice, chain themselves to sealing ships about to embark, or spray seal pups to compromise the value of their white fur. The groups also organized boycotts in the United States of all things Canadian, from tourism to fish products, while generating campaigns of pressure mail to Canadian officials that sometimes became barrages of hate mail to individual Newfoundland families.

I first paid attention to the seal hunt in early 1979, when some Canadian officials, threatened by the mounting pressure of mail and exhortations to boycott, held a press conference to defend the hunt at the prestigious National Press Club in Washington, D.C. The Canadians explained quotas, regulations, and seal biology to their audience. When it came time for questions, a sophisticated-looking woman rose to demand, "Do you mean you've come here to justify the clubbing murder of helpless babies in front of their mothers?" A young man who identified himself as the aide of a specific congressman asked badgering questions. No one addressed quotas or controls.

It impressed me that a roomful of supposedly objective journalists turned hostile so automatically. It further impressed me that many of these journalists came to enthusiastic life an hour later under the same roof at a rally conducted by the charismatic Cleveland Amory, author, founder of Fund For Animals, and godfather of the seal hunt protests. At Amory's right hand sat the congressional aide.

The Canadians, all of them respected scientists or officeholders, were nearly catatonic with anger over their treatment. I trailed them from the press club onto the windy street, and, after persuading them to stop for a moment, challenged them to find me a bunk aboard a sealing ship. I offered credentials as a writer and as a sometime commercial fisherman. If they truly believed their facts in defending the seal hunt, were they willing to chance my impressions if I pledged to report honestly? There was enough farm life in my background to accept that even a fast-food hamburger required the killing of a creature, but I warned that I cared for animals and would not put a gloss on real cruelty. Letters and considerations followed for the next six weeks. They finally found a single sealing skipper willing to take a chance on the prejudices of an American writer.

In early March, boots and thermals packed, I traveled to Newfoundland at my own expense. I sat out a three-day blizzard in the northern, snow-buried town of St. Anthony with media people, Canadian fishery officials, and protesters all waiting (in separate lodgings) to fly to the Front. The corps of reporters and photographers, staying in their small motel with a single bar, grew increasingly restless to get a story and picture so they could go home.

One night the grave members of Greenpeace held a press conference in the boardinghouse they occupied. They said there would be a symbolic action performed on the ice when the weather cleared, and then they described the cruelty of sealing and the way that it would soon wipe the herds of harp seals from the face of the earth. It was a quiet presentation spoken with earnestness and conviction.

They objected to the harp seal hunt on moral grounds, said John Frizell, a thin young man with a black beard who served as business manager of Canadian Greenpeace. The taking of young creatures like this was symbolic. "The attitude relates to how you treat everything on this planet, the way we treat the earth itself," he said.

One woman in the group had chained herself to the rail of a sealing ship leaving St. John's harbor during the blessing of the fleet the week before, while other protesters had buzzed the harbor in rubber zodiacs as the minister started to pray. When her chain was sawed free, the captain of the ship, veteran sealing skipper Morrissey Johnson, pushed her along the gangway. "Never in my life have I been treated with such brutality," she told the press group in a sad voice. "What is it that makes human beings act like that?" She refused to see, under the dry questioning of one of the reporters, how her nonviolent action could have resulted in such violence.

Finally, the sky cleared. Various parties piled into separate helicopters. The frozen land stretched beneath us, with small settlements in coves by the sea and houses buried to the windows in snow. We traveled north along the coast, across the straits that separate Newfoundland and Labrador and then, after refueling from drums in the snow at Mary's Harbor, we headed over the frozen ocean. Ice stretched before us from horizon to horizon. Some was solid and glistening. Then for miles it would be broken into sheets that fitted together like irregular tiles. An occasional iceberg floated in the broth of ice, its jagged edges catching the sun and a profound blue shining from its center.

Toward the end of the trip, packs of black specks appeared on the ice. They resembled mouse droppings in their shape, randomness, and concentration. "Seal!" someone shouted. Through binoculars, one could see a miniature yellow-white speck alongside many of them, the pups camouflaged by nature with white fur. The seals blended as part of the flat, white panorama, but at length the ice became narrowed by intrusive details. Irregular sepia trails led to patches of a darker color and then, as the helicopter homed toward the scattered silhouettes of ships, the trails turned progressively redder until they had the throbbing color of blood freshly let. There were men in small groups, some swinging their arms overhead, some bent forward as they pulled loads behind them.

The helicopter landed me on solid ice beside the 143-foot wooden-hulled *Gulf Star*, and the pilot waited only long enough to unload my knapsack before heading off on another commitment. The wind whined at twenty knots. I stood alone on ice atop ninety fathoms of water. A dozen men in blood-smeared oilskins were dragging tows of floppy crimson pelts that left a blood trail on the crags and nubbles of ice behind them. When I nodded, one or two responded in a cautious, grunting fashion. We might each have thought we were viewing the Devil.

I started toward the ship, walking granny-style to keep from slipping. Suddenly, from the deck above: "Who are you! Don't you come aboard here!" The angry man who shouted had a hostile glare on his rough, square-carved face.

"I had an invitation from Captain Frank Puddister," I began weakly, hoping he was not Puddister. The chill of the ice had already begun to penetrate my clothing and, while there were three other ships far away on the shining ice, and some distant circling helicopters, the only viable shelter lay in the black, scarred hull before me.

Captain Puddister, an easy-looking man with a smile at his own forgetfulness, appeared and made everything right. Oh yes. He had neglected to tell anybody that "some writer fella" might come aboard. Grinning men reached down hands caked with grease and blood to lift my luggage and help me up the ladder of slippery beams. Don Linfield, the mate who had done the shouting, apologized bashfully. He had thought I was a "Greenpeacer" come to harass them.

Elsewhere on the ice, the cortege of demonstrators had dismounted from helicopters beside a group of sealers. When I walked across the ice with the ship's fishery officer to watch them, the sun was shining with dazzling brightness and the men and women of the press, exhilarated with the adventure and with good weather at last, were treating the excursion as a picnic.

A member of Greenpeace, glum probably over the lack of seriousness, sprayed a seal pup. Waiting Mounties—heavy, authoritative, unamused men—promptly arrested him. Everyone took pictures. "Is this it?" one journalist asked, plainly annoyed despite the pleasantness of the day. It appeared to be, since the single demonstrator was in custody. "There used to be a hell of a lot more to these things." People climbed back into their helicopters and returned to the warmth of the St. Anthony hotel, mission accomplished.

The colorful, anger-provoking demonstrations to gain public awareness and funds had indeed run their course, to be replaced by a more subtle persuasion directed at parliaments. Paul Watson, the most flamboyant of the activists, no longer confronted sealers on the ice (while safely surrounded by media and police) to throw men's tools and pelts into the water and then chain himself to a moving whip-line of pelts. Brigitte Bardot no longer traveled north as she had in 1977, to pose while hugging a stuffed seal in the snow. (Later in Paris she told reporters that she had seen "adorable little bundles of wool"—actually seals are covered with hair—"that I held in my arms, and which I knew were going to die.")

Back at the *Gulf Star*, I settled in. My berth with the cook and his assistant gave me more privacy than most of the crew, who slept six or eight to a cabin. The entire ship had a sweet odor that turned out to be seal fat, but nowhere more than the corridor between cabins where the crewmen left their greasy oilskins and boots each night. Once aboard, I would have defeated my purpose by remaining a passenger. While I had no sealing license and no desire to kill seals, I turned-to on the ice with the rest, making myself useful by hauling pelts.

We rose about 4:00 A.M. each day to the bang of the cook's pan, and went out to stretch and urinate in the dark. The ice surrounding us on all sides had a bluish predawn glow like objects lit by black light. Frosty air puffed over the windward rail bearing a clean neutral odor. The other ships on the horizon twinkled like ornaments of no substance. From far below decks came the faint hum of the ship's generator, a sound usually unnoticed from its constancy. The ice scraped and groaned. From the ice, seal pups gave random cries. Nothing else disturbed the silence.

On the mess deck, we passed in line through the galley as the cooks slapped a huge bacon-fat breakfast onto our plates. The men washed it down with quantities of hot strong tea while Harry Brett, the chief cook, a big man in his sixties with a scowl formed from many years of squinting on the ice as a sealer, urged, "Eat more, b'y, here, finish it." Then we dressed for the cold and assembled. The worst part of the day was this wait at dawn on the main deck, muscles not yet limber, clothes still clammy from yesterday's sweat. A sweet-smelling slick of seal-fat-coated ropes, tools, coveralls, oilskins, everything. A cigarette here, even for a convinced nonsmoker, gave surprising solace.

The men, even the young ones, had faces cured to leathery creases from years of salt and cold, and fingers cracked and puffy like fishermen's hands the world over. They covered a gamut of personalities, all with a background in the Newfoundland outports: bashful Ross Etheridge of Brig Bay; Mercer Cullimore of Little Catalina, an aggressive veteran of many springs on the ice who complained about nearly everything but proved himself a formidably fast, neat workman; wiry Gordon Brown of Summerford who, with one withered leg, hopped boldly across the ice with a bird's lightness; the cheerful young White brothers Gordie and Arthur from Valley Field; taciturn Ross Slade of Ochre Pit Cove; Winston Fowlow of Manuels, a reed-voiced young singer of old sealing ballads on the mess deck, who was quietly thrilled to be starting his first year on the ice after going from ship to ship for three years to find a berth.

"Now, Bill me son, what do you think of we?" The question, asked often in different forms with a wary half-smile, embraced the entire seal hunt. Few outsiders they ever met, certainly no Americans, had anything but the worst to say about their work. The fact that I had gone on the ice for several days huffing and straining hundred-plus

[162]

pounds of pelts, getting as caked with grease and blood as the rest, might be forgotten in the middle of the day, but in the cold of early morning it appeared to them fresh that a man choosing to work on the ice for any but economic reasons must have something up his sleeve.

"Hard way to make a living, boy," I said, biding my time.

Aboard the sealing ship, it was the captain's responsibility to locate us within walking distance of seals. At first light, either he or the mate were peering to confirm that they were "in the fat" (helped by a lookout in the "barrel" high on the mast), or cracking the bow through the ice as necessary to search. Moving was easier said than done: Sometimes we had to dynamite the ice to clear a passage.

With fat sighted, the ship's whistle tooted several times. We grunted to our feet, tied hauling ropes around our waists, grabbed red flags and hakapiks (a steel-knobbed killing tool), traversed the main deck over piles of thick, blubbery pelts, and climbed down the side on boards roped together. Sometimes a gap of water separated the hull from firm ice and it was necessary to make a wide leap from the slippery, bumping ladder. Such a jump started the day of constant, wary alertness on the ice, which, for all its several inches of thickness, was after all only a fragile cover to an ocean that could freeze or drown a man in seconds.

The ice was different every day depending on the direction and velocity of the wind. It could be solid and glassy so that your feet skidded at every step or, with snow underfoot for traction, like a gravel path. Next morning, a swell would have broken the ice into "pans"—flat segments that could be as lordly as drifting islands, or a nightmare of small ones that dipped under a man's weight, separated by rivers of slush ("slob"). A strong blow might crush the pans against each other into "clumpers" several feet high that made the terrain as jagged as a mountain pass. Before becoming conditioned to it, I found the walk of a quarter mile a day's work in itself, even with the big-headed nails that Don the mate drove into my boot heels for traction as all the sealers had done for themselves. The pans never remained still, as wind and currents parted and merged them. An easy jump could change in seconds to a dangerously chancy leap across a widening gap. Sometimes the ice was loose enough to permit a sea swell, and the pans rode up and down. A large pan, riding the top of a crest, could split and separate between your feet.

'Only an occasional man fell in (none were lost this year), but many had wet legs by the end of the day.

Movement on all but the most solid ice required agility. Most of the sealers had grown up around frozen harbors and learned as boys to "coppy," the nimble skill of jumping from pan to pan.

The sealers traveled in groups, then separated in pairs for safety. Each group staked out an area informally, planted a bright marker flag and pole on a central pan, and scattered in quest of seals. We hauled the pelts to the flag, stacked them, and tied them together about ten to a strap. This was called "panning." The pelts themselves—"sculps" with the fur attached to a several-inch layer of fat—weighed about sixty pounds from pups and a hundred from adults.

The killing and skinning often occurred several hundred yards from the flag. Loosening a toggle rope from around his waist, the sealer would pass one end through the eye holes of two scalps, and place them fat-down to slide over the ice. The other end of the rope went over his shoulder. While pulling the pelts, there were blowholes to avoid (some covered with snow and not apparent), slob ice to circumvent, and gullies between pans to leap across. As I bent to the job, trying to keep 120 pounds of pelts in motion (since any halt meant a heavy tug to start them moving again), more than once a day my boot—even my leg—would crash into water. Soon my shins and knees grew black with bruises against the hard edges of ice. The smell of liniments and home poultices on the berthing deck attested to the commonness of such abrasions even among the seasoned.

Seals were abundant on the ice. The adults busily slipped in and out of their blowholes while the pups flippered and squawked. After the first week, more and more of the pups remained alone, testing the water until they had taught themselves to swim. As seal biologists will attest, the female harp seal nurses her pup intensively for fourteen to twenty days and then deserts it permanently. The Canadian government allowed only a small percentage of adult seals to be killed. Biologists consider one mature female left alive to be worth four or five pups, since her reproductive life spans more than two decades. Most of the dams deserted their pups immediately when the sealers approached. (One of the old timers said that only a dam with her first pup defended it.) When a female challenged them, the sealers attempted to drive her off and usually did. When she per-

Sealers descend a ladder to disperse on the ice in search of seals. The ice this day is relatively solid and clumped, despite large openings in the foreground.

A sealer leaps across a gully of "slob". His ship is far in the distance.

Sealers "coppy" from one ice pan to another, testing as they go. A fall through the ice could lead to drowning, as the weight of wet clothes quickly pulls a man down in the frigid water.

Fishermen deliver seal pelts in Twillingate, Newfoundland. The harbor is iced so heavily that they returned home in the wake of an icebreaker. The outport depended on seals for a major part of its income. Fishermen suffered permanent hardship when animal rights activists succeeded in outlawing the hunt.

sisted, they sometimes killed her along with the pup. (By law, they could kill a nursing female only if she threatened them by being "belligerent.") Or, with a laugh, they spared both dam and pup and continued on.

During the pups' nursing cycle, they grew explosively, from fifteen pounds to nearly a hundred, most of it fat to protect them against the cold and to provide nourishment until they could catch their own fish. Their fur was as white as the ice, nature's camouflage against predators: hence their name, "whitecoats." The white fur began to shed at the end of nursing as the pups learned to swim, giving way to gray-black adult fur. In another week, they had become swimming, functioning youths—"raggedy jackets," with coats of greatly reduced value. Whitecoats thus needed to be be taken quickly. It was the white fur (easily dyed), an abundance of fat, and their tender meat that made them commercially desirable. Also, the truth of it was that only the whitecoats could be hunted in large enough numbers to support the ships, since they could not escape into the water as did the adults.

The pups squawked day and night. It could hardly have been a function of fear, of which they had no experience, but the noise did resemble the crying of infants, which made it easy for protesters to characterize them as babies. On the ice, they were little sausages of white fur, their cute faces and liquid eyes just as heartbreakingly beautiful as those in the "Save A Seal" photographs. A snapping blow to the head changed all this—the eyes glazed instantly and blood crept from the mouth. Before the hunt on each ship, the fishery officer checked out every sealer to ensure his ability to make the decisive initial blow, which, properly delivered, caused immediate, irreversible brain damage.

During the hunt, one or two fishery officers per ship spot-checked skulls on the ice to make sure the job was being done properly. Canadian law since the later 1960s required three blows. For the sealers, who knew from experience that one firm blow did the job, this counted out wryly to: "One nog on the head to kill 'im, one for the fishery officer, and one more for Greenpeace."

No normal person would find it pleasant to see a furry seal pup banged on the head and skinned to a bloody carcass. The sealers closed their minds to it just as do the workers in slaughterhouses. The fact that the creatures displayed no anxiety and died quickly did not alleviate the grimness. For perspective, I needed to visit commercial abattoirs and see the assembly-line killing of apprehensive cows and pigs that society accepts with few questions. It was also reassuring that a study by veterinarians commissioned in 1971 by the U.S. Commerce Department confirmed clubbing as the quickest and most humane method to kill seals.

Immediately after striking, the sealer rolled over the brain-dead seal and cut an artery in its chest to ensure biological death. Spurts of blood covered ice and boots. The "sculping" followed—cutting fat, meat, and hide away from the bone structure in a single piece. I worked into the sculping only gradually, under instruction. False moves reduced the pelt's value and could also sever a finger.

The sculping knife, worn on the belt in a wooden sheath usually carved and decorated by the sealer himself, needed to be honed frequently to keep it razor sharp. Each man also wore his own "steel" for ready sharpening. The blade must follow the rib cage closely as one hand grips an edge of thick blubber and peels it back. The trickiest steps of the sculping were the cut around the skull, and the deft slices required to free the meat of the two flippers from the fat so that on deck later they could be separated with a final cut.

Cleveland Amory, an aggressive and dedicated whistle-blower on cruelties to other animals through his Fund For Animals, has declared with sweeping judgment: "This clubbing is the cruelest single mass event that goes on in the entire world." Cruelty, used as an emotional jab, was certainly the major platform of the antisealers, the one that brought in donations and inspired letters. Grade school teachers rallied entire classes to write to Canadian officials. "The sealers are like vampires . . . " began one schoolchild's diatribe. Then there were letters from individuals to names provided on lists. "You dirty rotten son of a bitch . . . I hope you die!" read one of these, from a man in Miami, which a shocked and sickened Newfoundland fisherman's wife opened one day. Another was from a woman in Santa Cruz: "I pray that the death you harbor in your heart sinks into your groin to render you impotent." The ultimate curse of the righteous followed: "May your children die in the same way as you kill other helpless babies."

The most harrowing accusation voiced in fund-raising brochures was that seals were being skinned alive. The despicably false old Artek movie might have been proven staged, but the image had been

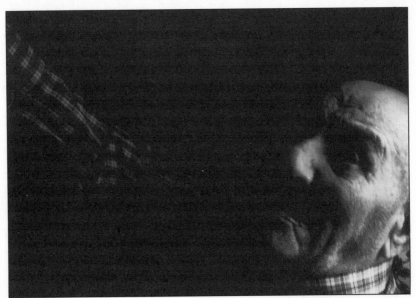

The late Hughy Mouland, eighty-eight in 1979 when this picture was taken, re-enacts the horror of his experience on the ice when eighty-five men froze to death around him. The 1914 disaster occurred when sealers from the ship *Newfoundland* became stranded on the ice during a blizzard.

Anti-sealing slogan displayed aboard the original Greenpeace ship *Rainbow Warrior*. The activist group had wedged their ship into pack ice off Newfoundland to spray seal pups in protest against the seal hunt.

Sealers aboard the ship *Terra Nova* wait under shelter in the cold early morning until the captain signals for them to go out on the ice for the day.

Crewmen of the sealing ship *Gulf Star* finish dinner after a day's work. Another two or three hours lie ahead to hose and store the pelts. Button on the cap of the man at right is his Canadian sealer's license.

established. I did see exceptions to the orderliness of the seal killing, as the men grew numb and tired after hours in the cold. However, I witnessed no instance in the course of several hundred killings, of a seal skinned while conscious or alive. The sealers were workmen with pride in their skill, faced with days of heavy labor. As one of them declared pragmatically: "I'd got enough work sculpin' 'um dead widd-out a live animal jumpin' under me knife besides."

The general mess was as bad as that in a farmyard at slaughtering time, except that among the seals, despite the claims of the protest groups, there was no parallel to the screams of pigs who knew something was wrong. My participation certainly required personal adjustments. Sometimes the carcasses twitched under the knife from involuntary muscle spasms—an ugly feel akin to that of seeing a decapitated chicken continue to scramble. The dead seal was still warm, the knife slippery with grease and blood, the pelt and carcass heavy to maneuver apart. I started out wearing sunglasses—ice glare blinds even under a gray sky—but sweat soon had them slipping off my nose. The sealers had a trick known in another form by football players, to slash a half-moon of seal blood under each eye. The dark patch absorbed the glare, and their eyes functioned without even a squint. But to a reporter spending his hour on the ice before flying back to a motel such a blood smear did give sealers a brutal look, and one that projected on camera.

In one move to palliate world opinion, the Canadian government banned the traditional but sinister-looking "gaff," which was said to be used for gouging the seals. They replaced the gaff, a curved hook combined with a pointed spike mounted on a pole, with a "hakapik," the head of which combines a straight hook with a blunt knob. The hakapik is a heavier instrument for hitting the seals squarely on the head, although sealers claimed the gaff was just as effective. The hakapik might also have been used for gouging by anyone who was determined to do this, although I never saw it happen since the blunt side was many times more efficient for delivering a death blow. The compulsory change of tools appeared at least in part to have been cosmetic.

Either hook was a basic tool of the sealers, used to pull objects or grip into the ice. Unfortunately for the sealers, the hakapik held pelts less firmly than the gaff and made the hard work of dragging them even harder. As for gripping ice, the difference between the two hooks nearly cost me my life. At one point I leapt a gap between two pans, failed to make it, and immediately sank waist-deep in frigid water that filled my boots and began weighting me down further by the second. I had been maneuvering alone, between groups, so that no one was close enough to help or even to hear if I had wasted energy on vain shouts. I beat my hakapik into the nearest ice, a glassy hummock, but it kept slipping. I found out later by trying one that a curved gaff would have held.

With luck and adrenalin, I thrashed my way to a handhold and struggled back onto the ice, then crept in a trembling shiver to the nearest sealers several hundred yards away. With chuckles and out-right laughs over how I'd "ga' a grand wettin' " (in the way they joked over their own misadventures), they helped me remove my boots, pants, and thermals in the biting wind and wring out the water that was already turning to ice against my skin.

When I complained how poorly the hakapik point had held the ice, they turned serious. "If they's any'ting you writes, Bill me son, you write how wit' no gaff a man's got n'er chance h'at all. You tell people that, now, who's never goin' to work on de oice and don't under-stand." We took a breather in my honor, which I prolonged beyond the others, nursing a rare cigarette down to its butt. Why explain to them that the world was indifferent to their dangers, having judged their work unacceptable?

After being panned, the sculps needed to reach the ship which could be half a mile or more away. The men dragged steel whip-lines from the ship to nearby pans, and a winch pulled the strapped clusters of pelts back over the ice by the flopping ton-load. Others layered the sculps on deck, too warm yet to store. (Residual heat would have started the fat turning rancid.) After gathering from an area, the ship headed for other pans, easing or crashing through the ice. Canadian law forbade pelts to be left on the ice for more than twenty-four hours. It was also common sense to collect the harvest daily since a sudden storm could sink a day's work. At dusk all sealers returned aboard for dinner, first placing lanterns on the flagpoles of any remaining pans.

Newfoundland ships served three traditional meals that the men considered home cooking. "Jigg's Dinner" consisted of fatty salt beef with boiled cabbage, potatoes, carrots, and turnips. Then there was "fish and brews"—boiled salt cod and soaked hard-tack biscuits with the above vegetables, covered with the fried skin of pork rinds ("scrunchions") and its liquid fat. The last of the three was "flipper dinner." Harry served seal flippers—each a thick hock of meat with no appearance at all of a flipper—in a heavy brown natural gravy with boiled dumplings and the vegetables. The dumplings also doubled as dessert when slathered with black molasses. Seal meat has the color of pumpernickel and a strong sea taste that is not fishy. Its texture after the fat has been sliced and soaked away resembles beef, although the flavor is richer and the protein content higher than beef. My friends in St. John's prepared seal as gourmet food, cooked in dark rum and accompanied by a full-bodied cabernet, but on sealing ships under a good "blacksmith cook" (the fishery officer's affectionate term) it was just the stuff for cold men with big appetites.

The work continued after dinner, first to recover any remaining pans on the ice with the aid of searchlights, and then to clean and store the pelts and meat. To move on deck over the layers of fatty pelts was like jumping on hills of Jello. Several men cut flippers loose from the fat—two to five pounds of meat apiece—and sorted them in storage bins along with the carcasses. Others hosed the furs with cold sea water to wash and chill them

Blizzards often passed over, coating oilskins, pelts, and tools with snow. It grew cold enough in the black darkness for eyebrows to frost, and for the water, blood, and grease on deck to turn a crusty slush. Thud went each sixty-pound to hundred-pound sculp as it dropped into the hold after being dragged across deck. A group stacked them below. Depending on the hunt that day, the deck work ended between nine and midnight. The men peeled off their greasy clothing, and either crawled to bed or went to relax a bit on the mess deck. On early nights, we often fried up a late supper of seal hearts and livers gathered that day on the ice.

Life on a sealing ship in 1979 was rough and messy by urban standards, but luxurious compared to that which the young Hughie Mouland experienced in 1914. Sealing crews used to be sixfold bigger on ships of the same size—some two hundred men compared to thirty-five—and this meant unbelievable crowding with minimal washing and sanitation facilities. Newfoundland outport men, among the poorest in the Western world, had learned to ask virtually nothing of life except work to keep their families from hunger, and sealing provided the only possible work during the ice-bound winters. No benevolent government worried about whether they made it, and they took discomfort for granted. Men slept in the hold, and as the hold filled with pelts they simply slept "on the fat." The stench after a few days, to city nostrils, must have been formidable. Food consisted of fresh seal, salt beef, hard-tack biscuits, molasses, and tea. Their wiry bodies delivered prodigious amounts of work from such limited fuel. It was a greasy, unsanitary existence that most survived in hearty good health albeit with rotting teeth, boils that the saltwater never allowed to heal, and faces weathered into wrinkles by forty-five.

Through the 1920s, steamships needed large crews because the early marine engines could not generate sufficient power to push through pack ice in search of seals. The sealers themselves had to do the traveling. Moreover, deck machinery lacked the power of modern winches to pull whip lines of pelts for hundreds of feet across the ice. It meant that each man needed to walk far over the ice—sometimes miles—for most of his "swiles" (as they called the seals) and had to drag back his own all the way. Under these conditions, a man delivered only a fraction of the sculps he could today and his share from the trip divided among so many was pathetically small. There was good Newfoundland money made from the seals, but it went to the merchants and owners.

During the final years of the harp seal hunt, individual ships' quotas ranged between eight thousand and eleven thousand animals depending on the size of the ship. The ship and the crew received set shares from the sale of the fur and fat. However, the crew divided among themselves all money from the meat, which they sold from the ship when it reached port. Often, this "flipper money" approached that from the sculps, so the crewmen wasted none of the meat. And, since dockside bargaining hinged on quality, they took good care of it.

On board the *Gulf Star*, Wilson Kettle, the fishery officer, tallied each pelt and then radioed the day's haul to his chief aboard the Canadian Coast Guard ship that accompanied the sealing fleet. Each ship had a quota from the overall allotment for the area, and when it was reached the crew abruptly stopped hunting. Having the quota safely aboard gave everyone a good feeling—in bad ice years, it could be far short by the time whitecoats become raggedies and swam away. The men washed and changed into fresher clothes. And, for a day, the mess deck stayed generally deserted while the berthing deck

[170]

reverberated with snores. We started toward open water, trying to maneuver between pans. When an ice shelf blocked the way, the captain and mate backed the screw carefully through our wake to gain enough forward clearance, then rammed ahead. The bow rose on the ice, shuddered, and settled in newly cleared water to the splitting sounds of broken ice, as yard-thick, ton-weight slabs of ice tumbled sluggishly into new patterns around us.

A two-day cruise south through open water outside the ice brought the *Gulf Star* home to St. John's. We arrived near midnight on a Sunday to find a few people waiting on the quay to buy fresh seal meat. Next morning, the sale started in earnest, with the sealers in their boots and oilpants turned merchants. Each crew had its own way of selling the flippers and carcasses—ours straight over the rail, some inviting customers aboard, others with a table on the street. (The St. John's quay is a main thoroughfare where cars can drive straight alongside the ships.) Families came to fill a drum in the back of a pickup truck. Individuals carefully picked a single flipper or bought several in a plastic bag. Jobbers bargained for them by the hundred. It was a gay, busy scene similar to market days in many places, as people stocked up on affordable meat. By dark, the bins were empty and a sizable egg of money had been divided among the crewmen.

Next morning, the ship sailed around the peninsula to the sealskin plant at Dildo to deliver the sculps. Here the hides were cured after scraping off the fat, and eventually shipped to Norway. In Norway, I later saw whitecoat pelts being dyed, and in stores I saw jackets for sale that were made from the dyed pelts. The fat was rendered at Dildo into a clear oil still valued as a lubricant because it holds up under higher temperatures than do petroleum oils.

I returned to St. John's by ship after the 1979 hunt and by helicopter after that of 1982. By ship, we encountered dozens of surviving seal pups in patches wherever we moved, while from the elevation provided by a chopper we saw whitecoats and raggedy jackets by the hundreds. Such random sampling provided no scientific count, although it did throw into question the claim of animal rights organizations that the Canadian sealers practiced genocide against the harp seal pups.

In 1977, the United States Congress passed a resolution against the Newfoundland seal hunt—an action much resented by

Canadians—based on data given it by protest groups that ninety percent of the young of the year were being killed. (This number would indeed have soon decimated the seals.) Responsible sources placed the percentage rather between forty and forty-five percent, a reasonable cull to manage the herd. A typical year's quota was 180,000 killed of an estimated 380,000 to 450,000 or more whelped. When the Canadian government provided this data to Congress, it was grandly ignored by the committee that initiated the resolution.

According to a report published in November 1982 by the International Council for the Exploration of the Sea (ICES), the number of harp seals had increased from 1.2–1.6 million in the late 1960s (when the whistle-blowing started in earnest) to 1.5–2.0 million in the late 1970s. The report also found the Canadian seal hunt to be humane. ICES is an eighty-year-old independent body of marine resources experts supported by eighteen member governments. The report was prepared by scientists from West Germany, the Netherlands, the United Kingdom, Norway, Denmark, Canada, and the United States.

In 1982, the final year of the Canadian seal hunt as it turned out, I returned to Newfoundland for a second look at sealing to check my earlier impressions. I first visited the ice in the Gulf of St. Lawrence (where the Greenpeace spraying and arrests that I observed took place) and then went to the fishing town of Twillingate to join inshore fishermen who were sealing from their longliners. Twillingate, population about a thousand, regarded sealing as part of the annual fishing cycle that in poor cod years made the difference between bills paid and hard times. In the old days, in fact, Twillingate and nearby Fogo had been major ports from which sailing schooners departed for the Front.

The harbor was locked in thick ice. On the night I arrived, a tug had just broken passage for several inbound longliners stuck outside the breakwater. With scant room dockside, they lined gunnel to gunnel and bow to stern as each waited its turn to unload its pelts. Some 300 to 450 sculps were removed from the hold of a sixty-foot boat, representing a trip of about a week for a crew of five.

The town of houses nestled in high snow barely showed a light, but the harbor had turned as lively as a city. Boat lights gleamed in green and yellow traces all across the ice, and people walked everywhere. I followed others more confident of the weight harbor ice can hold, straight over deep water to the rail of a friend's boat. The friend was

Don Linfield himself, the mate who had shouted me off from the *Gulf Star*. I had since fished with him, pulling and picking gill nets for turbot in the summer, but we had not seen each other for nearly three years and he did not know I was coming.

"Bill, b'y, have a piece?" he said as casually as if the separation had occurred three hours before, and offered part of something he was eating. He and his men looked tired and unshaven. Their faces had the darkness of weather burn and ingrained grease, and their bulky home-knit woolens, frayed around thick wrists, were not too fresh after a week in cramped quarters. Greasy clothes lay in corners of the wheelhouse, and the smells of seal fat and bilge were strong to nostrils just come from town. But the scene was loud and carnival-like, the hold being full of pelts. Earnest small sons and cousins crowded aboard for any errand to help share the glory. In junior-sized rubber boots and woolens, the boys were strutting miniature men, rehearsing the day when they'd go to the ice and the nets themselves.

The longliners had berthing space for only the four or five men who each had to pull his weight, but, asked Don, "You're comin' with we, next trip out, aren't you now? I'll just sleep on deck, it's no problem." We argued about who would take this place of discomfort a day or two hence when the pelts had been unloaded and another ice-breaking convoy formed, shouting over the noise of half a dozen men trading anecdotes in high good humor.

I stayed at Fanny Smith's motel, which in Twillingate served as the gathering place for fishermen and everybody to do with them. "Greenpeace got their way this time, eh?" she declared the next morning in her sandy, energetic voice as she served me tea strong enough to dissolve a spike. "Greenpeacers don't even need to go out, spray seals, and beat their boat up on the ice, no more."

The others in the kitchen, men in heavy work clothes (snow-caked boots left in the vestibule) nodded glumly. Fanny had driven a sealer friend to his boat at 4:00 A.M. to make a convoy through the ice. They had met a driver fresh in from the plant at Dildo, owned by the Reiber Company of Norway that bought all the sealers' pelts. The plant manager had just announced that, in light of a possible EEC boycott, he would pay only half the previously agreed price, and this retroactively from the start of the season. The Reiber Company was not merely being callous. Following the EEC ban, its plant in Dildo closed as did its tannery in Bergen, with the loss of many jobs in both Canada and Norway.

Longliners in Twillingate started no second trip. With the high price of diesel, the lowered price of sealskins reimbursed no more than expenses and nothing for grinding labor. Gone overnight were payments, not for Florida vacations, but for new boat engines and groceries. "Some little them Greenpeacers u'd care now, see, if seal pups was ugly as alligators," said Fanny bitterly.

In its Canadian edition of March–April 1983, *International Wildlife Magazine* published an assessment of "The Northwest Atlantic Sealing Controversy." The magazine, a respected membership publication of the National Wildlife Federation, might have been expected to defend the seals rather than the sealers, and its article had been researched with more than usual diligence. The following are excerpts:

> Is the harp seal an endangered species? The answer is definitely no: it is the world's third most abundant seal species numbering more than three and one quarter million animals. . . . Projected pup production in 1981 was close to 500,000 [indicating] that a harvest of 239,000 to 285,000 animals could be taken [although] the 1982 quota was held to 186,000 animals. . . . Veterinary and scientific observers have concluded that dam-pup relationships are predominantly hormonal in nature and cease rapidly with either the weaning or the loss of the pup. . . . Is the clubbing of seals humane? The answer to that question is unequivocally yes. . . . It is necessary to recognize that the East Coast seal hunt is a slaughtering operation, and there is no way that it can be made a pretty sight. It is, however, neither cruel nor a massacre. . . .

The article continued:

> In 1981, 211 crewmen from the nine large Canadian sealing vessels earned over $4,000 each in less than four weeks. For many it represented about one third of their annual income. 759 crewmen on small boats, and 4,300 landsmen earned incomes of $2,763 and $711 respectively. . . . When the harp seal population was at higher levels in the 1950s, scientists observed a high incidence of fighting wounds and poor condition in moulting males. Heavy parasite infestations were also noted, typical of overcrowded populations. . . . Harp seals are estimated to consume 1.5 metric tons of food per animal annually . . .

their consumption [now] roughly equals the catch of all fish species taken by all countries in the Northwest Atlantic. Uncontrolled expansion of the seal population can be expected to seriously curtail the supply of fish available to all countries now fishing the region. . . .

It should be no surprise that some nations with seals along their coasts have begun to consider the need for a regular cull to keep down the populations. In fact, Great Britain has done this for years to protect the Hebrides fisheries from becoming extinct. Such culls necessarily waste the animals, rather than making them available for income and food.

The abundance of seals on fishing grounds and in nets since the halt of commercial sealing may perhaps give the protesters satisfaction for a job well done, since these are all beautiful creatures who have been saved from a gory death at man's hand. Inshore fishermen living on a slim margin are the people left holding the bag. Seals unable to find enough food in the ocean because of their numbers come inshore to compete for the rest of the fishermen's livelihood. Then there is the fact, mentioned in the *International Wildlife* article, that overpopulations of seals develop parasites, which, expelled in feces and eaten by surrounding fish, are transmitted to the fish.

If parasites lower the desirability of fish fillets and fishburgers, or scarcity prices them too high, most of the tens of thousands who heeded emotional pitches to save the baby seals will have no problem filling their protein gap with brisket and hamburger. It requires only killing more cows. Tough luck for the fishermen.

The forced closing of the seal hunts was engineered by idealists and opportunists. They gained the fervent support of a large urban population that never needs to shed blood for its meat and tacitly accepts whatever cruelties occur in abattoirs. How many who sent money to "Save A Baby Seal" treat themselves to the veal and lamb, even suckling pig, that are babies of other animals? Seldom has there been such a dramatic triumph of those with high moral purpose and nothing to lose, over a small, vulnerable group of people in modest circumstances who have lost a major portion of their income and self-sufficiency.

[175]

12

Chesapeake Bay

Not all of the world's aquatic creatures roam the high seas. Many stick to the rivers, estuaries, and near-shore waters three miles from land, which, in the United States, are the regulatory province of the individual states. One of the great such inland systems is that of the Chesapeake Bay, an estuary that intrudes from the sea into the states of Maryland and Virginia. The men who live by fishing the Chesapeake Bay call themselves "watermen," and their commitment to working the water equals that of the salty seafarers.

The three basic crops for the watermen, who fish by the day in boats seldom longer than fifty feet, are oysters in the cold months, crabs during the summer and soft-shell clams the year around. The lower bay also supports a seagoing fishery for menhaden, worked from large seiners. This is not the end of it. Biologists report 2,700 different living species of fish, mollusks, and crustaceans in Chesapeake Bay, from large ones down to lesser planktonic forms that provide feed for the others. Watermen fish at least a half dozen of these to sell as prime, world-class table fare, along with others which provide food for everyday tables.

It is easier to humanize a body of water surrounded by land than it is the open sea, and the Bay, as locals call it, acknowledging no other, is an integral part of their lives. The place inspires a devotion that outsiders find difficult to understand. William W. Warner provided a reasonable explanation in his Pulitzer-winning "*Beautiful Swimmers,*

[177]

Watermen, Crabs and the Chesapeake Bay" when he wrote, "The Chesapeake Bay does not impress those who know it best as the grandest or most of anything. For all its size and gross statistics, it is an intimate place where land and water intertwine in intimate varieties of mood and pattern." There are no mountains or roaring seascapes for inspiration. Rather, the terrain is flat, in many places marshy. The murky green-brown water fills with sea nettles and plankton by midsummer, and often ices during the bleak, blowing winter. But those who work the Bay's waters have adapted to the seasons.

On a typically biting, frosty January morning with not a trace yet of daylight, Captain Lester Lee and his son Don headed toward a cove near Kent Island, Maryland, in their pickup truck. At the pier, Lee started the engine of his thirty-four-foot *Merts*, a boat named after his wife. It had an open deck except for a small cabin. A slick of ice covered everything. During the drive in the truck, we had discussed men who make their living fishing the Bay, and the conversation continued. "Watermen don't have no whole lot of money," Lee called cheerfully over the noise of the engine, a "motor" converted from an Oldsmobile car. "I don't know, reason they don't have none, they get paid every day." The statement brought on a rumbling, easy laugh. "Get paid every day, they spend it!"

Captain Lester, in his sixties at the time, was a chunky, gentle, warm man with a face beginning to resemble a Toby jug. He started at age nine to "follow the water" as Chesapeake Bay watermen put it, working with his grandfather. "I been captain of my own boat ever since I was eleven or twelve, arsterin' and crabbin' mostly." His sons became watermen, most with their own boats. As for himself, he still worked crab lines in the summer (Warner has described Lee's crabbing most agreeably in *"Beautiful Swimmers"*), but now left oyster tonging aboard the *Merts* to Don.

By first light, we reached the oyster bar and anchored. A chilly wind blew, and the sky, streaked with pink and gray, had its own coldness. Don kicked the ice from a set of shaft tongs and climbed with them to a balancing position on the narrow gunnel. Oystering tongs are toothed rakes, connected to a pair of poles fastened at the center to operate with a scissor motion. Don lowered the rakes into the water by their thirty-foot wooden shafts, then worked the shafts with his hands on top closing the two rakes over objects on the seafloor eighteen feet below. As with most skills, tonging has a touch. A good

Waterman Jack Webster of Deal Island on the Chesapeake Bay swings in a rakeful of oysters. To operate the heavy wooden shafts, often in freezing weather, requires balance, strength, and endurance.

Lester Lee of Kent Island, culls oysters as his son hand-tongs them aboard. Keepers must be alive and of a legal size.

Shaft-tonging for oysters on a river of the Chesapeake Bay. Local watermen divide their time between fall-to-spring oystering and summer crabbing.

John Dize (left) stops work between pulling strings of pots aboard his boat *Lisa Ellen* to compare for-. tunes with a fellow-crabber. Most fishermen relish visiting each other on the grounds.

The rim placed on the basket prevents feisty crabs from crawling out. Despite the small size of these females, Dale Marshall needs thick gloves against their claws. Skipper John Dize controls the boat and raises the pots.

Chesapeake Bay watermen have a pre-dawn breakfast at Gorden's eatery in Crisfield, Maryland, before setting out for a day of crabbing or oystering.

operator can feel the scrape of sand bottom, the slick of mud or the scratch of rock transmitted through the thick wood, and then (with acquired skill) feel out any clusters of hard oyster shell.

Don usually made three or four digs to seat the load. Then he lifted the shafts hand over hand, striking a rhythm with his back and legs. When his hands reached the fulcrum of the shafts (marked by a metal tab), the equal balance allowed him to swing the rakes to the surface and lever a dripping load of muddy shells and stones over to his dad.

Captain Lester had set up a scarred wooden trough. He hammered apart the crusty mollusks, knocked off barnacles, and tossed the keepers—the living oysters of legal size—into a pile on deck. With a sweep of the hand, he sent rocks, undersized and dead oysters, and empty shells back over the side. Live oysters have a feel, a weight, and a heavy sound if thumped, while an open shell clearly indicates a dead oyster. Captain Lester's hands flitted like good machines at work even though under his oilskin apron he was bundled and hooded to stiffness against the cold. He nodded toward Don and declared, "Hard work out tongin' arsters, there. I can't stand that cold on my hands no more. Used to hold onto them shafts all day long, but . . ." There was nothing of gloom in what he said, just a fact.

Every few hours they broke to sit around a small stove, in a cabin barely big enough for two men to huddle knee to knee. Over a thermos of coffee and a package of cakes, the talk turned to oysters accumulating slowly on deck. "I'll tell you what, they're nice and fat," said Don tentatively. "But ain't no whole lot of them, is there?" What of only one, two, three keepers in each rakeful, and the rest dead, compared to a dozen or more live ones in better days? Just a few years ago, you'd get twice as many oysters, no, three times as many, with no greater work. Men who follow the water say that if you haven't made it oystering to pay expenses by Christmas you're not going to make it. This year, Christmas season had come, but nobody was making it.

Captain Lester boiled it down to this, in the slow drawling accent of a Bay waterman: "Well, it ain't no more money into arster business now. It takes so much to operate with, you know—about twenty dollar before you untie the boat what with sandwiches, drinks, coal oil, gasoline—and arsters is scarce now besides. But ain't nothin' you can do about it."

The pollutions of the world may be entering the open seas with more or less persistence depending on which scientist voices his concern, but everyone agrees that sheltered, estuarine waters like Chesapeake Bay are definitely in trouble from the effluents of civilization that pour into them. The oyster scarcity appears to be due to two factors: a parasite that flourishes in years of low rainfall, and the disappearance of dissolved oxygen caused by the effects of excess nutrients washed from land. However, the adverse changes in Chesapeake Bay are not confined to the oyster bars.

An estuary like that of Chesapeake Bay is defined as a semi-enclosed body of river-fed water that meets the ocean and is affected by its tides. Because of the bay's size—it flows into the Atlantic Ocean from nearly two hundred miles to the north—the fresh water that pours from its rivers meets the saltwater entering in tides from the ocean in a great variety of patterns that change seasonally. The variety makes the bay one of the most complex and productive marine systems in the world, and one of the most difficult to treat with simple solutions.

The network of water that feeds the bay includes nine major rivers and some forty smaller ones. They have evocative Indian names like Potomac, Patapsco, Rappahannock, Choptank, Nanticoke, and Wicomoco, and colonial names like York, James, and Chester. Baltimore, Washington, Richmond, and Hampton Roads-Norfolk all have rivers of the Chesapeake flowing through them, but these cities only head the list of towns, villages, developments, and farms that draw from the vast water system. Including its rivers, the bay has a water area of 4,300 square miles that laps against a shoreline of over 8,100 miles. The rivers drain from an area that extends more than 64,000 square miles to embrace approximately ninety percent of Maryland, sixty percent of Virginia, a long swatch of eastern Pennsylvania, and fingers of West Virginia, Delaware, and New York.

All the tributaries—and remember that each river builds from dozens or hundreds of streams—carry into the bay whatever has entered their waters, whether naturally or through the intervention of man: eroded soil, sewage, chlorine from treated sewage and from power plant biofouling systems, industrial chemicals and other industrial wastes, nitrogen and phosphorus fertilizers from farms and lawns, acid rain from power plant stacks, farm manure and suburban pet droppings, car oils, detergents, and pesticides. Adding to this, many pleasure boats, work boats, and ships on the bay itself illegally dump trash and waste there, while the biofouling paint on many of their hulls has recently been found to release toxins destructive to marine life.

The damage caused by all these additives began to show up in the 1960s, but it was not until the mid-1980s that public alarm grew strong enough to make the job of cleaning the bay politically popular and to cut loose state and federal money for the job. By this time, most of the bay grasses were gone that had provided a habitat for all manner of the Bay's young shellfish and invertebrates as well as its wildfowl, while those species of fish dependent upon freshwater spawning had declined drastically or disappeared.

According to studies by the Environmental Protection Agency, the Bay's water had become dangerously "enriched," principally from excessive amounts of nitrogen entering the system through sewage plant discharges and farm runoff. Such enrichment stimulates algal blooms to grow in overabundance so that they block sunlight from shallow water and, in dying, absorb the oxygen out of deeper water. In deeper water, the result was a growing absence of the dissolved oxygen essential to most life forms. Crabs and fish could move, but oysters could only stay put and smother to death. The result of overenriched shallow water was the loss of the ecologically vital submerged vegetation.

The EPA made an even more sinister discovery when it put all the existing research together. Bottom sediments contained substantial amounts of toxic wastes, particularly metals from industry and synthetic organic compounds. Contrary to the general supposition before the EPA studies, tidal flushes from the Atlantic Ocean had not removed these toxins. Instead, they became fixed in bottom sediments, leaving the bay a sink that collected and recycled pollutants.

The fishery most immediately affected was that of the striped bass, the beloved "rockfish" of Chesapeake sportsmen and consumers. The striper, with its rich but delicate flavor in the pan, has always been valued by those fortunate enough to find it in their waters. Stripers are a basic haul for freshwater commercial fishermen along the eastern seaboard, and apparently have been so for a long time, since income from a striped bass fishery funded America's first public school in 1670 at the Plymouth Colony. Sport fishing for striped bass usually occurred in the summer, aboard all manner of small boats from skiffs to cabin cruisers. As might be expected, commercial fishermen did not wait for the balmy days.

Around Rock Hall, located almost due east of Baltimore on the other side of the Bay, the stripers used to fill nets from November into the summer. By the early 1980s they had dwindled to a mere ten percent of their volume a decade earlier. In addition Lewis Cain, who started fishing with his dad and had been at it commercially for more than thirty years, found that he needed to set his nets for striped bass progressively closer to shore. "The fish have been trending toward the shallower water," he said, giving support to concerns of the scientists that the areas of anoxic water where fish could not live were growing.

I myself remember fifteen years ago to nearly fifty, the basketfuls of fat rockfish my dad, grandfather and I could count on catching from a casual day's trip on the Bay with hook and line. The last time I took my son and daughter fishing, the stripers were so scarce it was hardly worth the trouble except for the pleasure of a day spent on the water. A Maryland seafood broker put it this way: "I couldn't stay in business if I relied on local catches anymore."

In January 1985, Maryland closed the striped bass fishery to both sport and commercial fishermen. The action sent watermen seeking alternate species on which to make a living. The closure was a significant act of responsibility for the state to take, because Chesapeake Bay rivers provide the spawning grounds for ninety percent of the striped bass that subsequently school along the eastern seaboard from New England to the Carolinas. Marylanders had no guarantee that other states would follow with a similar protective ban, so that to many watermen the closure meant simply delivering the fish to somebody else's nets. This indeed happened in some cases although at length, in action coordinated by the federal government, other states joined in the moratorium as a common cause.

Crisfield, located on the eastern shore of the Bay so far south in Maryland that it practically touches the Virginia state line, sustains a population of watermen who earn much of their living from the crabs that migrate past from late spring to early fall. A typical summer's day started at 4:00 A.M. with coffee and eggs at Gorden's, the local eatery that keeps watermen's hours. Men in T-shirts and scuffed jackets sat at the counter or in the booths, talking and joking quietly. Most were thickset men, the kind who ate so many starches (and sometimes

ate youth the muscles they developed
n in an overlay of flesh. They wore
'ing to oil companies or marine
ps that had settled into a com-

diner to wake and digest, John Dize and
er and traveled in the dark aboard his forty-
first line of his three hundred crab pots. By
ringing them in. The air was fresh and humid, full of
oolness that presages heat to come. Out on the open
e breeze turned southwesterly, and an acrid odor filled the
was the distinctive harsh smell of fish rendered in steam vats
or meal and oil. We were crabbing downwind of the menhaden
plants in Reedville, Virginia, a reminder of Chesapeake Bay prox-
imities and interactions.

A small hydraulic block raised the crab pots from ten feet of water.
The pots—essentially wire cages with a narrow opening—weighed
about thirty pounds when empty. Most of them contained between
one and two dozen crabs. Dize, a burly man in his late thirties, lifted
each pot aboard from the starboard rail while maneuvering his boat
with levers connected to the rudder and engine. His helper, young
Dale Marshall, opened the pot, shook the crabs into a shallow trough,
and knocked out the old bait. Dize rebaited the pot with two whole
menhaden, and returned it to the water with its individual line and
floating marker. Dale sorted the male and female keepers and tossed
them in separate baskets. The cycle took a few seconds less than a
minute. It was followed at once by raising the next pot in the line.

Chesapeake Bay blue crabs are noted for feistiness. A few pinched
into Dale's thick rubber gloves. He handled them gingerly enough
that they did him no harm. When a basket filled enough for the crabs
to start clawing over the rim, he placed another half-basket on top to
hold them in. The least desirable crabs were the smaller, less meaty
females, the "sooks." The best of the males, the big "jimmies," had a
tangible heaviness. As the sun rose, the day grew hot and the two
peeled to their undershirts. The sun had baked their arms the color of
earth. They moved in a steady rhythm, the sweat darkening their caps
and dripping from their faces. Even the breeze was hot.

The Chesapeake's human history goes back far. In 1607, the Bay

provided the setting for the first permanent settleme
America when the English established Jamestown on the J
a lower Bay tributary. Captain John Smith, one of the colo
ders, declared in his "*General Historie of Virginia*" after exploring
peake waters far up into what is now Maryland, that it was "a fa
. . . with fruitful and delightsome land" where "heaven and
never agreed better to frame a place for man's habitation."

The English were not the first to discover the Bay. Captain John (
local watermen would now address him) recorded the presence o
more than two hundred Algonquin settlements of twelve to fifty
dwellings each on his "Map of Virginia." He noted that the inhabitants planted fields of "green wheat" (corn), and plots of tobacco,
beans, and pumpkins; they hunted such "beasts" as squirrels, turkeys,
and deer, caught fish in weirs and with bow and arrow, and harvested
crabs and oysters.

Nor did the parvenu Algonquins come to virgin land. Archaeologists excavating near the confluence of the bay and the Potomac
River found oyster and clam shell middens that they dated to 2155
B.C. The digs showed that these early humans roasted the bivalves in
pits before eating them. They already had the knack of leading the
good life from Bay seafood!

If Captain John were to return, he might still recognize some of the
quiet marshes and inlets but, along with his Algonquin neighbors, he
would be startled by much of the rest. More than 12.7 million people
now inhabit the region, a population which has grown from 8.5
million in 1950. Statisticians project there will be 14.6 million by the
year 2000. Much of this settlement depends on the contributions of
the Bay to agriculture, heavy and light industry, world shipping to the
ports of Baltimore and Norfolk, food processing, power plants (of
which thirty rely on the bay and its tributaries for coolant), and
sewage disposal. The Bay is also much used for recreation. Maryland
and Virginia issue together more than 300,000 powerboat licenses a
year. On a calm summer's day, high-speed craft dart everywhere on
the water like insects, competing for space with watermen's pots and
nets. Many more vessels needing no license appear on the water
propelled by sails. On a bright, breezy Saturday, triangular white
marconis and billowing multicolored spinnakers are as numerous as
flocks of low-flying birds.

City people who delight in waterfront charm have begun spending their city incomes to build condominiums along waterfront property, and they pay enough to convert fishing boat piers to yacht marinas. Smelly old fish plants and storage sheds are becoming the target of complaints from these new citizens, who like to keep their local color visual.

Chesapeake watermen are faced with changing realities. One option when oysters or crabs or stripers grow scarce is to charter out to city people. The chartering life is not very independent, but neither is the work particularly hard for a man accustomed to following the water. As the hot sun cooks up an odor in the bait, the waterman affixes it with gruff cheer to the hooks of paying guests who would rather keep clean hands. A pleasant standoff prevails. The party members (especially the men) carefully call the skipper "Cap'n," as they (especially the women) enjoy his drawly accent. The waterman in his turn feels free to growl and be a bit salty as long as his talk contains nothing worse than "damn" in front of the ladies, whom he addresses as "Ma'am" with no loss of dignity. The day at its best ends with a nice batch of fish (bluefish these days rather than rockfish) and everybody cheerful, although often some of the guests nurse an overdose of sunburn.

A century ago, with catches at their peak, the succulent Bay oysters were such a commodity for the Delmonico's Restaurant crowd that hundreds of sail-powered dredge boats operated in bay waters. It was a fishery of heavy labor, big profits, and brutal frontier competition characterized by scuttled boats, piracy, and bloodshed. Today in the insular fishing communities of the Bay, some watermen still fight a bit, shout at their crews, carry family grudges, and drink heavily. But life is tame now by comparison. A vestige of the past remains in the aging wooden sailboats called "skipjacks." By state law, these are the only vessels allowed to dredge oysters on Maryland bars.

The skipjacks are work boats and little else. A bucket in the bilge serves as the toilet on most. Ranging in length between thirty-five and fifty-five feet, they were designed specifically for the conditions of Bay oystering. Other Bay boats like the bugeye have not survived. Only some thirty skipjacks remain in the Maryland oyster fleet out of hundreds of vessels, of several designs, that dredged oysters into the 1930s.

Marylanders romanticize the skipjacks with their heavy raked masts and sloop-rigged sails, both for their jaunty appearance from a distance, and for the independence of the men who work for them. Many are in poor shape up close, with patches inserted over patches and machinery held together by bailing wire. I once asked a skipper if they need much maintenance. "Oh yes, oh my goodness yes, " he answered.

The only power permitted aboard is a "donkey" engine to raise the dredges. A "yawl" boat with an inboard motor can push the skipjack to the grounds, but the dredging itself must be conducted under sail, except on Mondays and Tuesdays. Powerboats could scrape the bottom clean in a fraction of the October–March season. The restriction keeps the fishery inefficient, but alive and in the hands of local watermen.

Wade Murphy owned the forty-seven-foot skipjack *Sigsbee*, built in 1901. At 4:00 A.M. on a December morning at Tilghman Island, Maryland, he checked lines as three of his four crewmen, clumping about in heavy boots and padded coveralls, lowered the yawl boat astern, and started its sputtering engine. Monosyllabic grunts were the closest thing to conversation. There was a bit of a moon, and the chill penetrated to the bone. Below in the small after-cabin lined with narrow benches, Sonny had already begun frying sausages. The warm odor beckoned whenever we passed the hatch.

Captain Wadie was competitive. His lean, rosy face grew redder and his eyes narrowed at the thought of anyone beating him. On the water, he liked to be first out, and didn't mind declaring "If you're lazy you won't make it." Soon we were off through the narrows, passing other boats in the dark that were still moored with only a single light spilling up from each hatchway. As we entered open water and the wind started to bite, kicks of spray turned at once to ice on deck. Murphy at the wheel pulled a hood over his red visor cap and squinted into the spray, looking for buoy lights.

In his late thirties with a young family ("I married late, already twenty-four"), he had owned and skippered the *Sigsbee* for twenty years. Repairs were constant for a boat that age—recently five thousand dollars each for new sails and a new mast, eight thousand dollars another year for marine railway fees and general replacements. And skipjacks were good only for oyster dredging, so that you needed to keep another boat to work crabs, eels, clams, and finfish.

"Skipjacks pay for theirselves most years," Murphy conceded. (This was in the early 1980s, before the most precipitous declines in oyster harvests.) "But you don't make much clear money. Other than doin' what you want to do and being captain, you'd do just as well hand tonging."

At daybreak on the grounds, we raised the thick canvas main and jib, and the same twelve-knot breeze that had us shivering despite thermal underwear filled the sails nicely. You could feel the tug of wind power all through the wooden boat. Howell's Point was the location of the day's work, a three-hundred-foot oyster bar in shallow water close to a tree-lined shore. The point could be worked only once or twice annually, when a very high tide brought its depth up to five and six feet. (*Sigbee's* draft was three and a half feet.) Unless the high tide fell on a Monday or Tuesday, when engine-powered yawl boats made maneuvering possible, it required a northeast or south-west wind to tack across the bar.

The wind today was southwest, second choice. "See," explained Wadie in the particular wording and cadence of Tilghman watermen, "It would have been more better if it had been the other way, northeast. Then I'd have no chance of going ashore, ever, because the wind would have blowed me right back offshore. But you never get a time, very seldom, when its northeast and a high tide." As it was, we needed to come about fast at the end of each lick, one man holding the jib into the wind with his full weight, to prevent a deadwind that might stop the turn. With practically no maneuvering room for a second come-about, the wind could quickly drift us to shore and grounding. The fact was, with oysters scarce, it was worth taking chances on a good bed of them if you knew your boat. Captain Wadie stayed tense and alert the whole day, and the crewmen jumped to commands barked from his place astern where he controlled the wheel and mainmast boom. This was not relaxed fishing like that of the hand tongers who worked at individual paces.

Over with a splash went the port and starboard dredges, 125 pounds each, and the *Sigsbee* under sail power dragged them along the bottom. At the end of the lick, the donkey engine raised them. Two men grabbed each dredge as it came to the rail, hauled it aboard with a swing of their bodies, and emptied it in a single motion. Out tumbled mud, rocks, shell, and oysters both alive and dead. A shovel sent the obvious trash back overboard at once. Some of the rocks

[187]

weighed as much as forty pounds. The men knelt and culled until a shout sent them to the sails to come about and then to lower the dredges for the next lick.

The oyster shells were so grizzled and porous that some resembled weathered rocks. Many had fused together and needed to be hammered apart. The minimum keeper size was three inches, and notches along the rail provided a measure for any doubtfuls. Since the limit extended to the farthest thin edge of the rough oyster shells, everyone avoided stepping on oysters for fear of chipping off the vital fraction that might make them keepers.

Kneeling grew murderously painful, hour after hour, and those without commercial pads tied rags around their knees. Oilskins became covered with mud that dried gray in the wind. Despite insulated rubber gloves, the cold of the water and fresh mud penetrated to the fingers. Given a moment's pause, we went over to the wooden box amidships that housed the donkey, the car engine rigged to drive the winches, and lowered gloved hands against the hot exhaust pipe. Meanwhile, the rough, clean, glistening gray oyster shells rose in modest piles fore and aft. From their size, it was clear that we were working a choice bar.

At delivery time near dusk (the boats could deliver only until one hour after dark to ensure their working nothing but the daylight hours), Murphy cruised under yawl-boat power past the oyster buyers' sheds along a creek, shouting with the owners to compare their prices. We tied alongside a pier with a conveyor belt that carried oysters into a truck, and the checker sent the boom over to deck with a metal bucket that we filled.

The man examined the bucketful—they were big, hard-shelled, quality oysters—walked inside, and came out a moment later to announce that the manger wanted us to take them inside by wheelbarrow to be custom shucked. "Heyll with that!" Wadie declared, his voice rising. "Why should my boys work that extra just cause we brought quality oysters? You want to pay 'em extra, okay." He started to cast off for a rival pier. Within two minutes, the manager, his beefy face unsmiling, had the barrow handles himself. Wadie muttered about it to anyone around as he simmered down. But soon, under the pleasure of handling fat oysters, everybody joked, even Wadie, even the manager who soon found a kid in overalls to take over the wheelbarrow.

Captain Wade Murphy of the Chesapeake Bay skipjack *Sigsbee* sets out for the oystering grounds at 5:30 A.M. on a cold December morning. Maryland law permits the skipjacks to travel under engine power from a skiff astern, but dragging for oysters must be done under sail.

Crewman kneel to cull a dredgeload of oysters aboard the *Sigsbee*, near shoals marked by a lighthouse. A pile of "keepers" rises behind each man.

Research in waders. Marine biologist Ron Klauda of the Johns Hopkins University Applied Physics Laboratory (right) works with a technician to capture spawning blueback herring in order to remove and fertilize their eggs. He uses the hatched larvae in a Maryland power plant siting program, to determine the effects of acid rain and dissolved aluminum on the eggs and juveniles of fish that spawn in the Chesapeake Bay.

Skiff men "harden" (pulled taut) a seine holding tons of menhaden. The mothership drops a suction tube into the pocket of the net and pumps up thousands of the small fish a minute.

The buckets, punctured with holes in the bottom to allow drippage, were a legally regulated bushel size. With several going at once, I grabbed a shovel to help load them. "Hoo, Bill, shush, go 'way," muttered Traverse beside me. When I jumped back, the others started to laugh, especially Traverse and Lankford, the two blacks in the crew. It furnished an easy topic for joking. You didn't fill a bucket by dumping in the whole shovelful at once. You slid them in along the side so they didn't pack down. "That way, you save out one, two, three arster a bushel and maybe make up a whole extra bushel or two." With a crew share ten percent of the gross, we were talking money. On the pier, Sonny stood beside the checker, and followed to stand at the window of a little heated shack the size of a phone booth as a man registered the loads. It never hurt to keep your own count. Fishermen in Smokey and Gloucester and Stamsund did it too.

The initial legislation resulting from the EPA report on the dangers to Chesapeake Bay emphasized physical efforts. Maryland focused on control of critical areas, dechlorination, sewage treatment, sediment, shore erosion, fishery management, and stock restoration of finfish, oysters, and wildfowl. Virginia emphasized control of urban and agricultural runoff, sewer lines and septic systems, toxic chemicals, and fishery data and management. Pennsylvania (whose Susquehanna River, running through hundreds of miles of farm country, contributes half the Chesapeake Bay's water and at least half its excess nutrients without enjoying an inch of bay shoreline) concentrated more modest funds on controlling farm runoff through education, financial assistance, and manure utilization.

Research received relatively little from the states' budgets. Research is a tedious investment, because it requires monitoring and gathering facts for long enough to recognize patterns, while usually the immediate problems continue. There is a constant standoff between research scientists and the men on the line. As waterman and politicians would avow in rare prejudicial agreement: "We've had research. Seen you fellows out there every year taking samples long as anybody can remember. Now let's do something to bring back the fish and oysters!"

Dr. Reginald V. Truitt, now in his late nineties and the recognized father of Chesapeake Bay research, recalled urging the Maryland Legislature in the mid-1920s to raise the legal-size catch of oysters "to give the little oyster a chance to go through the winter and spawn the next spring." When he testified before a Maryland legislative committee, a senator from one of the Eastern Shore watermen's counties "took me to task. 'Here's the man!' he shouted. 'Here's the man coming before us, pretends to be a friend of the waterman, and he's taking their livelihood from them. Taking their very livelihood!' "

The scientists insist otherwise. "The data we have emphasizes the magnitude of man's input into the Bay, and makes it imperative to restrain these inputs," explains Dr. Eugene Cronin of the Bay research leaders in the generation following Truitt. "But we have to learn more about the effects through continued disciplined research, so that we can set limits intelligently."

Although more than a dozen laboratories in universities and other organizations have contributed basic research in specific areas, most of the sustained involvement in Chesapeake Bay research has emanated from four large institutions—the University of Maryland, the Virginia Institute of Marine Science of the College of William and Mary, the Johns Hopkins University, and the Smithsonian Institution. The bay research of the four institutions is funded variously by the states of Maryland and Virginia, and by grants and contracts from government agencies and private sources.

Specialized research and monitoring activities, of a complexity to make a waterman remove his tractor cap and scratch his head, have begun occurring all over the water. Each spring in recent years, a set of researchers from the Johns Hopkins University's Applied Physics Laboratory has evaluated the water quality and contaminant conditions in ten different striped bass spawning habitats, while another team tested the actual effect of specific contaminants and acid levels on fish larvae. Others from the university's Chesapeake Bay Institute have cooperated with scientists from the University of Maryland to follow the cycle of phytoplankton in two adjacent tributaries that produced markedly different sizes and quantities of the same oyster.

Further south at the Virginia Institute of Marine Science, near the mouth of the Bay on the York River facing historic colonial Yorktown, a scientist wearing a wetsuit dove in freezing winter water to dig up mats of eelgrass to take back to his wet-laboratory on the end of a pier, in order to study the declining submerged vegetation of the Bay. Another group from VIMS, wearing oilskins against the cold spray, bounced out in a boat to take water samples at five selected sites of bay grasses both growing and depleted. They had been doing this biweekly for over a year to record the conditions relating to the growth of the grasses—temperature, salinity, dissolved oxygen, light at different depths, suspended solids, and nutrients.

Elsewhere, up and down the bay, other researchers were assembling different pieces of the same great puzzle, counting oyster spat, measuring sediment plumes that washed from the bay into the ocean, testing the toxicity of boat biofouling paints, recording the seasonal patterns of anoxic water in specific water columns, examining sediment cores to determine the deposition of materials entering the bay, examining the properties of runoff from the land, testing for the minimum amounts of chlorine required to prevent biofouling in power plant systems, easing little yearling crabs from the mud of a mosquito-ridden marsh to tag them and follow their migratory course. And much more. It was slow work that required time, whether the watermen had time to wait or not.

"Bunkers!" declared Chuck Williams from the spotter plane, using the Virginia waterman's word for the sardinelike menhaden that school by the millions in the lower part of Chesapeake Bay. As soon as the message came over the wheelhouse speaker, Captain Earnest Delano of the 166-foot menhaden ship *Northumberland* pulled a single long blast on the whistle. A wiry man in his sixties who had worked everything on the Bay from shaft tongs to crab pots in his day, Delano kicked off his slippers and in the same motion stepped into boots, and pulled up the oilpants opened around them fireman-style. His motion continued from the wheelhouse, down the ladder, aft on the boat deck. Six crewmen had the starboard purse-boat ready to lower as did others by the portside boat. Captain Delano gripped a guy line and jumped aboard, and down both boats slapped into the water. Off they sped, joined together like Siamese twins by the 1,300-foot net with attached floats and weights they held in common. Delano had pulled the whistle line only sixty seconds before.

Delano steered his own boat and hand-signaled his athletic young mate, Mark Dameron, who stood with feet braced apart steering the other. Williams in the spotter plane circling overhead called maneuvers that crackled over the captain's sputtering walkie-talkie, and Delano changed direction as he pursued the school of menhaden that only the plane could see. "Okay, set," declared Williams from the sky. Delano threw down his raised hand and the boats parted. The seine gear zipped and clattered off the two decks as the boats set the net in a circle.

In purse seining, two boats unfold a surface net between them to encircle a school of fish, then purse-string it shut under the fish. The *Northumberland* men worked with speed and precision. Within a minute of the spotter plane's command, they had surrounded a sizeable school, tied their boats back together, and begun pursing.

A raised hydraulic power block on each boat did the heaviest hauling, as the two six-man crews stood beneath to stack the net with its floats and sinkers in place for the next set. Ugly blood-filled sea nettles flopped from the net as it passed high through the power block. The August sun might have been steaming hot, but most chose to sweat in oilskins and curse with resigned cheer rather than take the acid stings.

The water enclosed in the net began to stir as the circle drew tighter. You could see fish milling in clusters, just beneath the surface. Delano signaled the ship and it came to meet us. On the ship's deck, crewmen dropped a thick suction hose into the fish as those in the boats hooked fingers into web to "harden" the net by drawing it up taut. The bag of the net tightened and hundreds, then thousands, of foot-long silver fish rose to the surface in a boil of frenzied flapping. The hose pumped them at the rate of ten thousand a minute into the ship's hold, continuing for a quarter of an hour. That made a tally of approximately 150,000 fish, fifty tons. Only a medium-sized haul, no more, said Mark. The cycle had taken twenty-five minutes. The men secured the purse-boats alongside the ship, and redistributed the net between them, ready to go again.

A half hour later, the pilot plane spotted another school and the boats were off in seconds. It went like this all day. Captain Delano was an easygoing, soft-spoken Virginian (as were most of his biracial crew), but he drove hard. "You're not doing anything as a captain," he said during a quiet period on the bridge, "if you don't catch enough to make your crew some money."

The bridge radio crackled with talk from other menhaden ships. All of them in the area were based in Reedville, Virginia, located on a Chesapeake Bay tributary just below the Potomac River (which, about one hundred twisting miles upstream, runs through Washington,

D.C.). The radio speech had a different cadence than that of the Maryland watermen, more southern. During a slow period when nobody seemed to be catching anything, one radio voice declared cheerfully, without conviction: "Wo, big fish in front of me, flyin' along, turnin' side to side. Never heard so many shad down here. Doin' real good." (Shad is another local term for menhaden—like bunker and alewife—even though shad is also the name of a specific Bay fish.)

The *Northumberland* fished for three days around Mobjack Bay near the mouth of York River. At other parts of the year, the fleet moved to sea as the bunkers moved about. Other watermen in more modest boats fished around us, some in nothing but punts under oar. These traveled to a "pound net" held stationary in the water by stakes driven into the bottom. Circulating chilled seawater in the *Northumberland*'s hold kept the fish from spoiling. Menhaden is an oily small fish, not considered good eating, but the crewmen spent time between sets bending into the hold with a long hooked pole. They speared out the more desirable by-catch of croaker, spot, perch—all of them small white fish—to clean, wrap for the freezer, and take home.

When the ship headed back to the Zapata-Haynie pier in Reedville, you could smell from miles away the steam cookers that were rendering menhaden into oil and meal. Menhaden has been the business of Reedville for over a century, yielding fortunes around the turn of the century and still capable of producing a good living. The fishery itself operates from New York to the Gulf of Mexico, producing nearly half of all U.S. seafood landings. The Reedville fleet delivers about twenty percent of this as it pursues the migratory little fish in the Bay and along the Atlantic coast.

Delano, who had sailed with the Reedville fleet for thirty-four years, started "on the water" at age fourteen. He still dredged for oysters in the winter after the spring-to-fall menhaden season ended. Delano had seen the fishery evolve toward its present mechanization from the days when twenty or more men lined up in each purse-boat to hand-haul the net while singing chanties to ease the work. But the fish kept coming. Even with the evident problems of other species in Chesapeake Bay, the menhaden showed no signs of falling off. They spawned in the sea, and thus did not encounter the bay pollution during their vulnerable larval stage as did the river spawners like shad and striped bass. At least the bay still provided for some of its watermen.

Apart from pursuing research and regulation, the governments of Chesapeake Bay country have for years funded certain practical, immediate projects. One of these began on an April morning back at Tilghman Island, two hours before daylight in a hard rain. Oyster shells, the ubiquitous debris of oyster country, crunched under the tires as our cars converged on an isolated pier reached through sand and scrub from around a weathered dark house where a dog started to bark. The crewmen donned oilskins hanging inside a little gear shack, then stepped to the slick deck of the skipjack *Kathryn* owned by Captain Russell Dize. The September to March oystering season had ended, and the day's work would be to seed a new bar with oyster spat for harvest in three years.

The rain intensified as we prepared to leave the pier. Will Ridenour started the yawl boat motor, but it sputtered out. Damn, and checked yesterday! By flashlight, he and Dize investigated the fuel and ignition systems. Accompanied by the putt-putt of another yawl boat, a pair of red and green running lights emerged from the dark narrows, then the dim white color of a mainsail furled on its boom. A big number 5 on the side of the boat showed it to be the skipjack *Sigsbee*; the man in red visor cap at the wheel was Captain Wadie Murphy. Murphy peered straight ahead at rain-slanted blackness, fulfilling his urge to be first man out. Other Tilghman boats followed—tongers, patent tongers, skipjacks. With a reassuring sputter and thrum, our motor started and continued turning over. We cast off and joined the procession.

By daylight, we had arrived at the spat bar in Broad Creek. Spat, tiny young oysters, require a rough surface to grow on, and each year Maryland seeds millions of them on discarded oyster shells. Then, at the point of appropriate growth, the state hires watermen to dredge and tong the seeded shells and transport them to new sites. The work helps to keep the bay productive (assuming MSX and anoxia do not reach the mature oysters before the watermen) and also provides a few weeks' guaranteed spring income to men who rely on the vagaries of nature the rest of the year.

In the blue, rainy dawn, black shapes of skipjacks glided ahead and astern of us, each maneuvering for position. The lack of collisions was remarkable since the bar covered only a small area. Off on an edge of the bar in their own designated spot, the hand tongers balanced on the gunnels of smaller boats, their high poles criss-crossing as they dug the rakes into mounds of shells on the seafloor. Captain Wadie's *Sigsbee* glided past with a deck load high enough to hide the legs of his crewmen bent over shovels. ("Already got his drudge boat drudgin'," as Captain Russ put it when we first arrived on the scene.) Soon our own winch began raising dredges. It meant constant shoveling of heavy loads that had to be distributed all across the deck— hot enough work that, despite the blowing chilly rain, first one oilskin jacket flew aside and then another.

Eventually, the rain stopped and the sun sparkled on the water. The scene turned bright, almost gay. Wide sheets of sail glided by at close range. Crews competed with each other and skippers shouted jokes from stern to stern. The skipjack men were good enough sailors to make a sport of buzzing a neighbor without smacking him.

A full load delivered early meant the chance for a second the same day, so it paid to hustle. Spat shells rose head-high all around us. When the gunnel had been weighted as close to the waterline as good sense allowed, we headed slowly around the points of low-lying land that led to the Choptank River. The site designated by the state biologists lay more than an hour upriver, beyond the town of Cambridge to an area known to be free of the killer parasites. Overboard went the spat shells by the flashing shovelful as we cruised the bar. Then we hurried back downriver, racing some of the others. Captain Wadie had already started his second deckload.

13

Lofoten Rorbu Country

W hen in 1937 Artur Nilsen first fished the great traditional cod runs of Lofoten, his big treat during the three-month season was a piece of beef on Sunday. The Lofoten fisherman's diet consisted principally of cod fresh from the nets, boiled in a pot with the liver and roe. This diet was supplemented with home-baked loaves packed by wives at leave-taking that, as they hardened, might be gilded with a bit of butter or a drop of molasses.

Most of the fishermen had small farms back home. Each carried in a sea chest his own supplies, which included, depending on his prosperity, a smaller or larger slab of salt beef. On Sunday he would slice off the piece with which he could afford to indulge himself, and drop it into the common pot. No one guessed about ownership. Each man had sewn yarn of a different color through his meat so that he could claim it without question. A man without beef to spare was out of luck. Dangers might have been the common lot, but there was no giddy sharing of the luxuries.

The improvement in the lot of Norway's fishermen approaches the stuff of dreams. Many a Petersen, Olsen, and Larsen now working Alaskan or New England waters owes his American citizenship to a dad or grandfather who emigrated to escape the grim poverty of his homeland, in days like those of old Lofoten that are still vivid to all but the youngest generation.

|197|

Nilsen remembers certain Lofoten seasons, with their routine twenty-hour days of work in wet and cold, when the coins he brought home barely filled a pocket after settling with the merchants who advanced supplies in return for his catch. To Greta, one of Nilsen's grown daughters, Lofoten meant childhood apprehension. She speaks quietly of her father's tearful sadness as he prepared to leave, knowing the poverty in which he was forced to leave his family and the dangers ahead that always meant some would not return. They had a small farm of a few acres and four cows that her mother, Sigrun, cared for in Artur's absence. One year, there were only twenty crowns in cash to see them through the three months. But Lofoten was the place fishermen went, "the only way to manage," the place of mythical abundance where lay the sole hope of deliverance from the cycle of hard times.

The Lofotens remain grounds of legend among Norwegian fishermen, from the deadly whirlpools of the Maelstrom at the southern extreme romanticized by Edgar Allan Poe (actually boats make it through them routinely, with care, at high tide), to the Trollfjord in the north where fish and boats dead-end together at a sinister barrier of towering stone. The mountains of Lofoten have the very feel of lore and ancient hardship. They appear over the water from the mainland as a barrier of peaks, the "Lofoten Wall," glowing blue in the cold Arctic light, a sight few fishermen who have approached them slowly aboard small boats in stormy weather can forget. Artur Nilsen has retired after fishing for half a century. Does he miss it? "No indeed!" he declares. But at Lofoten time, Sigrun and his daughters say he becomes restless.

The Lofotens are an eighty-mile chain of five major islands and many smaller ones lying about fifty miles off the Norwegian mainland. They spread out above the Arctic Circle on either side of sixty-eight degrees north, a latitude that in North America brushes the frozen top of Alaska but in Canada lies several hundred miles south of ice-locked Labrador. The Gulf Stream keeps Lofoten waters free of ice. The islands' topography is nearly all vertical, with a few narrow waterways between mountains and enough harbors around flattened rock to accommodate several fishing towns and villages.

For as long as Norsemen have kept records, vast schools of cod ready to spawn have migrated here annually from the ice reaches of the Barents Sea above Norway, and fishermen have converged from

coastal villages hundreds of miles around to catch them. The fish—
big ones—move down the Atlantic Ocean side of the islands, turn the
corner at the southern tip, and swim close to shore into the waterway
called Westfjord that separates the islands from the mainland.
"Skrei," the spawning cod, dry well in the crisp Lofoten air, and the
tradition of harvesting them covers no mere century or two. A monu-
ment stands in one Lofoten town to Øystein, a Viking king who died
in 1123, which recognizes his role in the formal development of the
Lofoten fisheries—but artifacts show that mainland fishermen had
sought the cod long before this.

There is a novel by the Norwegian writer Johan Bojer, published in
1919, set among the Lofoten fishermen of the 1880s. Schoolchildren
in Norway are still required to read it. *Den Siste Viking* is largely
forgotten by the rest of the world, although it was once read in
English as *The Last of the Vikings*. Bojer writes, from experience in his
youth, about one Lofoten season with the crewmen of an open "six-
oar" propelled by sail and human muscle.

Bojer's book tells an accurate story of rugged, poor men who
endure hardships without question that few could face today. By the
time Lars Myran, the sixteen-year-old "scaurie" (first-year apprentice)
sees home again with his skipper father, one of the six crewmen has
died of pneumonia in a fishing area too remote for a doctor, while
one in a companion boat has drowned in a terrible storm that nearly
sank them all. Lars himself has changed from a boy to a man under
conditions that could be called romantic only from the safety of an
armchair.

These were the days before fishermen had marine engines.

Lars' hands were blistered with manipulating the heavy oar all day,
but he did not notice it until the nets were put out again and they
began to row back in the dark. There was a good seven miles to row
against the current, and with a heavily laden boat. . . . It was anything
but pleasant to go on rowing and rowing, and rubbing up the raw flesh;
but for the moment the one important thing was to come ashore and
set to work on the fish. . . .

The next thing to be done was to stand on the rocks through the
greater part of the night, and by the light of a lantern clean fourteen or
fifteen hundred cod before there could be any question of eating or
sleeping. . . . However long it took, they would have to finish it, at any

rate by the time they had to put to sea again. Lars found the smarting of his hands became almost unbearable with the handling of the sea-salt fish, and he could have danced and howled with the pain; but this was not the time for childish whimpering: he was a Lofoten man now. [Translation of this and subsequent passages by Jessie Muir, from the 1922 Century Books edition of Johan Bojer's *The Last Of The Vikings*.]

Lofoten fishermen today can still relate to the old days, even though engines and hydraulically powered winches have delivered them from the hardest pulling. Nothing about the mountains has changed, nor the chilly cod, nor the weather with its sudden, deadly storms, nor the need to clean fish with a sharp knife before delivering them. The men still leave home far behind for an enforced three-month bachelorhood, although these days, with less rough conditions, some wives and girlfriends accompany the men to keep house. Most crews still live in seasonal shacks called *rorbus*, and the first rorbu system is credited to the same King Øystein of the twelfth century.

To Bojer's fishermen, the Lofoten mountains "were like an army of stone giants that had crossed the sea and had stopped here to consider." The men approached Lofoten in an open boat, drenched by icy seas as they beat their way across the Westfjord in January:

They danced and swung their arms, half mad with the icy cold in their joints and limbs. The dusk was beginning to fall when suddenly . . . Lars gazed and forgot that he was cold. . . . "Look there!" he said to Kaneles.

"Yes, that's Lofoten," said Kaneles. . . . "It's the Lofoten Wall. There'll be a dram for us this evening.' " . . .

The banks of cloud between sky and ocean turned into solid mountains, a long chain of blue mountains running southwest, streaked with snow, and with snow-drifts on their summits. . . . This was Lofoten, about which he had heard ever since he was a tiny boy, a land in the Arctic Ocean that all boys along the coast dreamed of visiting some day, a land where fishermen sailed in a race with Death. Through hundreds of years they had migrated thither, and many of them had lost their lives on the sea. A few returned home with well-filled pockets, but the greater number sailed to the end of life in poverty. Yet they went up again and again, generation after generation. It was their fairyland of fortune. They had to go.

[200]

Spurred by Bojer's book, I went to Lofoten in February 1980 and joined the crew of a longline boat. There it was as we approached: the Lofoten Wall, a line from horizon to horizon of jagged white mountains rising straight from the sea. Few of the glacier-sliced peaks are higher than 2,500 feet, but they seemed grander with nothing but flat water for comparison. As we came closer, the peaks separated into individual mountains, with buttresses of black-gray granite protruding through heavy snow. The peculiar quality of Arctic air reinforced their mystery. Although clear, the air softly hazed objects even at a middle distance. The mountains appeared powder blue under the sun, flat gray under the more frequent overcast, but always pale, blended with sky and sea, the stuff of dreams. I was old enough not to be stirred, but I was.

The longline boat I joined worked out of Stamsund, a town of small, snug homes set against bluffs and mountain slopes facing the sea. Its population of 1,600 doubled during the winter fishing months. The permanent residents and the transients lived in separate worlds, even though the same fish supported them both.

The residents' town centered around a single road that dead-ended at a slip for the coastal steamers that called once a day in either direction. This town included a small modern tourist hotel with a swimming pool and a bar-restaurant (the only place in Stamsund that served alcohol), and a modest snow-slippery square that contained stores for notions and groceries as well as a low office building. The office building housed the Johansen family company that owns and runs most of Stamsund. Inside, removed from the informality of the docks by carpeting and a receptionist, brisk men in business suits phoned and corresponded with cod buyers as far away as Italy, Nigeria, and the United States.

Fish drying racks occupied any open space including that across from the stately Johansen home facing the ferry slip. They consisted of multiple poles attached horizontally across basic A-frames. Men on ladders, their orange and red oilskins bright against the snow, carefully draped the floppy carcasses of headed cod in rows along the racks. Tied in twos by the tail, these would be left hanging to dry from March until June, steeping the town in a mellow, richly fishy odor.

The people of southern Lofoten are particularly committed to drying cod into boardlike "stockfish" rather than salting them—or selling them fresh since the advent of refrigeration—because nowhere else in the world is the weather more suited for this slow, natural process. It requires dry winds that never freeze but which never turn too warm to rot the fish. In a commerce that has flourished for centuries, south Lofoten stockfish fetches a higher price than any other cured cod, from Mediterranean housewives who know. Its strong flavor when soaked to limberness, a flavor that holds its own with garlic and tomato combinations, has kept it a traditional dish in Italy, Spain, and Portugal despite the Catholic Church's cancellation of Fish Fridays and Lenten restrictions.

Not all Stamsund fish still go on the drying racks. At one far end of the harbor stood a modern Johansen fish-filleting plant, with refrigerator ships at the adjacent quay waiting to receive its product. Inside, the workers wore white caps and smocks, and shiny machinery conveyed glistening cod fillets from cutter to sorters to packers. At the other end of the harbor, a few snowbanks from the square, stood the weathered fish delivery sheds and the red clapboard rorbus, the fishermen's seasonal quarters.

I arranged to meet the fishing crew at the Stamsund Fiskerheimen, fishermen's home, just across from the rorbus. Bojer mentions these church-run institutions as part of the 1880s' Lofoten fishing scene— the place where missionaries preached in their efforts to wean the rough fishermen to godlier ways. The Fiskerheimen vestibule was wet from boots stomped free of snow. In an adjacent small television room, a few people watched an old American movie in Norwegian. The big dim central room had a counter on one side, and several tables at which men in boots and scuffed woolens sat talking gravely. When I tried to order a beer in halting Norwegian, speaking across the counter which displayed only soft drinks and a few cakes, the woman in charge gave a reproachful frown. The Fiskerheimen was still a churchly domain.

No one paid a stranger particular attention until about an hour later, when two men who had been talking all along—they had even begun to clown at one point, setting off a wave of laughter in the otherwise silent room—studied me and then came over. The oldest was a husky man in his late forties with grey hair and clear eyes, Ole Olsen. The other, a gangling and rosy-faced boy, was Rune (pronounced Roo'-nah) Grovassbakk. The two had come to meet a stranger, but apparently I did not fit their mental picture. Despite their previous lively mischief, they became very reserved.

|202|

Stamsund harbor, in the Lofoten islands of Norway. A small wooden jigging boat returns with its auxiliary sail still hoisted. Fisherman go out early each morning during the dramatic late-winter runs of spawning cod, after traveling in boats such as these from the mainland in January across forty miles of rough water. The Lofoten cod have drawn fishermen since Viking times.

Racks all over Stamsund gradually fill with cod hung to dry for "stockfish", a staple of Mediterranean kitchens. The Lofoten air is particularly suited for the three-month drying process because it remains cool without freezing. During this time from March to June, the town remains steeped in mellow, fishy odors.

The crew of the *Arsteinvag* in their one-room rorbu. The meal centered around boiled cod and potatoes. L-R are Edmund Sandholm, Borgny Larsen, Rune Grovassbak, Torstein Sandholm (back), and Ole Olsen (couch). Note Borgny's flowered plates and curtains are part of Borgny's effort to make the rorbu as homelike as possible.

Stamsund rorbus, where fishermen live during their seasonal stay in the Lofotens. L-R Torsteiñ and John-Arve. Note the braces of cod hung to cure.

They led the way in the dark across the road, into an unlighted maze of slippery paths and long red frame buildings banked with snow, the fishermen's world of Stamsund. It turned out to be completely removed from that of the town residents. Stores and offices, for example, all opened and closed again each day before fishermen returned. Heavy old stone steps connected the rorbu buildings to piers and fish sheds below. Fishing boats bobbed in neat ranks tied beam to beam, their masts little more than black lines in the dark.

At one of the long buildings, whose sloped roof dripped icicles, we walked up plank steps to a door of boards held shut with a bent nail, into a frosty, raw-boned vestibule that smelled of dampness, oil, and fish. It seemed unpromising.

Then we removed our boots and entered a place of warmth and color. It was a big, clean room, fresh painted in glossy blues and buffs like a toy house, laid with unscuffed linoleum flooring. Curtains hung at the windows, and the central table had a cloth and plastic daffodils. An orderly hand was evident. Ole and Rune washed at a small sink by the door, then dried themselves on bright-colored towels hung atop one another on a nail nearby.

Three men looked up from the table, but a woman baking waffles at a counter by the stove stayed at work. One of the men rose, smiling shyly, and introduced himself as Edmund Sandholm. The others, each rising to shake with a fisherman's hand that barely squeezed, were Edmund's younger brother, Torstein, and Rune's older brother, John-Arve. The woman was Edmund's companion, Borgny Larsen, quiet, sweet faced, so reserved that she could barely nod when introduced. (And, in fact, despite many hospitable acts, she did not address me directly for at least three days.) Everyone had finished dinner, but Borgny heated some leftover cod and potatoes. Probably no one had really believed that a strange American would arrive to bunk in and fish with them.

The turf-covered rorbus that the men in Bojer's book occupied a century ago had uncaulked siding that let in piles of blowing snow. Each hut contained only two rows of triple-tiered bunks to accommodate the six-man crews of two boats, so that the twelve had to sleep double in a bunk. When the fire died each night, the frigid wind took over through the cracks. The fishermen wrapped themselves in skin rugs as they huddled alongside each other. By dark early morning, when they rose to face the oars and nets again, frost had covered their beards and still-damp leather boots.

Bojer describes a poorly timed Sunday visit to a rorbu (Lofoten fishermen still observe Sunday as a day of rest) following a run of cod that had kept the crews working around the clock for days. The station doctor had come to "teach the fishermen cleanliness" and the preacher to encourage temperance: "The floor was one confusion of wet seaboots and leather clothing. The table was covered with half-empty cups, spilled coffee, and fragments of food. Round the stone-cold stove hung damp oilskins and woolen vests; and the odor of fish oil, leather, damp wool, and exhalations from human bodies made the two gentlemen gasp for breath." To their credit, "they turned and stole softly out, with a peculiar feeling of respect for the sleep they witnessed, and carefully closed the door."

Our modern rorbu had a coal stove for heat, and a new four-burner electric stove. For sleeping, a stair ladder at the far end of the room led to a bunk loft, while a curtain off the kitchen screened an alcove filled almost completely with Edmund and Borgny's bed. My own bed was a board-mattressed couch against the wall, for which Ole brought quilting from the Fiskerheimen.

The toilet—a luxury beyond dreams in former days—was located directly beneath the rorbu, but accessible only outside down stone steps slick with ice and around through the crunching snow. Each rorbu had its own private stall (our key hung on a string over the stove) and the concrete basement also had a communal shower and a laundry tub. This was true comfort. Bojer's men had needed to shovel snow from their rorbu floor and start the fire each night when they arrived exhausted from the boats, and their trips to relieve themselves (not described) must have been frosty experiences.

My self-taught basic Norwegian turned out to be a strange lingo for these Northlanders, whose own speech was slurred and rapid-fire. ("You'll never understand Norlanders," my friends in Oslo had declared. "It is difficult even for us because they do not speak so clearly.") My strange Norsk gave young Rune the chuckles, but Edmund hushed him. Edmund's own English was well-pronounced and American-accented, and he had enough vocabulary to see him through an exchange of information. Halting at first, it improved day by day. Torstein, closer to his school days, soon began to revel in exercising a second language. Ole, older than the others and thus part of another generation, neither spoke nor understood a word of English. Borgny, if she did, never gave it a try.

Rune and John-Arve had studied English in school more recently, but had never used it face to face. It took the outgoing Rune two days to essay his first word. John-Arve, painfully shy, did not take the plunge until I gently cornered him after several days. But he had been yearning to try, and whole sentences began to tumble out. We all settled into a cheerful bilingual relationship in which, if the words of one language failed, a path could be charted through the other.

Edmund and Torstein soon began explaining the set of their cod longline gear. The talk turned to the cost of gear and the price of fish, areas that concern fishermen the world over. The market price of fish in 1980 had risen with inflation. However, said Tor, the five kroner per kilo that Lofoten fishermen received for dressed cod had remained the same since 1974. Somebody profited, but not the fisherman whose fuel and equipment costs had never stopped rising. "We have to take more and more fish up from the sea to make a living. That's the wrong way. Soon it comes so little fish in the sea that no one can get on with it." Tor rolled a cigarette and drew on it carefully, delicately, husbanding the small treat.

Edmund Sandholm was a lean, tired-eyed man of only thirty. Everything about him appeared scrubbed even though he wore the frayed flannel top of his thermals. His thick hands were pecked with salt sores and cuts from hooks. Edmund owned one of the largest fishing boats in Stamsund, and he already had the gravity that even a small command produces. He had bought the forty-two-foot *Arstein- vag* for about $137,000 and needed to meet an annual mortgage payment of about $25,000 for ten years.

The size of the *Arsteinvag* gave him an advantage this season—the cod had not been abundant close by, and he could travel a longer distance than could the thirty-footers to seek them out. But all his expenses were higher with a large boat, especially the cost of fuel. It might have been expected that as a longline fisherman he would receive a better price for his cod than those brought in by gill nets (which leave net marks on the fish). This would have helped compensate for the extra miles and the cost of the bait not required in gillnetting. But a marketing organization to which all northern Norwegian fishermen belonged dictated a uniform price. His only compensation was thus a larger boatload of fish.

Unlike many Lofoten fishermen who returned to small coastal farms in time for spring planting (as had all of Bojer's men a century before), Edmund and Tor fished year-round aboard the *Arsteinvag*. They traveled north into the Barents Sea after Lofoten, first to fish for cod, then for shrimp. Ole was the only crew member who followed the traditional pattern, returning after Lofoten seasons to his farm in the village of Vandve. John-Arve had fished full-time for three years, while Rune at eighteen was just beginning. Neither had yet accepted fishing as his career, especially Rune. Norway offered greater options for their generation.

I joked that when the price of fishermen's catches finally caught up with the general economy, they would be rich at the rate they worked. Tor answered seriously, "It's good to have so much to live well, ja, but we don't need more. We are not interested in working so hard just for more than we need. It would only be to pay it in taxes." Norwegians, indeed, are taxed at a progressive rate that quickly discourages people without empire-building ambitions from overworking themselves merely for money.

I had arrived between dinner and dessert. It was a period of one or two hours during which the fishermen napped, or visited other rorbus. What with the warmth after a long day of traveling, I became drowsy, and they left me alone in the room to doze.

Suddenly, the door flew open and a woman entered as if she owned the place, trailed by a man. This was my first meeting with Artur and Sigrun Nilsen. Sigrun exhuded snappy good nature as she poured coffee, drew up a chair, and rolled a cigarette. Where was everybody? she asked in Norwegian, and then began to question me. Lethargic from sleep, I shook my head and declared in English that I understood nothing. She cocked her head and raised an eyebrow. No one ever sat straighter, but she also swayed to her words with cheerful mockery. "*Du maw snakk Norsk*" she declared—you *must* talk Norwegian—and continued her quiz with no quarter given except a slower and more exact delivery.

I sat up and started to apply myself. She was a natural teacher from the no-nonsense school, insisting on the correct word and pronunciation and—important thing previously neglected—the precise intonation. Wrong. Do it again. Patiently, firmly, she demanded each sentence be repeated until I had it right. With such bright involvement, the lessons became enjoyable.

[206]

Back home in Brønnøysund, on the mainland coast, Artur and Sigrun knew Edmund and Borgny as longtime friends—the two women were in fact cousins. The Nilsens had reached a point in their lives when their daughters were grown enough to care for themselves, and Sigrun accompanied Artur to Lofoten as mate on their small net boat the *Sigrun-Margrete*. In Lofoten, she made a home of the rorbu, in addition to picking nets and cleaning fish.

During my interrogation, Artur remained as unobtrusive as wallpaper, a quiet supporting presence and nothing more. A small man, he appeared frail, although this was far from the truth. Actually he was a highline fisherman with all the tough drive this required, one of seven sons who had first fished with his father in the 1930s. His face, smooth except for wrinkles running in a crescent from his balding forehead to his cheeks, had a perpetual pleasantness about it, quizzical, alert, with half a smile. It was only later that Artur's strong concerns abut man's overfishing the sea, voiced in an expressive north-Norwegian patois to which the others listened respectfully, emerged in translated conversations.

The others returned—Edmund and Borgny from a friend's, Ole and Rune from the Fiskerheimen, John-Arve from his upstairs bunk. Borgny laid out a service of dishes decorated with red hearts, and a platter with the waffles she had been making earlier. We ate the waffles cold with butter and jam—the butter knifed on thick—and drank the coffee black. The two skippers listened attentively to the weather forecast on the radio. Then the adults fetched their individual tobacco packets, rolled cigarettes, and leaned back to smoke them with quiet, obvious pleasure. We all retired around eleven.

14

The *Arsteinvag*

Next morning at 2:30 A.M., the alarm rang. Edmund shuffled in from his alcove and started the coffee pot, working by nothing but a dim bed light to allow me a final minute of sleep on the couch. Shortly, the others descended from the loft, yawning as they tucked thick shirttails over their longjohns. The banked coal stove had kept the room mildly warm through the night. Breakfast was a quick, informal affair of thick bread slathered with butter, and of leftovers like cod roe (cold, grainy, mild-flavored) and a sweet brown rice pudding made with buttermilk called *gomme*.

We put on boots and coveralls in the chilly vestibule. Outside it was snowing, dark and cold. We headed down icy steps and a path between high snowbanks to a padlocked baiting room just off the pier. The room, which smelled of dampness and fish, contained twelve tubs of coiled and baited line, the Saturday's work of three crewmen. We carried the heavy tubs through the snow and lowered them to the boat, where Edmund lashed them securely in a covered space on deck. In our longlining procedure, three men stayed ashore to bait a new series of line for the following day. I joined Edmund and Ole aboard the *Arsteinvag*.

We kicked the deck free of snow, battened for sea, and cast off lines. Since we were tied in a row with smaller boats which would not leave for nearer grounds until daybreak, Edmund had to maneuver through a web of other mooring lines. By 3:15, we had cleared the harbor, picking with a searchlight around seas that crashed against the breakwater and exposed black rocks. The only other lights were those of a sister boat skippered by a friend of Edmund's, Einar Fristo, who traveled with us to the same grounds.

The *Arsteinvag*—Arstein is a Lofoten island and *vag* means bay— began to pitch and take cold spray over the bow. It felt good to be inside the sheltered little wheelhouse as white water leaped from the darkness to stream down the windows. Ole climbed below to a compact galley with bunks in the forepeak, made coffee on a single-burner stove and handed it up, and then rolled a blanket around him and fell asleep in one of the bunks. We had three hours of cruising ahead. On the return trip, Edmund would sleep while Ole steered. The trip lay through waterways between the mountains to the side of the islands facing the Atlantic (technically the Norwegian Sea). Here the cod—on an earlier leg of their spawning journey—were bigger and more plentiful than in the Westfjord where most of the boats were forced by limited cruising speed to wait.

A ribbon of northern lights flickered across the sky, resembling green gauze in a wind. They silhouetted the jagged black mountains, which gradually took on a dark blue cast with the approach of daybreak. It was wild and lonely country. An occasional lantern flickered ashore from some fisherman's hut set alone by the water, only accentuating the solitude.

When skies at sea are overcast, the morning sun still may shine briefly during the initial minutes of its ascent between the horizon and the cloud ceiling, bathing every object in reds and pinks. Around us, the color gleamed on mountain snows high over our heads and reflected in the smooth sheltered water. Soon after, we were tossing in open water so rough that we needed to brace ourselves on sea legs or hold tight, and the sky had become a mass of gray.

We approached the float of our first line, moving with the wind astern so that it would propel us along the gear. Longlining, as the name implies, involves fishing with an extended line—in our case three *stubbs* each of which was two miles long, or six miles altogether. The collective lines bore a total of 3,840 hooks spaced about eight feet apart.

When we paid them out astern, the lines were arranged to sink to the seafloor. Unseen to any fisherman, the gear would unfold in the dark water so that the baited hooks dangled a few inches above bottom, held in place by alternate attachments of hollow plastic floats, to raise them, and rock weights (*skankas*) to hold them down. After we pulled a stubb aboard and gaffed off the fish, we coiled the line with its attached hooks into a tub (each stubb filled four tubs) and sent over a fresh-baited stubb in its place. The new line would then be left to soak for one or two days.

Edmund was permanent *kortmann*, manning the most tricky position by the hydraulically powered roller that brought in the line. He needed to gaff each fish neatly as it surfaced—cod are soft-mouthed and can squirm easily from the hook—while making sure that the floats cleared the roller and that the line coiled properly in the tub. As skipper he also raced to the wheelhouse occasionally to correct the boat's heading.

The other jobs kept one or two men on the run, bleeding and storing the fish, shifting and stacking the tubs, detaching floats and sinkers from the incoming line and preparing them to be tied quickly to the new one as it payed out, hosing offal from the deck. I assumed the duty of *bløgger* (bleeder), cutting the main artery of each fish as required both by Norwegian law and by common sense. This action drains the blood before it penetrates the meat. Aboard the *Arsteinvag*, I stood over a low wooden bin into which Edmund threw the fish with a single swing of his gaff. Edmund's able gaff began to pile the fish high. The principal harvest was gray-green cod ranging in size from five to forty pounds, but it also included smaller black haddock, viciously spiked redfish, occasionally even a glinting silver salmon.

Indeed I had fished before, but never with this particular gear. Every job has its skills to be learned. The slippery cod kept eluding my grasp. Ole showed me how to grip a cod in the throat and eye with one hand as I held the sharp knife in the other. After a hundred such operations, the cold began to stiffen my hands so that the fish became more difficult to hold. What with the heavily rolling boat, and my knees pressed into the boards of the bin as I crouched over it, I soon had a sore back and was in a thorough sweat. Cold spray blew around us, and colder wind. And, my lord, we had barely pulled half a stubb. Five miles of line to go!

Eventually, we brought the first stubb aboard. Ole and I readied four tubs of the fresh-baited line. Soon the new stubb clattered over the stern chute, hooks snapping dangerously at high speed. With the timing of a dancer, Ole attached floats and sinkers at proper intervals and made sure the whole apparatus paid into the water without a snarl.

At crucial points in the operation, Ole would flick off his gloves for greater freedom. They lay in the deck slosh until he slipped them on again, wet and cold, and cleared them of water with brisk slaps against his thighs. These were thick woolen gloves of a village kind that Ole's wife had knitted for him. I have seen similar ones on the hands of sealers on the ice who come from Newfoundland villages, made three times oversize and then shrunk systematically in hot water to a near-waterproof density.

In the village Bojer describes, "even the old grandmother, with spectacles on, was busy, and sat by the stove dipping the new woolen gloves and socks into hot soapy water, and rubbing them upon a fluted board, so that they would become matted and be thick and warm."

So it went aboard the *Arsteinvag*, without a stop or a meal except for black coffee between stubbs, from dawn until early afternoon. After we had finished the final stubb and laid a new one to soak, Ole and I hosed the deck and battened gear while Edmund steered a straight full-bore course for home through the choppy waves. Cold water broke over our hooded oilskins and helped clear the deck of baits that had flown off the hooks. Finally, we could seek shelter in the wheelhouse, turned slippery-wet from boots, then down below in the dry, warm, compact galley. Food came out at last—a repeat of breakfast more than a dozen hours before, with *gomme* and cold roe on slabs of bread.

On the way home, Edmund slept and Ole steered, as they had done in reverse coming out. As we approached the mountains, they seemed truly a wall, without entrance. Then a passage opened, and another, leading a course from the Atlantic Ocean to the Westfjord. Under gray skies, the Arctic haze made the slopes and peaks appear as flat as cardboard. Numerous little houses stood solitary or in clusters, with no apparent access except by sea. Since the ocean side took most of the prevailing winds, it must have been a bleak life. According to Edmund, smaller boats that had been bouncing with us on the same horizon all day were from these little harbors. As in Newfoundland, sometimes the proximity to fish determined the placement of a home more than any considerations of comfort.

When we entered the Westfjord, the water became rough enough to have been the ocean. Eventually we passed through the Stamsund breakwater along with numerous smaller boats returning from nearer grounds. The boats accumulated around the delivery sheds where those closest to the pier delivered their catch into open bays located above mast level. Men stood around bins in each bay, their knives slicing vigorously at fish piled on tables in front of them, as buckets of glistening fish rose by pulley from the boat decks below. Other boats milled everywhere, jockeying for place, putting out fenders, switching positions with a more-or-less orderly handling of lines.

A flurry of snow whitened everything, and then an intense bath of light shone as the sun set between the clouds and horizon. The varnished natural wood of the boat hulls glowed gold. Some boats had small auxiliary sails of white, dark red, and blue. The red and orange oilskins of the men on decks and in the bays throbbed against the brown pilings. After the solitude of the fishing grounds and the gray passage home, the bustle and color were exhilarating.

Delivery proved to be the best part of the day. Not only did a hot meal, warmth, and rest await, but a chance to socialize as well. At the fish piers, we relaxed as part of the community. While waiting to deliver, Edmund and Ole chatted across the gunnel with other fishermen, comparing grounds and catches. Artur maneuvered the little Sigrun-Margrete alongside. Sigrun herself was there, in orange oilskins, silent for once amid the men's shop talk. The smaller boats that were forced to fish within sight of shore all reported poor catches along the Westfjord that day, information that justified our long trip to the ocean.

When our turn came to deliver, Tor, John-Arve, and Rune waited to catch our lines. Each crew cleaned its own fish. Rune, the youngest, had the job of unloading the hold, and soon he stood hip deep in cod and haddock with only the top of his head showing above the hatch. I lined up with the rest above, flanking the bin where our catch thumped out from the buckets Rune filled. We passed a hone and sharpened our knives. Tor and Edmund instructed me with grave care. Onlookers gathered to watch. Sigrun joined the group, her mouth pursed critically. No one spoke until I had grasped enough of the job not to ruin the fish. By sticking to the smaller fish, I began to manage without disgrace. The others soon began an easy round of talk and laughter in Norwegian. This was the time to compare catches

[213]

and to pass tales and jokes, a time anticipated during the monotony and discomfort of fishing.

After the cutters headed the fish, the carcasses passed down the line to Ole and John-Arve, who eviscerated them with a sweep of the hand through the open belly. They threw the roe and livers each into separate barrels and tossed the heads into a pile. Each of the three parts was a saleable item along with the fish meat itself. At the end of the fishermen's assembly line, a plant employee washed the cod carcasses, weighed them, and tied them by the tail in twos ready to be draped on a drying rack.

The cod heads, strung out to dry about twenty to a line, would eventually make it to Nigeria. First they went through another subharvest by the gutting bins, where a busy group of young boys speared each cod head we threw over, and sliced out the throat or "tongue." The boys, known as "tongue millionaires," worked free-lance after school as an accepted part of the scene.

Everyone's knives flashed through the fish by second nature as they talked. I began to feel so in tune that when the pulley raised a bucket load I grabbed to empty it, confidently but too soon. Fish flopped back down to the boat, some into the water. Since they floated Rune retreived most of them. None of my crewmates seemed upset (although some of the onlookers frowned). After apologizing I returned to the work with doubled vigor. Presently, from the deck twenty feet below, a cod slapped my head, then another, as Rune sent up the overboard catch with sure aim. His grin stayed tentative until I laughed. Then everybody laughed.

With the catch delivered, we hosed the gurry from our oilskins and then walked stiffly up icy paths to the warm rorbu. Borgny had a simple dinner waiting, but she served it in whopping quantities and refilled each bowl over and over as we heaped our plates. The staples were potatoes and fish, the embellishments bread, butter, turnips, carrots, and cheese. Boiling was the basic preparation. On subsequent days, she added an occasional bit of ham or pork, but sparingly, as little more than a seasoning mixed into mashed potatoes.

Despite the heartiness of the eating, everyone displayed fastidious table manners. Edmund, for example, cut his bread carefully into pieces before popping them into his mouth. Each hungry man took the time to peel his potatoes. Bojer reported the same habit among

Edmund Sandholm removes a large cod from the longline aboard his boat *Arsteinvag* fishing off the Lofoten Islands in Norway.

Ole carries a heavy tub of baited line to the boat for a 3 a.m. departure.

The buoys and anchor that mark the end of a "stubb" of baited line go over the stern of the *Arsteinvag*. Note the small auxiliary sail.

Edmund chats with another skipper at the end of the day as he waits for his crew's turn at the gutting tables in Stamsund.

Longline drudgery. In the baiting room, Rune clears the 320 hooks in a half-mile length of line, rebaits with slices of mackerel, and coils the line in a new tub. The job, which takes a skilled man three hours, must be precise to avoid snags as the line races out from the boat. Each baiter is responsible for four such tubs a day.

his fishermen a century before and, custom or whim, everyone stopped to watch (very discreetly) whenever I ate my potato skins.

Borgny prepared fish in a variety of ways. There were delicately flavored haddock (*hyse*) balls in white sauce (*fiskeboller*); round haddock bits fried brown and served with a rich brown sauce and tart berries (*fiskekaker*); leftover cod in a creamy mush (*plukkfisk*); salmon served with a light sour cream (*laks med romme*); and of course cod (*torsk*), boiled first in vinegar water and then washed in heavily salted water.

Heavy salting seems to be the prescribed seasoning for cod in the places where cod is both the basic harvest and the basic table food. In Newfoundland, lovely fresh cod is soaked two days in brine, then served in such a coating of salt that it burns the mouth. The taste has been acquired from generations of preserving cod in salt. The ancillary products of cod are each distinctly different, and while they bear the taste of the sea, none are fishy. Tongues, the meaty section from the throat, become rich as butter and hypnotically delicious when fried, or stewed in sour cream. They have the chewy texture of small clams. Borgny served cod at its best with the roe and liver, which we would deliver to the rorbu straight from the boat. (This was our Thursday night meal, the way some Americans used to have chicken on Sunday.) The roe, boiled whole for about twenty minutes, had a lighter flavor than most rich roes. With its close-grained texture, it was something like a dumpling when hot, and a smooth spread when cold.

Bojer described the ultimate treat a century ago:

> Someone said "Melja!" and instantly there was a chorus of "Melja." That was a dish to set before a king, and they had not had it yet this year; so of course it must be "melja." . . . Henry brought in several plates of broken-up flat-bread, and then, taking in the saucepan full of boiled, steaming hot cod liver, he ladled out a liberal helping into each plate. The oil glistened as it flowed over the piles of flat-bread, and over it was strewn grated goat's-milk cheese, after which treacle was poured all over in long, golden-brown, sinuous lines. The next thing was to stir it all up with a spoon, and there you had a mixture that was worth tasting! . . . This was not simply food; it was like a wedding! The plates were emptied in an incredibly short space of time. . . . Faces, beards, fingers, shone with oil, treacle, and cheese. . . ."

Most of the men ate at least three heaping platefuls of food, this being the only full meal of the day. Then they settled back, rolled cigarettes, and relaxed. Ole, a great talker when not confronted with a stranger, launched into a monologue with gestures and vigorous inflections. I didn't understand a word, but he did it with such high humor that I knew I was the loser. It turned out to be the account of a movie he had seen. When Ole shed oilskins and greasy coveralls each evening to scrub and put on a dressy Norwegian sweater, the hooked nose and shock of gray hair that made him look the classic old fisherman on the boat became accents to mischievous eyes, and ten years dropped from his face.

Rune talked expressively in his husky adolescent voice, bandying words with his skipper who answered in quiet amusement, joking head-on with Ole who had children his age. Their laughter erupted often. When Rune played a slapstick trick, Ole chased him up to the bunk loft and then stood guard at the ladder, winking and grinning at the others. Some Norwegians might have grim natures. This is certainly the impression one gathers from the claustrophobic atmosphere of Ibsen's plays and the anguish of Edvard Munch's paintings, while there is a basic type of Norwegian fisherman I have encountered in Alaska who is silent, stingy, and hard-eyed. Not here.

Despite Rune's horseplay and the bond that comes through working together, language still kept me apart and the table talk swirled over my head. But it took no special acuteness to know that one recurrent subject, first at the gutting bins and then at dinner, was the clotted gash on my forehead from a blow I had accidentally received from a gaff out on the boat. After mentally rehearsing each word, I cleared my throat for attention, pointed to my forehead, and declared; "Jeg var doven." The announcement that I had been lazy stopped everybody. They began to chuckle expectantly. And, I continued, banging with an imaginary gaff, Edmund had yelled, "Du! Arbeide!"—"You! Work!" Bob Hope never had a better audience. The first collective laughs were satisfying enough. Two hours later, when Edmund told a visitor my magic words, the guffaws reached roaring proportions. I had settled in.

The days repeated themselves, with occasional variations. On bad-weather days ashore, we all helped bait. More hands on the job allowed us to yawn and take more time with coffee before descending the snowy paths to our baiting room, the *egnebu* (pronounced ahn'-bu). Inside the cinder-block room, the oily odor of mackerel combined with the damp chill of the concrete floor, while the air frosted with each breath despite small electric heaters kept low all night. A knee-high bench lined three of the walls. Each man lifted to his part of the bench one of the heavy wooden tubs containing line brought in by the boat the night before, and placed a clean empty tub beside it.

The first job was to transfer the line into the clean tub while straightening it and removing old bait. Then we began the main job of returning the line to the original tub while putting fresh bait on the hooks.

We baited with fresh frozen mackerel, greasy and rubbery to the touch, that we sliced into diagonal chunks. The job also required replacing hooks and gangions (a short line that connects each hook to the main line), and straightening other hooks. The hooked baits were laid around the rim of the tub in scrupulously even circles, with newspaper scraps separating layers, so that on deck when the line paid into the water it would not bunch or snag.

One tubful of line, or *stamp*, was 2,625 feet long and contained 320 hooks. Each of the men in the *egnebu* was responsible for baiting four stamps (which equaled one stubb or complete set of the longline we fished on the grounds) with a total of 1,280 hooks. Picking old bait from each stamp took about an hour, while fresh baiting took another two hours. This worked out to a twelve-hour day in the *egnebu*.

The stationary nature of the baiting led to quiet conversations, but a radio also played most of the time. The single national station provided learned discussions and classical music in greater abundance than the jaunty popular music that would have gladdened everyone most, but as a spin-off of their captive listening Lofoten fishermen were unusually well informed on world affairs. Edmund, Tor, and Rune, for example, asked questions about United States politics from a base of knowledge more sophisticated than that of the average American.

By the time each morning that our three *egnebu* men had normally cleared and rebaited their first stamp, the piers directly outside had become busy even though the sky was just turning light. Masts swayed as fishermen in orange and red oilskins jumped from deck to deck. One group of men relayed a half-mile of green gillnet on their boat from the shed where they had been mending it late into the night. Few spoke.

Engines began to sputter. From the rows of boats tied together, some in the middle tossed lines and moved out, then others, until the rows disintegrated and most boats were gliding free. In such buzzing numbers, with auxiliary sails hoisted and wooden hulls glistening, they resembled big dragonflies on a pond. The sky had puffs of pink in it when the boats all started in lines toward the two breakwaters on opposite ends of the harbor. By now, the collective engine noise was enough to rattle house windows along the high rocks where early light had brightened the snow. The boats traveled so close, gunnel to gunnel, that men could be seen poking their heads from wheelhouse windows to call back and forth.

Young Rune watched the departure restlessly. He confided, when we came to know each other, that if to be a fisherman meant standing all day in a baiting room he would soon find other work. His attitude reflected the new options for Norwegians. With the discovery of offshore oil, rural Norway was no longer simply a land of farmers and fishermen. Among the *Arsteinvag* crewmen, only Ole retained this double occupation. The two boys were still undecided, and could afford the time to try something else. Edmund and Tor had made a full-time commitment to fishing. They followed the cod north after the Lofoten season, and pursued other fisheries with different gear during other parts of the year. Edmund had little choice, in order to make a living and still meet payments on his boat.

On one relatively calm day aboard the *Arsteinvag* Edmund and Ole conferred, then handed me the gaff and sent me to the roller. Suddenly I was *kortmann*, in charge of bringing in the fish. Responsibilities come in many forms, and I felt at once the weight of this one—answering for the rorbu's income. I watched the incoming line. Gradually, a flip-flopping patch of white underbelly rose through the water. When the full cod emerged, I gripped a handle by the roller as I had seen Edmund do, and leaned far down with the gaff in the other hand. I missed, struck again, missed, while the fish rose slowly to the gunnel and shook free. Fortunately, cod in cold water is a sluggish creature, and Ole retreived this one neatly with a long pike.

Tensely, I watched the slow emergence of the next white patch. He was huge. I made contact, and swung him aboard with a back-cricking sweep of muscle and a triumphant yell. Edmund and Ole watched it all with amusement.

Next came a small haddock which I barely snagged. The obvious became apparent, that little fish provide less target area than big ones, even though they might be easier to lift over the side. At the end of the stubb, my knees were bruised from digging them into the metal side as the boat rolled, and I could barely see for the sweat in my eyes.

Edmund's calm ninety-nine percent gaffing average earned my new respect. Over the next few days, my own average reached about eighty-five percent with four times the expenditure of energy. Ole continued to save the rest by remaining a cool hand at the pike.

Back at the rorbu that night, Edmund told the others gravely that I had something to announce, and then prodded me into saying in my best Norsk that I was now a *kortmann*. I delivered this limited truth with no conviction, and explained how little of a *kortmann* I amounted to unless Ole was there to help. Just the same, everyone applauded. Then they began a laughing discussion that quickly rippled over my head.

15

A Norwegian
Bash Remembered

One day Kalle Larsen of the twenty-eight-foot *juksa* boat *Ferder* invited me along. (*Juksa*, pronounced yook'-sa, is the Norwegian term for jigging.) I joined him by stepping rail to rail over several boats of like size moored in a row. We started late by *Arsteinvag* standards, with a cup of coffee at 5:30 A.M.

The brave little jigging boats were the smallest in the Lofoten fleet, usually less than thirty feet long, operated by a single fisherman who often lived aboard as did Larsen. About twenty of them fished out of Stamsund—which meant that they had negotiated at least forty miles of rough open water to cross from the mainland in early February—and as many more fished around the *Arsteinvag* from scattered, completely isolated little houses on the bleak west side of the Lofotens where we traveled daily. With their honey-colored round wooden hulls, they bobbed around our forty-two-foot steel-hulled vessel like bathtub toys, riding seas high enough to hide their masts completely in a trough.

After a few minutes, to the noise everywhere of engines coughing and then taking hold with a roar, we unmoored and peeled off from the row. At 6:00 A.M. sharp, a fishery patrol boat moved clear of the main exit from the harbor, where it had been holding the juksa and gillnet boats in check like so many puppies, and the whole fleet headed toward two passages between high rocks.

Lofoten law requires the boats that fish Westfjord grounds to remain in harbor until 6:00 A.M.: in fact, until 7:00 A.M. during February, with its late sunrises. A version of this law had already been passed in 1816 as a means to keep order in a fishery of hungry, driving men who might otherwise never rest, and whose boats carrying no more light than a lantern would often have rammed each other in the dark. Other laws first passed long ago designated exclusive areas for different gear types. It is no new thing for hooks to snag nets, and for nets to drag off baited lines.

The exodus of all boats together made for a grand parade through the breakwater as the rising sun etched the bows and masts in blinding ruby light. We rode so close to other boats that Kalle had only to raise his voice above the engine noise to carry on a neighborly conversation. The *Sigrun-Margrete* pulled abreast for a moment, and Artur waved while Sigrun called over, but their slightly larger boat with its heavier engine soon outdistanced us.

Out beyond shelter, the boats—many no longer than twenty-five feet—started a swinging pitch and roll that would last all day. We had entered the fisherman's element, where it was bruising work merely to maintain balance. The concept of a starting time leads naturally to that of a race. Many of the boats took off full bore as their skippers leaned into the spray. Kalle, a placid, short, stocky, unflamboyant man of sixty-six, seemed detached from any such competition. He remained in his wheelhouse the size of a telephone booth, peering at the water as if examining every wave for the fish underneath. But his hand rested full down on the throttle, and nobody left us behind.

The rough cold water separated us further and further from land. The houses ashore diminished to spots of decoration beneath the snowy Lofoten peaks, nothing more than incidentals to the sweep of mountains and sea. Kalle stopped his engine abruptly. Perhaps he had raced with an eye on the water, but he also had been watching a point of triangulation between two of the mountains where, over the years, he had known good fishing.

We dropped our unbaited hooks in thirty fathoms of water, lowering each line from a hand-cranked reel on deck until the sinker thumped bottom. Then, holding the line, we raised it about five feet (much higher off the bottom than is the practice in Labrador) so that the hook floated free in the area where the cod swam looking for food on the seafloor.

We needed to keep the line in motion. Kalle did it with a steady upward sweep of his arm to make the hook move below with a glint of life. His fisherman's feel made all the difference in keeping the hook positioned, distinguishing between vibrations on the 180-foot line from current, bottom, fish, and friction. A cod would telegraph its presence on the hook with a heavy jerk, but then subside into dead weight or at best no more than a twitch. The line with a hooked fish had to be kept taut. The reel made this easier than hauling hand over hand, but nevertheless my arm ached by midday from cranking in response to false alarms. When Kalle reeled in, he always had a fish.

Fishing with Kalle had precision and order. The fish came up one by one, and after each bleeding washed the deck immediately. The orderliness extended below decks. To appreciate it fully, one needed to experience the drubbing the bathtub-shaped *Ferder* took at sea during even a normal day of fishing. Kalle had a curtain at his porthole, and a vase of artificial flowers anchored tight against the bulkhead near pictures of his wife, children, and grandchildren. Every utensil, every piece of equipment, had a place either in a rack or drawer. When we finished coffee after fishing, Kalle wiped the mugs and stored them again immediately.

Kalle led an even and frugal personal life. He spent his evenings at the Fiskerheimen, talking with friends—with whom he also compared notes at sea as they bounced alongside each other—and watching TV, sometimes affording himself a small treat. He drank no alcohol, and refused politely an invitation to the hotel bar for something to warm us after the long day's jigging. But he did have one small weakness.

Once we were sitting with Tǫrstein at the Fiskerheimen, and Tor persuaded me to order the specialty dessert of the house. It turned out to be a large and relatively expensive concoction of sugar and pink gelatin that I abandoned after a single spoonful because it was too sweet for my taste. Kalle had finished a more modest dessert (costing perhaps a sixth as much), but when I pushed aside mine he became restless. Tor made a mild suggestion and, embarrassed, I offered it over. "Tusen-takk!" (a thousand thanks) declared Kalle at once, and without ado spooned it down with obvious pleasure, his sweet tooth and his innate horror of waste satisfied simultaneously.

Of the other gear types used in Lofoten, longlining had its practitioners aboard more than the Arsteinvag and its sister boat even though it was less common than gillnetting and jigging. Two men who berthed near us, for example, shared a small longline boat. They seldom lifted their heads to speak, and their weather-reddened, unshaven faces wore a permanently grim set. The single glance that I had inside their rorbu showed a bare and Spartan room, left chilly to save fuel, with a dark jumble of clothes and bedding in one corner and a single blackened pot on the stove.

The labor-intensive nature of the gear appeared to have them enslaved. They handled less line than we did—five stamps compared to our twelve—but they did all the baiting themselves after running from the grounds each night. There they would be when the rest of us walked down to use the toilet before going to bed, working beside their tubs in a little baiting shed. Dim lantern light cast a yellow slick over mounds of frozen cod heads just outside the steaming window. They had no radio, exchanged no conversation. They just worked.

The domesticated circumstances of the Arsteinvag crew put me in contact more with fishermen accompanied by wives and girlfriends who gave the rorbus a vestige of home, less with those who came to Lofoten as bachelors. The latter were in the majority, however. Borgny's entire day revolved around making our rorbu a home. Even though we left books in the vestibule, she scrubbed the floor and shook the scatter rugs every day. But she was no slavey. Edmund or someone else usually dried the evening dishes, and we took care of ourselves at 2:30 in the morning.

Sigrun must figure in any account of the rorbus. Though no other woman I saw worked on a boat (supposedly there were others), she never lost her femininity. She picked nets aboard the Sigrun-Margrete and gutted fish on the pier as easily as the men—declaring she liked doing it—then fixed dinner while Artur moored the boat and washed it down. The home she kept in their one-room rorbu (the beds were in an exposed loft) revealed a bright woman's whimsy. The walls were decorated with her own drawings sketched in graceful lines, as well as with crayoned houses and people done by grandchildren. The curtains and tablecloths bore vivid folk designs.

On weathered-in days, Sigrun would bake, and invite us over in the evening for strong coffee and big, light pastries. "Coffee-doctor cures everything," she maintained, applying a term to plain coffee that

Artur and Sigrun Nilsen, a husband-wife fishing team, put aside oilskins and forget codfish during a Saturday night dance for fishermen away from home. Elsewhere in the hall, lots of "homeburn" is being passed around to help unwind after a week of hard fishing.

Kalle Larsen visits with another one man jigging boat in sight of the line of mountains known as the "Lofoten Wall."

Against the majestic mountains of Reiñe in the Lofotens, a boat glides to harbor after a day's fishing, framed by cod hung to dry. Below a fisherman, still in oilskins, checks his gillnet for tears before going home.

colloquially refers to coffee laced with alcohol. All that she did had a positive stamp: a strong handshake, a look straight in the eye, an outspoken remark. "Bill! You scared the shit out of me!" she declared when I snapped a flash picture without warning. The word is nearly the same in both languages. She articulated with such distinction that it sounded proper to the circumstance.

One Saturday, the *Arsteinvag* crew rose at 2:30 A.M. and worked the usual full day. After dessert, however, Borgny darkened the room and lit candles. Edmund brought out a bottle of lime extract and another of vodka. Artur and Sigrun arrived, then some other friends. We rolled cigarettes and had a second round of drinks as everyone became increasingly cheerful.

Two hours later, we were dancing in a big hall to thumping polkas and waltzes as we gulped indiscriminately from bottles of vodka and "homeburn" passed mouth to mouth amid joking and shouting. Edmund pulled Borgny into a boisterous set of twirls that left them both flushed and gasping with laughter. It came as no surprise that Sigrun danced on light feet. She divided her attention between Artur, Torsten, and me. When Tor's turn came, they pranced a polka, straight backed, with particular style. Fishermen I knew slightly or had never met urged me to share their bottles. My back grew sore from being pounded, my throat numb from shouting and helping to sing over the noise.

Our dance at the Stamsund hall closed, but with everyone in motion who wanted to stop? The roar of songs continued along icy wharves and rorbu paths. In the middle of it, someone from another boat pestered Borgny. Edmund's friendly face became firm, suddenly. He said a few forceful, quiet words and held a clenched fist ready. The man's hand slipped from Borgny's arm, and he wove away.

From around a corner we heard brusque thumps, the sounds of a contention being resolved over a tangle of nets on the grounds a few days earlier. It had been rorbu gossip, how two boats each claimed their right to a spot and made simultaneous sets. This was private business among equals, and when I wondered if we should stop the fight everyone shushed me away.

A hundred years earlier, Bojer had described this Saturday scene: "The concertina player was sitting on a beam up under the roof, and the place smelt of fish, tar, and fish-oil. The faces of the men and girls were red with drink and dancing." However, the fishing station of

Bojer's story had few women, and the competition for their attention erupted into a free-for-all: "As he began to swing his great fists the women shrieked and fled toward the door. . . . Kaneles was not one to let a good fight pass unheeded. . . . At last the day began to dawn. It had been a lively night. The Ranen man had had one of his eyes knocked out. . . ."

A crowd of us stumbled along the road, falling once into a snow-bank like a chain of derailed boxcars and laughing the louder for it, singing mightily. At Sigrun's it was open house, passing the dregs of open bottles, consuming pastries she had found time to bake and endless *kaffe-doktor*. By about 3:00 A.M. (past time to rise on most mornings, including the one previous), many had collapsed or given up. Edmund and Tor, after a slump, revived to wander singing to Einar Frisno's rorbu and the crew who fished from a sister longline boat. Borgny followed to make sure no one came to harm on the slippery piers.

At Einar's we burst upon another party just winding down, and our arrival started it up afresh. I gave up in time to see the dawn. After wandering among some laden fish racks that smelled of drying fish, I watched the first pink light brighten the mountain snow above silent, respectable, permanent homes. An occasional shout or burst of laughter came from another of the long rorbus, but the town lay deserted like the scene on a postcard, the road glinting ice, snow banked high against stone steps and red rorbu boards, the masts of a hundred boats reflecting in the dark water.

That noon the whole *Arsteinvag* crew, subdued and cheerful, en-countered the faces of the night before around tables at the Fiskerheimen. A grin or two passed across the room while everyone waited soberly to be fed. The two crews who had fought sat close to each other, as friends will, their faces scraped with a purple bruise or two set in expressions of solemn dignity. The dinner plates came out from the kitchen (some of the men including Tor and Rune helped with the serving) heaped with pork and sauerkraut in opaque gravy. We downed the meal with the relish of people who seldom eat meat. Then we went back home and slept. Next morning at 2:30, after all, the alarm would ring again.

[226]

16

Myre Ascendant

The village of Nyksund appeared as a black presence from a bend of the mountain road skirting Myre fjord, where an autumn storm swept the water with trails of white scud. The twilight at 3:00 P.M. had already cut dark lines into the gray sky. A few dim caretaker lights glimmered among the towering old salteries that surrounded the harbor, but the lights did not extend to the small houses scattered on the rocks above. The causeway leading to the island community had splits where the foundation had eroded beneath, and spray broke over it to make the remaining surface glassy. On the other side, an unpaved road led around the U-shaped harbor. It passed through a canyon between the buildings and a face of rock, across a wet breakwater bridging the harbor, then up over rocks to boarded houses facing others on the opposite side.

A single figure moved on a pier below the road. He seemed old from the stoop of his thick shoulders under oilskins as he checked the lines of an open skiff. After a while, he walked up a path to the breakwater. His face was indeed wrinkled. His eyes met mine with a judgmental hardness that might have said: You don't belong here, wouldn't last five minutes on the oars.

"Hi, how are you?" I asked in Norwegian.

He walked past without answering, toward a hill of unlighted houses.

Nyksund was once the center of civilization in the Vesteralen, as this rugged coastal area of north-central Norway is called. Fishermen—there was no other occupation—lived in island communities of two and three houses. At Nyksund, the high fish sheds enclosing the harbor provided shelter like that of a mother's arms to boats beating in directly from the sea. The barnlike salting sheds themselves were a marvel of adaptation, with platforms built on several tiers so that boats could deliver at any stage of the twenty-foot tides. The company store here carried everything a sensible person might want. Nyksund even had a bakery, and a church. It also offered the stimulus of companionship. Imagine, houses by the dozen with a family in each!

The men who fished around Nyksund, like the Labradorians, originally settled on the farthest islands into the sea, since they could reach the fish in waters beyond the land only through the labors of oar and sail. The rocky islands held enough soil to grow grasses for livestock, and the small homesteads included a cow or two, a pig, and sheep from which the women would weave wool and make the family's clothing. It was no easy life. The greatest cod runs occurred in January and February as the fish swam toward Lofoten. This is a time of darkness above the Arctic Circle. A grudging twilight might appear in the sky for two or three midday hours, but the men set, pulled, and picked most of their nets by lantern.

People knew that they could ask little more of life than to fill their boats with enough cod to barter for necessities they could not produce themselves. They worked in an economy run by fish kings who set the price paid for their catch and merchants who set the price for the goods they needed. Often, as in Labrador, the station king and the merchant were the same man, or represented parts of the same organization, taking calm advantage of the situation to pay low and charge high. Given the isolation, the fishermen had no alternative, and for generations they accepted their lot.

During all these years, most Norwegians had only a humble opinion of themselves. For a land whose history included the Vikings, it had experienced centuries of humiliating unimportance. The Vikings emerged around A.D. 800 as magnificent seafarers able to navigate northern seas to pillage and settle throughout the North Atlantic community, and they left a permanent imprint, but their last raid occurred in 1066. There followed long periods of civil war. The Black

Plague of 1349 wiped out half the population and started a decline that sank Norway into a position of vulnerability. The small country, diffused by a mountainous coastline that stretches more than one thousand miles along the Atlantic seaboard, became little more than a colony governed from Denmark or Sweden, or exploited by German merchants of the Hanseatic League. Norway, in fact, did not become truly prosperous until the discovery of North Sea oil began to produce wealth in the early 1970s.

By 1866, the poverty had become so grim that Norwegians, like the hungry Irish, poured into North America. Further migrations ended on farm homesteads in Minnesota and Manitoba, and on fishing boats in New England and the Pacific Northwest. These remain places where the Sons of Norway still make a huge splash, where Hansens, Petersens, and Jacobsens outnumber Smiths and Joneses.

The Norwegian fisherman's acquiescence to hardship lasted until the upheaval of World War II. Legions of Norway's fishermen escaped their occupied homeland to join the Allied forces in England. They sailed, even rowed, across the churning North Sea in small boats that most men would find unsafe to take a mile from shore. What men these Norwegian fishermen were! In England at naval training camp, they rowed with such an iron pull that they broke the regular oars and had to be issued special ones with holes in the blades. Such men, soon risking their lives in combat, quickly lost any tolerance for the old exploitative monopolies. So did those who stayed home and stood up to the German invaders.

The Vesteralen region had escaped the worst of the Occupation, because it was remote and decentralized. The German army negotiated an agreement with the Quisling government to take sixty percent of the fish harvest in return for leaving the Norwegians forty percent for home consumption. Kaare Hagerup, a gracious man now in his seventies whom many regard as the father of the modern Vesteralen fishing industry, worked during this time for the Norwegian Department of Trade to ensure that his countrymen received their share of the fish. The coastal steamer system transported the fish for both German soldiers and Norwegian civilians. Hagerup knew the steamer captains as they knew him. Between them they could produce stevedores at most stops to transfer a few undocumented crates of iced fish in the dark. "And so, sometimes," Hagerup recalled in nearly perfect English, enjoying his words, "sometimes we sent fish to people that was not noticed. So perhaps the Norwegian people got more than forty percent."

After the war, Nyksund began to grow. As prices paid for fish acquired a more realistic relationship to the cost of goods, fishermen could at last afford boat engines. The engines enabled them to cover a further distance each day, making it possible to abandon residence on the bleak outlying rocks and move inshore to the amenities of Nyksund. Perhaps the town could be reached only by sea since no road connected it to other communities scattered among the fjords, but how else would anyone have needed to travel to a place whose business was fishing?

Then the government built a road, a single dead-end ribbon of graded gravel that skirted the mountains a few hundred feet above the stormy waters, to open Nyksund to the world. The planners intended to make Nyksund accessible, to help it expand. Instead, the road enabled people to continue their migration. First the older children left for school. The girls, having glimpsed an easier life than that of gutting lines and wood-stove kitchens, found ways not to return. The boys returned because they had work they knew aboard their fathers' boats, but how long could young men remain committed to a society that lacked young women?

The world began closing down on Nyksund in another direction. The major cod runs along the coast were too seasonal to sustain a year-round population that expected any level of affluence, and when fishermen acquired new boats they chose ones large enough to extend their season by following the fish along the coast. The turbulent water at the entrance to Nyksund was deep enough for a small boat laden with fish, but not for these larger vessels even at high tide.

The road to Nyksund, whatever the outcome it produced, was part of a larger plan. With the war over, the Norwegian government examined its coasts with a new appreciation for their strategic importance. The Germans had used the coast for submarine bases to decimate Allied supply ships to Russia. Now the Russian advances in central Europe made this country a frightening enough neighbor that in 1949 Norway abandoned its historic neutrality and joined the North Atlantic Treaty Organization. It became national policy to keep the coastal communities populated, just at a time when rural people the world over were heading for the easier life of cities.

|230|

The islands of Vesteralen, connected only by ferry and fishermen's boats, were a mass of fishing villages and small fish plants. Most plants lacked cold storage facilities, so that all fish had to be salted, dried, or sold fresh. Moreover, they had such a limited capacity that a fisherman might be forced to call from one to another before finding a plant able to take his fish. Certain men might be counted on to live by the boats whatever the circumstances, but the area needed a better system if it hoped for the stable prosperity that would keep a population in place.

The government began to make plans to ease life in the Vesteralen by funding some venture to improve transportation and fishing. It recruited Kaare Hagerup, who had continued to work in the fish business, and had remained a man respected along the coast for his resourceful wartime liaison. He and others envisioned a cooperative local institution that would aim for the strengths of centralization while keeping the traditional fishing patterns intact.

It came time to choose the site for the new venture. To use Nyksund would have required blasting a deeper channel through the rock seafloor, and reconstructing all the facilities from scratch since they were built exclusively for salting fish. With engines the few miles' trip to fishing waters meant nothing anymore compared to a better natural harbor and an easier topography for roads. Inevitably, Nyksund lost its boats and its fishermen to nearby Myre.

They named the new Myre fish plant Øksnes-Langenes Fiskeindustri after the old regional designations of the Vesteralen. The long, squared structure of steel and concrete was generations removed from the wood and stone fish houses of Nyksund with their gabled delivery verandahs. The government highway program began producing a network of roads and bridges emanating from Myre that connected the isolated islands, so that trucks could collect from fishermen in all the outlying villages. People stayed and continued to fish.

The tale of belated transition from the nineteenth to the mid-twentieth century might have ended here. But within a few years of opening the Myre plant, Hagerup and his board realized that Øksnes-Langenes needed a steadier supply of fish than seasonal fleets could provide if it meant to offer employment throughout the year. The local fleet was geared to inshore fishing. It consisted of forty-foot to sixty-foot boats that worked gillnets and longlines, fished within a few miles of shore, and delivered daily.

However, the cod and other species schooled off the Vesteralen coast in commercial abundance only from October through March. Then they migrated on, south to Lofoten in April, and north to Finnmark from June through September. Other boats were catching them to deliver for the prosperity of other places. A steady supply of fish to the Myre plant required large boats that the company itself controlled, which could follow the fish and bring them back iced or in frozen blocks.

These new boats would have to be geared with trawling nets, the only practical means to harvest factory-volume quantities of fish from deep water. But Vesteralen inshore fishermen hated trawlers—as do many longline and gillnet fishermen from Labrador to Alaska to New Zealand. Trawling is relatively new-fangled, since the method had not existed until marine engines became powerful enough to pull a heavy net along the seafloor. Trawl gear can tangle and ruin other gear. Worse, the method itself can be efficient enough to scoop up species and their young indiscriminately, leaving nothing in its wake for other fishermen but a seafloor disturbed and bare.

Hagerup knew the problem well enough: "Trawlers take the fish from other fishermens; they take the sea from them." But he patiently argued the realities of Myre's situation. There was nothing to be done except to join the competition. He put it bluntly, "Shall you beat them, you must have trawlers." After earnest deliberation the board of Øksnes-Langenes decided to build an oceangoing trawler.

Even though the local fishermen's association began to fight the decision at once, Hagerup's logic eventually reached the pragmatic Norwegians. Fishermen themselves bought most of the ninety-six shares of the company organized under Øksnes-Langenes to finance building, eventually, four big trawlers. It worked out. Fishermen had the opportunity to profit, and the new boats recruited their crewmen from among local fishermen. Nor did the big Myre trawlers compete on the same grounds that local fishermen could work in smaller boats with different gear. They entered the jungle of international waters north of Norway, among the ships of the Soviet Union, Great Britain, the Germanys, Spain, the Faeroe Islands, and Portugal.

Myre, grown to a population of 3,000 from 350 in 1954, has become the fishery center of the Vesteralen. The plant is one of the largest fish-processing facilities in Norway, its products marketed throughout the world. Large boats leave the plant pier to travel hundreds of

At the Marintek Institute in Trondheim, Norway, the owners of a new modern trawler study the performance of their projected hull under various simulated sea conditions. The design of more capable marine hulls has become a matter of keen interest to the builders of modern fishing boats. Similar towing tanks are available to test new designs at the U.S. Navy's David Taylor facility near Washington D.C. and at Memorial University in St. John's, Newfoundland.

Abandoned fish sheds lie open in the near-deserted village of Nyksund on the Vesteralen coast of northern Norway. The multiple levels permitted delivery at any time despite very high tides. Nyksund was once the home of station kings and the hub for dozens of small fishing communities on outlying islands. However its harbor could not accommodate modern boats with deep drafts.

Messdeck and lounge aboard the Norwegian deep sea trawler *Myrefisk-Two*. Foreground, bosun Asbjorn Wolden, a veteran of trawlers in Norwegian and foreign waters, and a young cabin boy.

Mending nets under deck lights aboard *Myrefisk-Two*. The complicated re-webbing, often done quickly in the worst weather, is one of a trawlerman's most basic skills.

miles up and down the coast. Smaller ones continue to deliver from close inshore. In Nyksund, the high sheds of the ghostly fish houses meet the sea winds and lose more planks each year. Myre's paved main street, flanked by stores, has enough commerce to support even two florist shops. Modern homes flank the foothills below the surrounding mountains, where, throughout the twenty-hour winter darkness, warm amber lights illuminate the snow beneath windows framed in lace curtains.

The story does not end with bells ringing in every direction. There are still more in Myre who fish from small boats than large ones, but these are fathers and uncles. The young prefer the easier life, higher potential pay, and greater security of the trawlers. To add to the inshoremen's problems, their gillnets have begun to come up with drowned seals tangled in them instead of fish. "In fifty years I have fished," said Tormond Kroknes, who now teaches fishery methods at a Myre school, "there was never seals into the nets. But now the Greenpeace people have stopped us hunting seals, and they come too many of them, hungry." Each year, Norwegian sealers had killed a quota of between 400,000 and 500,000 of the stock now inundating the Norwegian coast. The harvest had been part of many fisherman's living, and had also kept the population in check. The cod run into the Lofoten Islands have suffered similar devastation from the new proliferation of seals. The change is a legacy from the thousands of people in North America and Europe who campaigned and contributed to stop the killing of pretty young seals. Their efforts had high moral purpose and required no personal sacrifice.

On the happy side, in 1984 Myre saw, for the first time anywhere in Norway, a trawlerman elected to head the local fishermen's organization. With majority votes on the side of the more numerous inshore fishermen, the honor is more unique than it might appear to an outsider. Hagerup could declare with quiet pleasure, "Now we are very good situation between local fishermen here and the trawlers—*special* good here!"

17

Big Trawlers

By midnight in Myre, it had begun to snow, and the mountains surrounding the town were gathering clumps of white that defined their shapes in the dark. Mr. Hagerup came to escort me to the trawler *Myrefisk-Two*. A slippery path led behind the fish plant to the pier. This was no fishing boat but a fishing ship. Its black hull and superstructure towered above the other vessels moored and anchored nearby. The engine system made a distant, steady ship's hum, and, on deck, bobbins and chains and reeled nets of a size beyond anything that men could handle manually lay encased in an icy crust.

I climbed aboard, picked my way forward around the heavy gear, undogged a hatch under the main housing, and entered a changing-room lined with oilskins on hooks. A door beyond this opened into a passageway leading in one direction past cabin doors and in another to the galley and mess deck. A ship of this calibre would have been hosed, scrubbed, and disinfected after the previous trip and delivery, leaving no trace aboard of the old catch, and yet the very metal smelled of fish—an acrid, chilly, jolting odor to nostrils just come from a warm living room.

Crewmen began to thump across the deck carrying duffel bags and suitcases, most of them shaggy young men with little to say at this hour. One by one they gathered in the dim wardroom to smoke and settle in—they, too, had just left the warmth of homes, and the trip ahead would keep them at sea for at least a month, so there was no reason for high spirits. They snacked absently from a jar of herring and another of peanut butter. Someone inserted a cassette in the television set without bothering to switch to the beginning. It was the American movie *Equus* with Norwegian subtitles, a convoluted enough tale to watch from the start, that everyone generally ignored except for a puzzled grunt over some scenes of abnormal nudity. One of the men had flown to the mainland during his few days of holiday, and he spoke of the damned long wait at the Bodø airport coming back, with no place to lie down and sleep. The engineer, his clothes touched with grease, entered for a smoke. One of the condensers was down, he said, so maybe the 3:00 A.M. sailing time would be delayed. At this, those not on watch turned in, and *Equus* disappeared in midscene to be replaced by a jumpy comedy.

The ship finally departed in the half light of early morning with the captain, Tor-Eirik Bye, steering from the wheelhouse. We glided among the small boats in the harbor and made our way beneath grayish white mountains that had been brown only the day before. When we reached open sea, the ship began to pitch enough to require holding on. Tor-Eirik, an earnest, relaxed man in his thirties who comes from a family of Myre fishermen, set his course and confirmed it on an electronic plotter screen. We followed the mountains to starboard, traveling north along the coast.

Besides the captain and the mate, the ship's complement consisted of a cook and his helper (a silent boy on his second trip who worked through a daze of seasickness), two engineers, and ten crewmen who, in five-man watches, worked the gear and dressed the catch as do fishermen everywhere. Each man's workday covered twelve hours, divided into two six-hour watches either from eight to two or from two to eight around the clock. Mealtimes coincided with the change of watches. The cook served breakfast between 7:30 and 8:30 A.M., dinner from 1:30 to 2:30 P.M., and supper during the hour beginning at 7:30 P.M.

A fishing skipper must locate fish to be successful, and the closer Tor-Eirik could find them to Myre the shorter the time they would all have to spend at sea. The cod might be expected to reach the coastal waters off Myre by January as they headed toward Lofoten, but in early November these fish still usually schooled far to the north. The main fishing fleet, including the *Myrefisk-One* skippered by Tor-Eirik's brother Oddmund, had found large cod five hundred miles north of

Myre near Spitzbergen, and the ships were reported following the school slowly south. It was worth trying closer grounds on the way in case the migration had accelerated.

Long after dark on the first day but still near home—the ship averaged a speed of eleven knots—we reached the Tromsøflaket Bank and hove to for a trial set. This had been a good fishing ground the year before, especially for blue halibut, which fetched a higher price than cod, and the color echo sounder in the wheelhouse indicated fish patterns on the seafloor. The snow continued to blow as the watch appeared on deck bundled in thermal coveralls to work the heavy gear. In the warmth of the wheelhouse, Tor-Eirik controlled the operation from a panel installed facing aft so that he could watch the long floodlit deck. Everyone worked together, routinely, one step at a time.

Shooting took only a few minutes, but the action provided the final transition away from life ashore. The men returned to the mess deck with a snappier step and began to joke. Even the cook's apprentice perked up as the ship's motion calmed with the reduced towing speed. In the wheelhouse, Tor-Eirik whistled a tune under his breath as he prepared for the mate to relieve him. Whistled! An older generation of Norwegian fisherman would have considered this tantamount to conjuring a gale at sea. It illustrated the new order among fishermen. Did young skippers have any superstitions? I asked, and he laughed. "Only that I shouldn't catch fish, maybe. Not so much other."

I carried the subject down to the mess deck, where everyone ate at the same table. Significantly, each man's cup hanging from a row of hooks did not face the same way, a disorder that in other fishing times would have been an inconceivable goad to the fates. Asbjorn Wolden, the boss of the watch (seafarers in English-speaking countries would call him the bosun) said sure, superstitions were old-timer stuff that nobody bothered with anymore. But, he added, his hooded eyes serious as his mouth smiled, it was still just as good not to bring waffles aboard, or to mention, for example, certain animals on a fishing boat. He meant horses, voicing a classic superstition among Norwegian fishermen that probably relates to the animals' association with land, a place any boat had best avoid. As for waffles? No one could say why, but they also did not appear eager to pursue it. The sea deals arbitrarily enough with those who fish that many, especially those of an age to have worked in small boats with oars or cranky engines, would rather play it safe. In Myre, Mr. Hagerup had told how once he brought his wife aboard a fishing boat. As they left, he saw an older crewman waving fire around the deck to purify it.

Asbjorn, a man in his late forties, lean, balding, calmly assured, was older than any other crewman except the mate. (One of the men under him, in fact, lived with Asbjorn's daughter.) He had fished distant waters, including those off Labrador and Brazil, before his roaming stopped with marriage to a Myre girl, so he brought a wide perspective as well as enough command of English that he had no reticence about using it. "You like superstitions?" he said, looking around as he lit a cigarette. "I give you a crazy one." One trawler skipper he had worked under decided a certain net was bad luck and refused to fish with it. So the net stayed in a bin, occupying precious space on deck. "One night while the old man slept, we moved nets, switched that sonofabitch to another bin so he wouldn't know." After a few days, when the net had caught as much fish as any other, the secret was revealed: "Oh ja, he laughed when I told him. But not so much at first."

About three hours later, near midnight, the mate signaled to bring in the tow. Asbjorn and the others slipped quickly into boots and thermal coveralls, put on hard hats and inflatable life vests, and stomped onto deck through an accumulation of slush. The full panoply of gear from warps to doors to net took thirty minutes to bring aboard from a depth just short of half a mile. At last the cod end snaked up the stern ramp, disappointingly flat. It held about two hundred blue halibut rather than the thousands of a good haul. The echo sounder in the wheelhouse, while not an infallible gauge, had shown only small concentrations of fish after the encouraging initial signals. Another reason for the unrewarding catch became clear when the boom raised the cod end high to empty the fish down a chute leading to the factory, and a torn panel of net flapped loose in the wind.

That ended fishing on Tromsøflaket Bank. The mate set course for the next grounds northward. Two of the men went below to the factory deck to bleed and dress the few fish (which weighed one to two pounds each). They placed them with water in a freezer compartmented in vertical frames, to be quick-frozen into blocks. Later, they stacked the blocks in the main hold. In Myre, plant workers would thaw the frozen fish as needed for the processing line. Blue halibut was generally smoked, since under this method the flatfish became an attractive product of rich-flavored amber meat prized by the Japanese and paid for accordingly.

On deck, the others gathered a supply of flat mending needles from a gear locker and wound them with twine, then lined up along the torn net like ladies at a quilting bee and started to mend. Behind them, as the ship reached cruising speed and began to pitch again, the stern ramp plunged into the dark sea and dashed up water that hissed around their feet.

There are times, especially in blowing winter weather under pressure to set again when there is no spare net on deck, when trawler crews simply lash a torn net together with looping thrusts of the needle. In contrast, Asbjorn and his men patiently cut back web to the necessary starting point and recreated each damaged mesh. Although the air froze their fast-moving bare hands to a reddened numbness, the work could not have been performed more professionally in a heated shed ashore. Nothing special, said Asbjorn cheerfully. One January in Labrador it was thirty degrees below zero on deck and the nets froze the minute they touched air. That was sonofabitch hard mending! The relief watch appeared on deck at 2:00 A.M., took over the needles, and continued the job.

Asbjorn blamed the tear on a full moon whose presence overhead we never glimpsed through the gray mat of clouds. Two trawler skippers later confirmed his reason, that a full moon, raising the earth's surface by a few centimeters, softens the mud and clay of seafloors that otherwise remain hard. The softened mud on the bottom enters through the mouth of the net and accumulates in ton weights for the mesh to drag. Whatever the scientific credentials of the Myre trawlermen, they knew they mended more nets at full moon than at any other time.

Next day, we crossed another of the known fishing grounds and set with an equal lack of success. There was no question that the fish lay to the north and we would need to travel the full distance to tap into them. The Barents Sea (not to be confused with another seafood ground of world proportions, the Bering Sea that separates Alaska and Russia) is one of the northernmost bodies of water on earth. Its boundary extends from the north coasts of Norway and Russia to the Arctic Sea and the ice pack surrounding the North Pole. The Russian and Norwegian two-hundred-mile zones encompass only a portion of the Barents Sea—the two nations share with occasional unease a gray zone of convergence in the eastern part where they have not yet agreed on a permanent dividing line—so that the waters cover an international fishing ground of historically productive banks.

On Monday evening (thirty-eight hours underway), we crossed Norway's two-hundred-mile line and sent an official notification required by Norwegian law. Another message would follow when the ship started fishing in international waters. Norway accommodated some foreign fishing ships within its two-hundred-mile zone by agreement, as did the adjacent Soviet Union. But, like most other fishing nations including the United States and Canada, no foreign vessels were allowed within the twelve miles of territorial sea around its coasts, reserved exclusively for domestic fishermen.

Both nations retained the right to inspect ships fishing in its zone, and both were known to search holds minutely to make sure quotas were being observed. During the previous winter, the Soviets had boarded *Myrefisk-Two*, leaving Tor-Eirik to marvel at the experience. The Soviet inspector came accompanied by four armed guards, a photographer, and a commissar. They refused any refreshment except coffee, and insisted that Tor-Eirik drink the coffee first. He had also been inspected by his own countrymen. They had been absolutely businesslike, but nothing like this!

The days were shortening of their own accord as the year approached the winter solstice, but we accelerated the process by beating a course north. After fifty-two hours underway (a few of these spent fishing) we had traveled more than five hundred miles to reach the international fleet near Bear Island. At seventy-five degrees thirty minutes north latitude, we occupied a spot of sea 360 miles north of the closest Norwegian mainland. A glance at the world map will show that little exists at this latitude but the top of Greenland and a scattering of Soviet and Canadian islands, as well as the mountainous Norwegian island of Svalbard (Spitzbergen), where separate colonies of Norwegians and Russians mine the ore deposits while maintaining their respective strategic presences. The richest concentration of life in this part of the world lies under the sea.

By now the ship's routine had long been established. The door to the cabin where I slept flew open at 7:15 A.M. and a belligerently deep voice bellowed, "ALL UPP!" It was the fifteen-year-old apprentice cook, who hardly ever spoke a word otherwise, performing his head-line act of the day. Topside the stars shone for the first time during the trip. Ships' lights dotted the horizon. A breeze blew from the southwest, but the weather radio in the wheelhouse predicted a northeast gale within a few hours. Gradually, it turned light. The dark shapes of the fishing ships emerged around their work lights. Just after 9:30, a pale sun rose behind a scattering of clouds and glistened on the waves.

An exercise bicycle stood in the corner, secured to one of the bulkheads so that a ship's roll would not send it crashing. It indicated the physical inactivity a fishing skipper endures while everyone else uses his muscles. I asked Tor-Eirik whether the daily twelve hours of watch left him restless. "Oh yes," he admitted. "Often restless. But, you know, every time we are hauling the trawl it's very exciting. What will come up from the sea? Its always different." He did choose usually to spend more time on his feet than sitting in the padded captain's chair surrounded by consoles, even when chatting by radio with another skipper on the grounds.

I planned to transfer to another trawler nearing the end of its trip rather than spend an entire month as a passenger while *Myrefisk-Two* filled its freezers and hold. Ideally, the second ship would be the newest of the Øsknes-Langenes fleet, *Myrefisk-One*. While we were making our first drag on the grounds, *Myrefisk-One* drew near, and sent word for me to pack and get ready before the weather turned bad. We waited until the set came aboard. As the boom pulled the wings of the net high in the air, the sun added a rare edge of color to the dripping meshes that dramatized the usual poverty of light at this time of year. In another month, some sixty days of total darkness would begin. The cod end came up the stern ramp, fat enough with fish that the crew gave a cheer. At last they had begun the process that led to the next homecoming and payday.

Several hundred feet away, the other ship lowered an open life-boat. The sea looked placid for November, with little more than a chop along the surface, but waves seen from a ship tend to appear unimpressive until they reach a height that can be measured from deck to deck. The boat in water quickly disproved the illusion by disappearing for moments at a time as it slid from crests to troughs. The sea was already darkening. A dusky red ball of sun hovered near the water, flanked by the pale oranges and yellows of a far northern sunset that streaked the horizon beneath a gray cloud canopy. "Daylight" had lasted less than two hours.

Alongside us, the boat, its two coxswains in soaked floater suits swaying at the knees to keep their balance, rode a mean surge that scraped it ten feet against the hull. Asbjorn threw down my bags encased in plastic sacks. One nearly hit the water, as the small bow veered on a sudden rogue wave that sent spray as high as the ship's deck and drenched those in the boat. Then it came my turn. To transfer to a small boat from a ship requires one caution above all others: Enter the boat at the highest point of its surge. If you climb down further on the Jacob's ladder the boat's gunnel may rise and crush your leg. All eyes watched, the skipper and Asbjorn with particular concern. I had made such transfers while serving in the U.S. Coast Guard thirty-five years before, and I managed the jump (with relief) to land honorably on my feet and stand upright for a moment before the swoop of the boat knocked me down. To general cheers and waving, the lifeboat bounced safely toward the *Myrefisk-One*.

During the bumpy passage, I could compare the two fishing ships. Ahead lay *Myrefisk-One*, the pride of Øksnes-Langenes. It had been commissioned less than a year ago, replacing in name an earlier company trawler and in modernity the *Myrefisk-Two*. Externally, the two ships appeared alike, each with a black steel hull that culminated in a graceful bow, a wide forward housing that stretched beam to beam, an assortment of antennas atop the wheelhouse, a long main deck, and astern a squared steel arch for supporting heavy weights, the "gallows" distinctive to trawlers. On paper, in fact, the new 170-foot (51.5-meter) ship was only inches longer than its sister, and its beam was wider by only a foot.

After a wet few minutes, we came surging against the high black hull of *Myrefisk-One*. We ducked wildly swinging hooks as the coxswains secured them to the boat fore and aft, and the men on deck above raised us slowly in the davits. It was a relief, since this was a tricky operation in rough seas, when the boat at last reached a height where seas no longer slammed under us. If a big wave had lifted one end off its hook while the other end stayed attached, the lopsided plunge would have emptied the boat like an upended bowl, dumping its occupants into water so cold and rough no rescue was guaranteed.

Once I fell overboard, in Alaska, and the icy weight of soaked boots and clothing that pulled at my legs, while the cold sapped my strength, sobered me forever to the power of northern water. Thus in the balance, for a mere minute, sometimes hangs the difference between a life that passes to the next small incident and possible death or mutilation.

The internal difference between the two Myrefisk ships was apparent at once. Could a ship's architect really design so much more space from a single extra foot of beam? I followed the mate, John Danielsen, a man no older than thirty with an even younger face behind his three-day beard, to hang my oilskins and flotation coveralls in a large, heated changing room flanked by lockers. By comparison, the changing room on *Myrefisk-Two* was narrow and chilly.

Back in Myre, Hagerup and the people at the plant had all spoken proudly of *Myrefisk-One*, and it was obvious that the men aboard her felt the same. John loaned me spare clog slippers from his locker, because by tacit agreement no one wore boots in the living quarters. His orientation tour led through a series of passageways kept so clean (they smelled of scented polish) that they resembled more those of a tourist ship than a fishing boat.

The most spectacular difference between the two Myrefisk ships—and between this and most fishing vessels of any size—lay in accommodations. Aboard *Myrefisk-Two*, the crew slept two and three to a cabin and shared two toilets and showers in the changing room. These are normal enough living conditions on seagoing trawlers of the late twentieth century. Aboard *Myrefisk-One*, each man had his own private cabin, with adjoining private toilet and shower! Perhaps only a fisherman would gasp at such luxury, but luxury it is for a fishing boat. No wonder the old Nyksund men of Myre turned quiet when they spoke of *Myrefisk-One*, remembering how in their time men on fishing ships slept in shelflike bunks all crowded into a single fo'c'sle, sometimes shared a bucket for their toilet, and washed from a common basin if they felt the need.

The wheelhouse alone of *Myrefisk-One* was as large as Kalle Larsen's entire little juksa boat back in Lofoten, while Edmund Sandholm's *Arsteinvag* could have been placed comfortably in the combined galley/mess room/lounge. Belowdecks in the factory area, the heading and gutting machinery had been improved to eliminate an entire step of the usual processing, a fact that John mentioned three times.

In the wheelhouse, a bank of windows across the front permitted a half-circle vista of the water, easily watched from behind consoles that displayed all the ship's controls. By noon, bands of darkness were closing down the horizon for the night, and the lights of fishing ships began to blink everywhere. The captain stood facing a row of windows aft, working a panel of controls and speaking occasionally into a microphone as he made a set. His few monosyllabic commands in Norwegian at key points in the process—"net down," "doors out,"—barked out over outside amplifiers. He could watch the deck below with a view of all but the nearest portion of the floodlit fishing deck. Chains as thick as a man's leg rattled into the water followed by scraping steel bobbins the size of beach balls, while the watch stayed safely to the sides except when one of the chains snagged and two men leapt out gingerly to free it.

On both Myrefisk ships, a central encirclement of consoles made their wheelhouses cousins to the control room of the spaceship *Enterprise.* The array of electronic equipment permitted the watch to monitor undersea activity around the net as none in an earlier generation could ever have dreamed of doing. John showed off each console in turn. He or the captain could observe, through computer graphs and diagrams in bright colors, the location and density of schools of fish throughout the water column, the individual size of fish in the path of the net, the approximate volume of fish captured, the distance between the otter boards as they dragged across the seafloor, even the sea temperature on the bottom.

One console provided navigation with a choice of three different methods—satellite, Loran, and Decca—that could be used to cross-check each other. The computer that tied into the navigation systems automatically plotted courses between destinations and predicted the time and length of the passage. It could recall on the screen, for reference, the location and pattern of previous sets, and could furnish the location of charted wrecks and reefs.

With all these aids, I joked, did any work remain for a fishing skipper? "I think such equipment shall make it easy to catch fish," John said with a smile. "But then there still must be fish in the sea to catch, and no net to tear a hole in ever. These are things not always so." Captain Oddmund Bye, who had joined us, added that just this trip they had searched three days without catching a single fish.

As the darkness deepened by 2:00 P.M., the full moon danced a path on the busy water. This was to be the only clear night of the trip. The lights of the fleet around us took on a sparkle. There were nearly sixty ships, of all sizes. More showed up as radar blips beyond the visual horizon. Some of the largest—John identified one as a Soviet mothership—had so many lights along their superstructures that they had the gaiety of Christmas decorations. It could have been a festival. "Are you speak Russian?" Captain Bye asked me hopefully. He would gladly have eavesdropped on more than the Norwegian, English, and Faroese part of the international fleet around him.

Oddmund Bye, skipper of the *Myrefisk-One* and Tor-Eirik's older brother, led me to his cabin and indicated the most comfortable chair. He had spread ship's papers on the table in anticipation of my visit and now, lighting a thin cigar and puffing slowly, he leaned over them, leafed through until he found a diagram, slapped it, and, emphasizing each word, declared, "This are a very good ship!" I assured him that I knew it.

He warmed at once to the subject. Did I know the cruising speed of *Myrefisk-One*? Fifteen knots, compared to eleven or twelve knots for *Myrefisk-Two*, which was also a good ship and had been his command until the Number One arrived. Was I interested in fuel capacity? We could carry 260,000 liters, from which the daily fuel consumption (he referred to the record of a specific day) was 3,980 liters and the hourly consumption of the engine 240 to 260 liters. He had compiled many other statistics from the present trip if I cared to have them.

The company, said Bye, purchased *Myrefisk-One* a year ago for 42.6 (million kroner, approximately 6.7 million U.S. dollars) but due to the sudden rise in demand for trawlers the same vessel today would cost about 52 million kroner (8 million U.S. dollars). Cod, from the market report today, was worth eight kroner per kilo (about sixty U.S. cents per pound). Blue halibut, of which they had made a good catch for the trip, today fetched 12.5 kroner per kilo. "The ship," Bye declared, "must earn each day 63,000 kroner." (This is about 10,000 U.S. dollars.) "But *Myrefisk-One* each day *does earn*—he smiled—"average 84,000 kroner."

Each evening, Bye tabulated the catch and what it had earned, and left the figures in the lounge so that crewmen could calculate their day's earnings. A trawlerman made annually between 220,000 and 250,000 kroner (between 33,000 and 39,000 U.S. dollars). "This is twice what makes a working man ashore, average," Bye declared. "But there are twice work hours, more than twice, and it is working around the sea, not at home, so that for this money our families we see not very often." He added delicately, "For me personally, as captain, I make some more. But I pay more taxes too."

"We have a good social nation," Bye continued, "but the taxes are very high." The forty-five percent tax rate for an unmarried man in the deck hand's 220,000 kroner bracket graduated quickly to sixty percent for Bye himself. Back in Myre, in fact, a company official had confided a problem keeping fishermen on the trawlers for the final trips of the year, especially after profitable earlier fishing, because so much of their additional income disappeared in taxes. As one man put it, just in from deck with hands a purplish red and ice crystals melting in his mustache: "If I had get my money by talking telephone from an office, so it's all right, big taxes. But for so long at sea in bad weather. . . ."

Bye kept reams of statistics on the new ship's performance, far more than for a ship fishing long enough to have had its capabilities explored. He did it with an enthusiasm approaching passion, but the results were meant to be studied for possible improvements. His effort reflected the competitive approach that Norwegians now take to fishing.

Calmly walking the course of his wheelhouse with the erect arched back of a flamenco dancer, Captain Bye was the sort to study a new fishing ship in detail, to relish squeezing any final tuning of performance. In this, he typified the most aggressive of his generation, whom gains in technology and a diminished resource have forced into different pressures than those of their fathers who could hope that fishing sense and dogged hard work would fill their holds most days.

"I have only fish'-ed in my life," Bye said, to explain his lack of fluency in English. This was modesty. Although he sweated like a schoolboy over each sentence before he risked saying it, his words were more expressive than many who claim English as their mother tongue. One of six brothers and six sisters, Bye came from a fishing tradition. His father had begun fishing at age twelve aboard his own father's boat, and all of Bye's brothers have remained fishermen (five of them skippers in Norway and one the bosun on a large trawler in

The modern 170-foot trawler *Myrefisk-One* in the Barents Sea, north of Norway as the sun sets at 11:20 A.M. one November morning. The pale daylight lasted less than two hours, and some ships on the cod grounds did not bother to turn off their deck lights. Within weeks the sun disappeared altogether until spring.

Captain Oddmund Bye in the wheelhouse of the *Myrefisk-One*. Surrounded by banks of plotters and fish finders and computerized controls, Bye's post resembles that of a naval combat center.

Nets clogged with ice and covered by snow in the Barents Sea.

A medium-sized bag of large cod about to be opened.

Nova Scotia) as has Bye's twenty-seven-year-old son. Bye himself started fishing from Myre at age fourteen aboard his father's longline boat. He had a good example set for him. The boat, the Morild (a type of sea phosphorus), had earned enough respect as a highliner that the local Myre football team named themselves Morild in order, according to Bye, "to have some success." The Morild fished traditional routes from Lofoten to Finnmark, and in the process, Bye declared, "My father learn me the right feeling for fish."

Aboard the parental longliner in 1949, conditions were normal for a medium-sized inshore boat. Indeed, conditions inshore have changed only partially in the interim, since there is a limit to the comforts that can be crowded into a small space, and since most smaller boats lack the manpower to divide the work into shifts. "We have a crew of seven or eight, all fished at the same time. One six-day trip we had seven hours' sleep altogether. No cook, must cook for self, everybody in bunks together, wash hands and face from a basin."

Within a few years, Bye left Myre to work aboard a larger boat, a trawler, that fished farther from shore. "My father couldn't like it, that I left him. But he could see that we had to fish with trawl since Norway have big areas at sea that must be fished with big boats." Some trawlermen make no bones of the fact that the larger the boat the better the living conditions. "I couldn't like small fishing boats," Bye stated frankly. Aboard the first trawlers he knew they slept only two to four in a cabin and had the luxury of two bathrooms. He has been a trawlerman ever since.

After taking himself to navigation school, Bye drew his first command at age twenty-three, a trawler with a crew of twelve. In 1960, when Hagerup of the Øksnes-Langenes plant began to organize a trawler fleet, he persuaded Bye to return to Myre and captain the first ship. Given the feeling against trawlers at the time, especially in places like Myre committed to inshore fishing, Hagerup needed a local man of Bye's trawler skills to make his project successful. The first eight years back in Myre were grindingly hard, according to Bye, with no time ashore for his family "because I was so busy making trawler go."

During this shakedown time, Bye logged 4,500 work hours a year. (A forty-hour week, minus two weeks' vacation, totals an even 2,000 hours.) "And so the boat is bigger and bigger," as his commands progressed and the fishing technology advanced. At fifty-two, Bye's tousled, sandy hair had no trace of white, and his blue eyes darted with a youth's alert interest. But his face in repose had a puffy tiredness. "The ship are for five weeks," he explained of the present trips, "five weeks of searching out fish on the sea."

He told, enjoying it now, how during this trip *Myrefisk-One* had cruised the fishing grounds near Spitzbergen for three days, running a thousand miles back and forth scanning the seafloor for fish and making test sets, before they located the huge school of cod that the international fleet now followed. During the search, the fleet was scattered, either searching, or setting on small schools. After Bye found the school—"special big fish"—he shut down his radio and worked the grounds for two and a half days before revealing his location. "It was my reward for finding the fish, to catch them a little bit first," he said in mild apology. We both knew that he had simply acted like a fisherman, one who routinely paid his dues.

Bye was a man at ease with command, who never needed to raise his voice to gain attention. He could banter, yet stay in dignified control. One day in the lounge, two crewmen in their early twenties, after hauling a catch on the cold deck and icing it below, began commiserating over the difficult life of a trawlerman. Bye set them straight in good humor. He spoke without vehemence, listening to what they had to say more with the air of a big brother than a father, then saying his piece. As he told me later, "Many times we are talking about this. The young men speak of how hard a life. They don't know history, that for fishermen hard life is normal. How tough it is to shovel the ice, they say. In early days, ice came in blocks and had to be chopped first. Nowadays a machine at the plant chops it for them. Many little things like this, on and on. It's okay."

Bye had the credentials to argue, with the perspective to know that he himself had chosen the life of a trawlerman at least in part because it was a more comfortable life than inshore fishing on small boats. Myre, in fact, had experienced such a drain of young men to its trawler fleets that many considered the inshore fleet to be moribund. The men who made their living pulling nets and lines were growing older. While their sons chose to follow in the fishing occupation, they chose to do it in the security of a company ship (where there was even a guaranteed minimum wage if they caught no fish at all), and in the comfort that a small boat could never provide.

With efficient heavy equipment that brought in high-volume catches, young trawlermen's income ran consistently higher than that of their fathers who continued to pull nets. What they sacrificed was the independence that some fishermen in other places still find heady. And they sacrificed daily contact with their families. Yet, aboard the Myrefisk trawlers, everyone shipped two trips and stayed home for the third, so that they spent approximately every third month at home. Was that so bad?

"I am restless to go on the sea again," said a twenty-seven-year-old trawler crewman in Myre during his rotation ashore. "It is very little to do on shore after a few days of sleeping unless you make a journey somewhere. Too much sleep. And even your wife gets tired to see you so much."

18

The Barents Sea

The trip of the trawler *Myrefisk-One* had begun on September 25th, and it was now November 3rd. An equipment failure had required a return to port, so that fishing had only started on October 3rd. It took until November 1st to pack the main hold with frozen blocks. The blocks, each weighing 50 kilograms (110 pounds), together totaled 260 tons of headed-gutted fish, most of it cod. On November 1st, the crew also began icing fish in trays to deliver it fresh. This meant that the trip was nearing an end, although several days of work remained.

At the time I came aboard, 729 trays of iced fish had been stacked in the 1,800-tray hold. That left 1,071 boxes to go. Since a filled tray weighed approximately 92 pounds, we had some 50 tons of fish meat to pack before starting the two-day journey home. However, from the first icing the ship could take only nine days to deliver no matter how few boxes had been filled.

Nine days, for fresh fish? The consumer may be aghast when he counts the further days of unloading and shipment before a "fresh" fish reaches the grocer's or fishmonger's counter. The truth is, a fish bled at once and kept chilled just above freezing can remain wholesome for a very long time. A decade ago, the halibut schooners off Alaska made three-week trips, icing the big flatfish with care, and the meat remained acceptably fresh. The only way to be assured of absolutely fresh fish is to catch it yourself or buy from a boat that fishes day trips close to shore. Far closer to fresh, these days, are the fish that the big trawlers freeze at once, whose meat begins to harden in ice within an hour or two of flapping aboard.

Everyone began counting trays, since time now limited our productivity and profit. During the remainder of the day that I arrived, we added only 91 trays, while day four yielded 190 more. When the cod end floated astern and then snaked up the ramp, we looked and estimated, even those on deck who were racing with shackles and chains to get it aboard safely. Meanwhile, ship's life continued in the pattern—the comfortable rut—that makes long periods at sea bearable. The crew observed the same watch and eating schedule as practiced aboard their sister ship, the six hours on, six-off watches coinciding with mealtimes on either side of 8:00 A.M., 2:00 P.M., and 8 P.M.

The hours of watch passed slowly, at least for a newcomer freshly arrived from the outside world, where work dominated less of the day. When the net became a nightmare of rips that needed to be mended on the double, nothing could shield the feet and hands for long from the painful cold as frigid winds swept the open deck, but everyone stood his ground until the job was done. Belowdecks, the jobs of processing fish had as much repetition and machinery noise as any job on a factory assembly line. In the wheelhouse, the skipper or mate passed most of his hours in solitude, pacing, sitting, checking charts and consoles, talking by radio with other skippers of his own nationality.

Landlubbers can find that sea time hangs heavy, but seafarers over the ages have learned to slow their systems in order to cope with the monotony. The slowdown has its price. After a few days at sea, try to remember yesterday's dinner menu, or which day the wind blew seventy knots, or whether today is Wednesday or Saturday. This fuzzing of time explains the need to record events as soon as they happen. The entries in a ship's log must be written immediately each watch, not from recollection at a later time.

Trawler skippers with any sense of profession log the details of their sets as the work unfolds—the minute of setting the tow and the latitude and longitude (or the Loran coordinates), length of cable, seafloor depth, nature of the bottom, length of tow, size and species, distribution of catch. Such data kept by men who fish the same grounds year after year result in a personal literature, a kind of empirical textbook.

Fishermen are generally healthy fellows—they have to be—but the condition of their work leaves them vulnerable to terrible injuries. Just as keeping a log is part of a fisherman's professionalism, so is a rudimentary knowledge of first aid. Often the mate serves as the doctor, since emergency training is part of his way up the ladder. Aboard *Myrefisk-One*, crewman Are Andreassen sliced open his hand one evening gutting fish and came straight to the wheelhouse where John Danielsen held the watch. John took a box of medical supplies from a cabinet, carefully unwound the bloody towel around the hand, and bent over to apply disinfectant, then clamps. Are, a lean youth in his early twenties, frowned as he watched, grimacing now and then, as the two chatted. Small injuries were routine.

A few months earlier, the fate of Are hung in more perilous balance. That which men far out at sea fear most actually happened: a fire. It started, probably from a faulty electrical connection, in the factory deck laundry room located between Are's cabin and the changing room. By the time someone discovered the fire, it had poured a blanket of black smoke into the changing room and into the cabin where Are was sleeping. He woke in time to try for his door, but he collapsed before reaching it.

The bosun rushed to hook up a fire hose, but the smoke prevented him from moving beyond the door into the changing room. Meanwhile, the smoke had penetrated through three deck levels into the wheelhouse, where the captain, choking, took charge alone as all other hands made for air on the open deck. John the mate strapped breathing equipment over his face and went through the smoke. There were flames. The fire was spreading. When fire rampages through a house in minutes, occupants who escape can run from the heat. At sea there is no place to run. John dragged the unconscious Are from his cabin into a passageway, and also put out the fire. It all happened within the space of minutes. And then the fishing continued, along with the cleanup.

During tows aboard *Myrefisk-One* that lasted a full four hours and yielded only a few tons of fish, the work itself was sporadic followed by long periods of idleness. The watch passed its time in the lounge, a small room with homelike paneling, bookcases, and red upholstered settees where the tables had rubber matting to keep objects from sliding off in heavy weather. The curtained portholes viewed darkness so much of the time that nobody ever bothered to look out, but the video television set ran at least half the time, watched by men with half-closed eyes.

The repertoire of tapes consisted of four American movies with Norwegian subtitles. For lack of any other occupation, they received so many repeat screenings that the characters in them became part of the scene, even at three in the morning—an aspiring boxer and his loving pa, two rivals on the dirt bike circuit, an accumulation of people marooned in space, an empty-headed American family traveling abroad. Conversational banter flowed with easy predictability. You called home and nobody answered? Ahh, what must your wife be off doing? The young second engineer bent over the log of the day's catch, calculating his take for the day. "He's the richest man on his island," somebody said. "Well sure, he probably is, since there's only a hundred people living there and none of the others work on a trawler." "My dad, a carpenter, he's glad when he makes half as much as I do." "With this trip's pay," said a lean man in his twenties who had been studying catalogues, "I'll get me that new pickup truck."

We ate at two tables of four each in the room adjoining the lounge. The oncoming watch had first sitting and then relieved the others who took their places. The captain always sat closest to the door, in the chair also occupied by the mate since the two had alternate watches. Talk after weeks at sea was subdued and polite, occasionally jocular, never boisterous. Sometimes everyone ate in silence. People reached for dishes boardinghouse style. The rough weather and the long confinement seemed to dampen nobody's appetite for sturdy food.

One Sunday we had fried pork cutlets each the size of a dinner plate. The deck boss, a ruddy-faced youth of about twenty-five whose muscles lay beneath a coating that might have been mistaken for fat, prepared his plate deliberately. First he mashed down a bed of potatoes and mixed vegetables, and drenched it with melted butter gravy. He placed a cutlet on top and applied more gravy, then garnished the meat with creamy mayonnaise squeezed from a tube. This took a few minutes of steady shoveling and chewing to finish off, but, with plate clean, he duplicated the entire meal, then repeated it a third time with an even heavier topping of mayonnaise. His eating

Factory work aboard the *Myrefisk-One*. A crewman feeds cod into automatic machinery that cuts and cleans them for freezing. Cold seawater sloshes underfoot, and the man's ear guards indicate the high level of noise.

The blahs. About 3am, between tows during a six-hour night watch, after more than a month at sea.

Tiers and tiers of iced cod in aluminum trays rise from the hold of the *Myrefisk-One*. Trays store the fish without crushing them. The catch was iced "fresh" just prior to returning to port. Before this it was flash-frozen in blocks.

lasted fifteen minutes, after which he rose with barely a belch to go on watch. The variety of food that came from the pantry after more than a month at sea dramatized the difference between the Spartan life on a small fishing boat and that aboard a fishing ship. Most of the meals had a clear Norwegian origin, but there were also New Zealand green apples. It was a nicety to contemplate while pitching on dark northern waters. While the cod we caught near the North Pole could travel all over the world thanks to modern transportation, the ship fishing it could also carry aboard crates of fresh fruit that came from a country near the South Pole.

Breakfasts aboard *Myrefisk-One*, as Norwegian at sea as those served ashore, included boiled eggs, fruit juice, and sliced bread, plus an array of cheeses, and such strong-flavored seafood cures as smoked blue halibut and herrings pickled or swimming in mustard sauce. For 2:00 P.M. dinner, the main meal of the day, the cook brought out platters and then replenishments of steak, chicken, fish, or cutlets. There were always boiled potatoes and usually boiled carrots. Supper started with cold cuts, and there might also be a plate of smoked salmon as well as the breakfast herrings. It occasionally featured a hot dish like chili, sausage, or boiled knuckles.

A variety of delicious salads appeared fresh at supper, and then reappeared at every other meal until consumed. Norwegian salads are so steeped in creamy yellow mayonnaise that sometimes only the color of the main ingredient gives them away before tasting. The red salad contained beets, the orange one carrots, the yellow usually potatoes, the green one slaw. Fruit salad might be detected by the smooth shape of a grape or the fiber in a chunk of pineapple.

Within a day, the wind had changed, although the projected gale arrived only gradually. Under an increasing northeasterly, the waves rose with scuds of foam on top, ice began to form on the nets and shrouds, and ships passed us half vanished in troughs. The school of cod that Bye had located several days earlier continued a dynamic southward migration, but it did not move uniformly. Eventually, the pack of ships scattered as they followed its different branches. This lessened the pressure on any narrow band of fishing ground. It also made less tricky the captain's or mate's job to tow a safe course without snagging other ships' gear.

No brightness accompanied the two hours of sun on the horizon and the hour more of twilight. Clouds diffused it all to a cold gray that crept soon into blackness. The watch that quit at 8:00 A.M., ate breakfast, and then went below for a nap, missed daylight altogether. The constant darkness seemed to depress nobody but myself except that, when not on watch or eating, people slept. (As a corollary to this, the long daylight of summer in this same region and others of the far north seems to induce wakefulness, and people feel less need for eight hours of sleep.)

The weather turned steadily worse. So long as seas kept within limits, we continued to fish, although as the wind built all of the smaller ships stopped towing; soon the larger ones began to stop as well. During the brief daylight, the sky remained so dark that it never illuminated the sea beyond a hazy blue-black over which whitecaps moved like brush strokes. *Myrefisk-One*, a sea-kindly ship whose broad beam kept it more stable in rough seas than most fishing vessels, began to roll and pitch like a giant breathing heavily. The few lights visible from other ships, kept on as full at noon as at midnight, would sweep through the air and then blink off for long moments as waves rose to block them.

During the sixth day, we were icing fish in the hold when suddenly the ship took a violent roll that sent stacks of loose trays crashing down on our heads. The work space at this point of filling the hold resembled a deep ditch, with a wall of loaded trays rising to the ceiling on one side and a high bank of ice and loose trays on the other. The empty steel trays were heavy enough, as they free-fell several feet followed by others from the deck above that tumbled through the open hatch. But what if the ice lock broke on the full trays that towered above us twice our height, each weighing nearly a hundred pounds? We extricated ourselves and scrambled up the ladder. Then when the ship leveled off we returned to straighten the mess and finish the job.

The severe motion rendered inaccurate the sensor on the cod end of the net, which blinked conflicting empty/full signals to the wheelhouse. In my bunk, as I tried to sleep braced against the bulkhead while secured objects broke loose and clattered around, a sudden roll threw me airborne across the cabin to slam against the door.

More sinister, on deck the ice that had been a mere glaze waxed thicker and thicker. It made glassy shapeless masses of stationary gear, and coated nets so that they exploded with shattered particles when anyone handled them. Ice accumulated to an inch thickness on the smooth surfaces of the gallows and then blew off in the strong wind, plummeting to deck in wicked projectiles.

By the time captain Bye started his midwatch at 2:00 A.M., the sea had become a black stew of flashing whitecaps. According to the mate, the other Norwegian trawlers in his circle of communication had stopped fishing to ride it out. However, *Myrefisk-One* was larger than the others. Bye, a trawlerman for thirty-five years, knew the point of bad weather at which it would clearly become unsafe to fish. He considered the situation now marginal. Ironically, each successive tow had become heavier, perhaps from diminished competition. He called a meeting of the watch, the men who would have to bring the net on deck and risk falling trays below. Did they want to stop?

This close to the end, with fish coming in? They shook their heads, and the fishing continued.

A day later, the trays of iced fish filled so much of the hold that they blocked the overhead lights. The men worked in semidarkness with barely room to swing a shovel. After a tow that ended in early evening, Bye declared the fishing completed even though a few more trays might have been jammed onto the final stack. As soon as the watch emptied the net and chained the steel doors to deck, Bye started the ship on a full-speed course for Myre.

By now the storm had broken. On deck, the men hosed clear the ice, which flew apart in chunks, and continued with the nets, then stowed and tied everything secure. The factory deck below received the same pressure-hosing with seawater in its turn. During the two-day trip home, movie cassettes lay idle as the watch cleaned decks, stairs, and cabins, most of which would have passed cleanliness tests ashore without the single application of a mop or rag. The factory smelled of disinfectant and the passageways of scented wax. In the changing room, the deck-smeared clothing disappeared into lockers. At 2:00 A.M. you could find men scrubbing bulkheads.

The course led on a diagonal south. By the second morning underway, the daylight lasted longer and, more important, the sky had a greater brightness even under clouds. It had not been imagination, that oppressive darkness!

Oddmund Bye was a self-contained man. It came out only in conversation during the trip home that this was his final voyage with the Myrefisk enterprises to which he had given twenty-seven years of his working life. In partnership with two brothers (including Tor-Eirik

[257]

who commanded *Myrefisk-Two*), he had bought a factory trawler of his own. He had stayed with the company long enough to shake down *Myrefisk-One*, but now his time would be spent outfitting his own ship, then skippering it. Bye had earned enough community respect to become the first trawlerman elected to head the local fisherman's organization. At fifty-two, he could now begin looking to his future.

After five weeks at sea, *Myrefisk-One* made its landfall only a half hour away from home, at five in the morning. The blink of Anda Light shone first through the darkness, marking an unseen cape jutting into the sea. As we neared, mountains took shape like ghosts. A moon through the clouds cast a diffuse bluish glow on black ridges of rock dusted with snow, softening their shapes and details. It was a sight more solemn than could any be in bare daylight. Snow showers passed like layers of curtain, to erase the mountains and then reveal them again. The village of Stø passed as a stipple of lights beneath dwarfing mountains. Then came the dim black outlines of Nyksund, where life had once centered but where now only a single light shone to mark the shoal-clogged entrance.

As we entered Myre fjord, the mountains funneled in from both sides. Lights bounced from small pitching boats on their way to sea to start the day's fishing. Myre appeared in a lazy streak of moonlight, a sketch of buildings with the outline of mountains far above them. The town then vanished in a gust of snow to reappear a few minutes later with its full details of houses, bridge, and ranging fish plant. Imagine houses after five weeks on the ocean, their amber all-night lamps shining from windows curtained in arcs of lace!

The men lined the rail in the wheelhouse. A car light swept along the wharf by the plant. "That's your wife," said Are to the skipper.

"No," said Bye, "Maybe yours."

"Not mine, my dirty car. I could have smelled mine from here." Everybody laughed and laughed.

It would take two and a half days to unload. The *Myrefisk-One* would then put to sea again, at once. Nets out of the water catch no fish.

19

St. Peter's Fiesta

I t was 10:00 A.M. on a warm June Sunday in Gloucester. The main
square downtown had the look of a party catching its breath. The
streets were mostly clean, but rubbish along the curbs and bits of
torn streamers indicated that the tinseled arches and shuttered
carnival booths were not waiting to open for the first time. At the
harbor side of St. Peter's Square rose an elaborate facade that, viewed
head-on, appeared to be a mansion placed just at the waterfront
among the clustered fishing masts. While only an outdoor stage
setting propped in back by heavy beams, the illusion was a Mediterranean dream of a mansion, all maroon, with white columns, its
arches rimmed in sparkling little lights.

In front of the facade stretched a long stage with a line of chairs on
either side. A flower-decked niche in the center enclosed a statue of
St. Peter with his hand raised in blessing. Workmen were busily
straightening the hundreds of chairs that filled the square in front.
Bleachers closed in one side. The other side opened onto the carnival
booths.

This was the culminating day, the Sunday of St. Peter's Fiesta in
Gloucester, the Italian fishing community's annual celebration in the
name of the fisherman's patron saint. The three-day festival has
occurred for more than sixty years. While it draws tourists, it remains
a very local affair.

I expected to find Joey Testaverde at home, since nobody fished on Fiesta Day, but Joanne said I'd find him on the boat. She added that he hadn't been feeling well, that the doctor had said something about mononucleosis and he should stay in bed for three weeks. "But stay in bed? Joey?"

There he was indeed aboard the boat, his bulk filling a dark little compartment beneath the cabin ladder as he jiggled a greasy flashlight in one hand and replaced a wire of the refrigeration system with the other. He was pale and sweating. Oh sure, really laid out the week before so that it was a little tough going fishing, but now it was better, only like he had a perpetual hangover. He started at once to tell me about the pair trawl he and his brother Tommy on the *Sea Fox* were going to try out in a couple of weeks.

The other Testaverde family boats were moored in place, Tommy's *Sea Fox* aft and John's *Linda* B alongside. The two skippers, and others of the marketing association that owned Fishermen's Terminal, alternately visited on benches outside their big open warehouse or puttered on their boats. I had expected to see bright pennants and frills in all the rigging but, "Nah, not really, anymore. The party boats crowd the blessing so much its dangerous out there in the harbor."

On the *Peter and Linda*'s deck, Frankie "Munza" Catania mended web and Bobby Gross applied a coat of black paint to the windlass, but their talk had a fiesta brightness. "You don't want to miss the races," said Bobby. Last year he'd been a member of one seine boat crew—from the look of the bulges under his T-shirt you could guess his pull on an oar—but they were eliminated in one of the preliminaries.

Joey joined us, wiping his hands on a rag. I wanted to know more about the pole walk, the traditional scramble along a greased pole high over the water that sounded, from my reading, like a Gloucester fishing boy's right of passage. Had any of them ever walked it? "Twice," said Joe. "Walked it twice when I was a kid, fourteen. We'd practice all summer for the next year. Never grabbed the flag myself. But Big Munza, there . . ." Frank, now a heavyset man in his middle forties, looked up from the net. "You know, Munza got the flag one year, he's on the books, what year Frank? His nephew's walking for him this year."

"1959 was my year," said Frank, pleased. "Yeah, he's walking for me today."

Is it dangerous, I wondered. Oh, nobody ever killed. One kid yesterday cracked two ribs. Testaverde's brother Sal, the marine biologist, banged his ear falling from the pole and it gave him a permanent hearing loss. Things like that.

The sound of amplified voices testing a speaker system drifted sharply from the square two blocks away. One by one, the men dispersed. Joey's two youngest daughters came to walk home with him, and we arranged to meet back at the boat for the parade.

The square had filled in the hour since I left to visit the boats. There was not a seat left, even in the bleachers along the side, and standees encircled the wide seating area. On the stage to the left sat choir members and dignitaries. A cadre of Knights of Columbus, the white feathers of their cocked hats riffling in the breeze, occupied the right-hand side. At the altar before the statute of St. Peter a priest in a cream-colored cassock began the service. The cardinal regretted not being able to attend, he announced, but they were lucky that Bishop John Mulcahy had come to speak in his place.

The bishop, a man in late middle age wearing a red skull cap, rose. The breeze spread his splendid red robe. In a dry church voice, he got right to the point, stating the dual practicalities of a fisherman's religion. "The Fiesta was started by fishermen who wanted to ask God to protect them out at sea, and because they needed the help of Almighty God to make sure their nets would always be hauled in to the breaking point."

A half century ago, the people in the audience would have been grave-faced men in Sunday black, with their wives in sober church colors and young girls in fluffy white. A few girls still wore white, but everyone else wore casual clothes for a busy day which only began with the Mass. One woman with white hair stood praying earnestly. Her lined face and roughened hands indicated a life of raising a large family, but instead of the black in which an elderly Mediterranean woman would have been encased a generation ago she wore a lime green pants suit.

The choir of St. Ann's, the Italian church of Gloucester that houses the statue of St. Peter, began to sing. The open-air acoustics and amplification made it sound ragged, but the hymn brought home more than a sermon could the solemn heart of the day. Everyone joined.

FISH DECKS

Eternal Father, strong to save,
Whose arm has bound the restless wave,
Who bids the mighty ocean deep
Its own appointed limits keep;
Oh hear us when we cry to Thee
For those in peril on the sea.

Oh Christ, whose voice the waters heard,
And hushed their raging at thy word,
Who walked upon the foaming deep,
And calm amid its rage did sleep;
Oh hear us when we cry to thee
For those in peril on the sea. . . .

During the service, the vendors and carnival ride operators quietly unshuttered their booths just adjacent, while spicy and sweet odors from grills and ovens began to drift about. The people on stage received communion as the audience watched patiently. Then, with a final blessing, the service ended, and, slowly at first, the secular part of the fiesta began. I bought a charbroiled Italian sausage with steamed onions and peppers, since according to Joey, "You've got to eat at least one every year or it wouldn't be like Fiesta." A woman at a canopied cart began squeezing lemons from a pile that rose on both sides of her. In the concession area, booths opened for business where the lucky could win a fluffy animal doll or at least a lollipop, where a ride in a seat attached to a girder would suspend you upside down, where the hungry could buy aromatic pizza slices and baked pastries.

The parade began to make up as new lines of people converged on the square, many in costume. Beside a truck bed of papier-mâché clouds, one mother fidgeted with the wire that stiffened her young daughter's angel wings, while another mom straightened a halo. I joined Joey, and we walked up the hilly road from the square, past the columned American Legion Hall and a heroic equestrian statue to Gloucester's war dead. Enough boys had already scaled the statue's pedestal to have occupied all the spaces beneath the granite horse's legs.

From the loudspeaker below, a parade official arranging the marchers barked, "First the navy, then the priests."

Joey sauntered through the crowd gathering along the roadside, saying hi to people on the way. Near the intersection of a street that wound downhill among clapboard houses, others of the Testaverde clan had gathered around his brothers, John and Tommy. This was their corner, Joey said, where they gathered every year to watch the St. Peter's parade.

The navy led the parade, bearing the flag. Soon after came the six-hundred-pound statue of St. Peter, its palanquin with yellow and white carnations borne by men of the fishing community in uniform white pants and shirts. Women walked alongside selling St. Peter's buttons to benefit their patron's Church of St. Ann. A while later, the Portuguese congregation of Our Lady of Good Voyage escorted their own Lady of Fatima on a pedestal of red roses, as parishioners sold roses to the spectators. Many people bought one or two of each. The churches of the two nationalities used to have separate celebrations, but since the main Portuguese fishing fleet moved to New Bedford there were no longer the numbers to support a separate Portuguese fiesta. The parade now escorted both statues from the harbor back to their respective churches.

Bands followed, including one that strutted smartly back and forth across the road during frequent halts to clear the street ahead. The halts kept a truckload of singers in folk costume singing lively Mediterranean songs nonstop to fiddle and accordion. They clapped hands and enjoyed themselves as much as the spectators below who danced to the music. People on parade floats usually develop an institutional wave, but these were waving to friends. Another of the floats—the one that had occupied the anxious mothers down in the square—depicted St. Peter standing before the heavenly gates above a cluster of angels. During halts, the man who played the saint, sweating under a white stage beard, gamely kept his hand raised in the statue's pose of benediction, but the young girls in gold-trimmed white satin, wings, and halos let their gold cardboard harps tilt unstrummed as they peeked around at the crowd. Nor did the trumpets stay raised for long of the older angels behind the pickets of the pearly gates.

At Joey's home after the parade, Joanne served dinner for enough of the Testaverde clan that the breaded veal and spaghetti came from the kitchen in casseroles as big as pots, and the men gathered elbow to elbow around the table while the women sat in the living room with plates on their laps. From the porch, we could hear the amplified speakers as the Blessing of the Fleet commenced out by the fisherman's statue only a two-minute walk to the water.

Unfortunately, so many cabin cruisers now crowded the area that the fishing boats for which the blessing was intended stayed at dock. On shore, several hundred people craned for a look at the scarlet-cloaked bishop with his crook and mitre. The bronze fisherman in sou'wester peered to sea from his eternal crouched position against battering waves, as kids climbed over the figure to see better, digging a foothold where they could.

After the ceremony, the church entourage drove off in a limousine to deliver the bishop to a local whale-watching boat. He cruised the harbor and blessed some two hundred moored fishing boats. Later, by special request, he also went up the hill overlooking the harbor to bless City Hall, whose high cupola rises as a landmark to returning fishermen.

The fishermen's center of action shifted to the bars by the harbor. The pole walk would start in another hour. "See that red flag against the bar mirror?" Joey asked. The winner from another year had donated it to his hangout bar here. While spectators gathered in boats and along a bank overlooking the water, the participants psyched themselves in a process as traditional as the scramble through ankle-deep grease itself. Unlike the oarsmen chosen to race the three seine boats later, who stayed soberly to themselves and hoarded their strength, the pole guys drank and strutted. It required abandon to walk a swaying slippery telephone pole twenty feet above cold water.

In bounced a muscular young fellow wearing gold ornaments, white tights, and a red apron that he kept flipping up to reveal his bathing suit. One of his buddies wore a purple robe and Merlin cap, another red longjohns with a dark cape. Others who came and went wore stuffed brassieres, gold cardboard armor, checkered tights. Noisy, stimulated, they bear-hugged each other around the neck, and huddled to shout verses in Italian that ended with "Viva San Pietro!"

Only thirty young guys could sign up each year, Joey explained, from the hundred who applied. It used to be only fishermen, but now the committee allowed others also. Kids from families that had walked before got priority. A lot of them dedicated their walk to a relative, like Frank's nephew today. Once a girl tried to sign up. The

During the annual blessing of the fleet in Gloucester, kids romp over the fisherman's statue as adults listen to the priest at the waterside.

Men of the Italian fishing community in Gloucester carry the statue of Saint Peter, patron saint of fishermen. The parade follows an outdoor mass conducted within sight of the boats. Blessing of the fleet will follow in the afternoon, as well as a greased pole walk high over the water and pulling-boat races, all of it traditional among fishermen for more than six decades.

Bottomfish piled three feet deep cover a deck the size of a playing field aboard the Japanese factory ship *Soyo Maru* in the Bering Sea off Alaska. In back is another deckfull of equal size. At the time, July 1976, the 566-foot/173-meter-long ship was servicing the continuous catches of nine trawlers to produce up to 600 tons of fish paste and meal a day. A larger Japanese factory ship in the area had a fleet of twenty-four trawlers. It was this massive fishing pressure in U.S. waters by Japan, the USSR, Poland, Spain and other nations that led the U.S. to declare two-hundred-mile jurisdiction.

memory brought a chuckle to the men at the table. That really upset everybody. "Did she get to walk?" I asked. "Well, *no.*"

The pole, secured horizontally from a pile-driven scaffold, was a permanent fixture of the harbor. A red flag flapped from a stick at the far end, and the winner was the one who could walk out and grab it. The forty-two-foot pole seemed long enough to stretch the length of the harbor, and it had a wicked little warp at about the halfway point. Even from shore among a crowd of several thousand, you could see the thick topping of grease along its rounded surface. (The announcer gave the name of the marine supply house that had donated the grease, one and a half tons of it.)

Boats took out the participants, the loose parts of their costumes waving in the steady harbor breeze. They climbed a high straight ladder to assemble on a central platform and wait their turns at the top. The announcer called out the name of the first contestant, and that of his grandmother for whom he was walking. A cape blew back bravely in the wind as the figure dashed onto the pole, quickly lost its footing, and fell the long twenty feet to the water followed by chunks of dislodged grease. The crowd gave him a hand. When he climbed the ladder again, the cape was gone.

All the costumes had disappeared by the time their owners returned from the first dunking. Several reported later that the barnacle scrapes they suffered from pilings exposed at low tide, as they groped in the cold water for a hold on the ladder, were worse than any smacks the water gave them. In their few seconds on the pole, some walked deliberately, some with a run as if sheer momentum would take them to the flag. But by the end of round one none of the thirty had made it much beyond the halfway point. "Nobody expects to get the flag first try," said Joey. "Maybe not even the second." It was apparent that the clumpy grease had to be conquered inch by inch.

Even from a distance, you could feel the slipperiness of the pole, the curved surface without traction. Feet were simply propelled away from it. Every time a walker made it beyond the warp at halfway, the tapered wood (a standard telephone pole) began to sway. Some walked straight and others crept sideways. Either technique required absolute balance on the top ridge of the curve. "Those guys who go crabways never make it to the end," Joey declared. "They can't keep going fast enough." But it was a tempting way to do it since on the inevitable fall you could count on clearing the pole.

Some of the straight walkers banged a shoulder or hip so hard it seemed that you could hear the thump, even feel it, and as the crowd groaned the announcer would call for folks in the boats below to make sure the man surfaced and made it back to the ladder. But the worst were the unlucky ones walking straight whose feet flew free in opposite directions to slam them open-crotched onto the hard wood before they slipped around and dropped. The end of the pole swayed in an ever-meaner arc as feet pushed closer to the flag. It was rough play, the kind of contest devised by men whose work assumed danger and required agility. Young Newfoundlanders played at jumping ice pans in the same spirit.

At length, during the third round after several near misses, on a vibrating pole that now had only a final clump of grease guarding the flag, one boy made it in a straight line that careened him off the far end with the stick in his hand. From the water, he waved the flag as cheers rolled across the harbor.

The young contestants might have come out by boat to protect their finery, but now by tradition they each made a final assault on the pole and took a last tumble. (One even made it all the way to the end.) The swim to shore through cold water was the closing push. By ritual courtesy, they waited for the winner to arrive first, wave high his flag, and receive the extravagance due a winning athlete. Blackened with grease, grinning with the full-blown joy of the world in his hand, he rode the crowd's shoulders. Other spectators stayed to applaud the remaining twenty-nine, even hug them despite the black smudges, as they trotted from the water. They had all proven themselves.

The races followed of the three seine boats Nina, Pinta, and Santa Maria. The ten oarsmen and coxswains of each had trained and competed all year, and their work was disciplined, collective. It rounded the traditional requirements for a fisherman in harsh northern waters, complementing the gutsy individualism of the pole walkers.

Exuberant partying followed. Even the members-only St. Peter's Club had its doors open to anyone, and a wall painting allowed the saint himself to look down from the bow of a fishing boat. Winners and losers (but especially winners) all cut a swath as friends bought them drinks. After dark, in front of the mansion facade, winners received their awards while strings of lights sparkled everywhere. There were enough people to fill the seats, and also to crowd the noisy carnival area adjacent. Then, by the harbor, fireworks splattered across the sky and reflected in the water to choruses of "ahh!"

A few hours later, Joey Testaverde and his crew assembled on the pier at 2:00 A.M. as usual. So did others. We talked little, but with drowsy good humor. (On the way to the fishing grounds in time for a set at first light, only one man needed to stay awake by the wheel at a time.) In St. Peter's Square, workmen were disassembling the facade of the maroon mansion, and sweepers shoveled debris onto trucks, but the strings of dotted lights that outlined the decorations still sparkled. The only people around to enjoy it were fishermen going to their boats.

1

A Two-Hundred-Mile Fish Story

In April 1976, the United States passed a controversial law claiming jurisdiction over all marine harvests within two hundred miles of its coasts. By the time the law took effect a year later, Canada, Norway, and a host of other coastal nations had followed the U.S. lead in declaring their own two-hundred-mile fishery jurisdictions. The actions altered forever—or at least for the present generation—the rules of a coastal nation's rights within its contiguous waters.

Immediately before this drastic action, foreign factory fleets had dominated North American waters, and had taken virtually all the available fish. Most inshore fishermen—especially those along the eastern seaboard of North America—had as a direct result of this depletion been unable for years to make more than a marginal living. In Labrador, the ships intercepted offshore cod so efficiently that few fish survived to make an annual migration to the coast, and the traditional inshore fishery disappeared. Small fishermen's hard times left them unable and unmotivated to afford modern boats, and this exacerbated their inability to compete with the big new foreign ships. According to official statistics on Georges Bank for 1973, the Soviet Union took forty-two percent in volume of all species caught while its Eastern European satellites took another thirty percent. American and Canadian boats caught only eleven percent and nine percent respectively of the total.

I witnessed the extent of the foreign presence on Georges Bank one February evening in the early 1970s, only sixty miles from parts of the New England coast. In the wake of a winter storm, rolls of blackening water reflected glassy pinks and reds from a cloud-covered sunset. Big trawlers pitched over all the horizon, some with nets in the water, some in various stages of haulback, their square gantries crisscrossing the sky like railroad trestles. The natural ocean sounds became a background for the distant scrape of warps against steel ramps and the clank of winches. The salty breeze bore whiffs of sea mud and fish. Another odor, a stench, drifted by occasionally from processing ships downwind whose orange smoke carried the residue of rendered fish meal. Water was still the dominant element, but the scene also resembled an industrial city on a workday.

The ships' lengths varied between 250 and 400 feet, and the flags showed their homes to be the Soviet Union, Poland, Cuba, Bulgaria, Spain, Italy, Japan, East Germany, West Germany, Rumania. In contrast, there was only an occasional boat (not ship) from the United States or Canada, 50 to 80 feet in length—midgets by comparison. As the sky darkened, ships' lights began to blink while the fishing and processing continued to the muffled snorts of machinery. First, the superstructures showed in silhouette, and then the night absorbed each shape to leave a sparkling cluster of deck and cabin lights.

With naked eye aboard the U.S. Coast Guard cutter *Gallatin*, we counted thirty-seven such clusters on the horizon, but the radar scope in the wheelhouse showed nearly sixty blips the size of big trawlers within twenty-five miles. Each ship contained a community numbering sixty to four hundred people. The foreign fleet, which began its career in the Pacific with the entry of Japanese fishing ships off Alaska in 1952 and of Soviet ships off New England in 1960, had become monstrously healthy. According to U.S. Department of Commerce figures, in 1975 there were 2,339 foreign ships fishing, processing, and transporting the catch home off the Atlantic coast of the United States (1,347 of them Soviet and 293 Polish); 476 off California; 382 off the Pacific Northwest; and 3,477 off Alaska (2,616 of them Japanese and 729 Soviet).

Checked only by the accepted three-mile territorial boundary of a nation's waters, and after 1964 by a twelve-mile zone that the United

States timidly declared, the foreign ships harvested what they pleased, placed it in freezer packs, cans, and fishmeal bags, and took it home. Americans who fished the grounds in modest-sized boats, their take thus limited no matter how hard they pushed themselves, were forced to stand aside or risk having their gear destroyed—as it often was. To go to Georges Bank had become the equivalent of pedaling a tricycle down the middle of a zooming five-lane highway.

Worse, even the foreign catches began to dwindle under the intense fishing pressure. When the big trawlers found one species growing scarce under their efficient methods, they targeted another with no thought for the conservation they would probably have practiced in their own waters. By 1975, the ships had overfished and depleted ten major commercial stocks—haddock and ocean perch (neither of which have ever really recovered), halibut, herring, Alaska pollock, California sardines, Pacific mackerel, sablefish, yellowfin sole, and yellowtail flounder. "Raping the resource" became a rallying call for action among American fishermen, and it was close to the truth.

In the early 1970s, when angry cries from the coastal states began to be heard, the U.S. Congress started considering a plethora of politically expedient bills that declared jurisdiction over the marine resources within two hundred miles of all U.S. shorelines. The Nixon and Ford administrations opposed any such form of two-hundred-mile control. They were fielding enough criticism from the Vietnam War without courting further alienation from allies and adversaries among the fish-oriented nations. In echoing the concern of these administrations (and guiding them), the State Department contested the bills hotly and persuasively enough to delay for years their passage in any form.

At the time the two-hundred-mile concept was a disturbing one, even though some South American nations had begun claiming such rights. The United States had protested vigorously when Peru and Equador arrested American tuna boats that pursued migratory tuna into their two-hundred-mile waters, and the State Department abhorred the idea of ever giving legal sanction to the practice. State also feared to set a precedent that would interfere with the cherished freedom of the high seas that benefited every large maritime nation.

Indeed, the world at large did not appear receptive to extended national fishing rights. In the North Atlantic, Iceland had tested the concept by claiming a mere fifty-mile unilateral extension of its fisheries' jurisdiction, precipitating the "cod wars" with England, whose fishermen had gone to the Iceland waters for generations. In the summer of 1974, the World Court (the International Court of Justice at The Hague) had ruled against Iceland. John Norton Moore, a distinguished maritime lawyer who was serving as chairman of the National Security Council's Interagency Task Force on the Law of the Sea, asked during a congressional hearing called to consider U.S. two-hundred-mile jurisdiction: "Mr. Chairman, what would we do if this bill were to become law and another country brings us before the International Court of Justice?"

None of this meant much to fishermen. The halls of Congress resounded to the clump of big bearded fellows in plaid shirts and wool caps who spoke in loud, confident voices of the outrage they felt at being bullied in their own home waters. They wanted the foreigners out, and they expected a law that would do it for them.

However, the climate of official opposition forced the bill's sponsors (all from the coastal states) to go beyond an initial bill introduced in 1973 that merely expelled the foreigners. They realized that their congressional colleagues from the farm belts would not be willing to buck the administration for a mere fish bill unless it provided some appealing national mandate. A sense of stewardship began to enter the conventional legislative rhetoric. Between 1973 and 1975 the bill, aptly named H.R. 200, evolved into a vehicle for managing the seafood stocks as well as protecting them. At stake, after all, was a great protein treasury. Continental shelves are the only parts of the ocean where sea creatures congregate in commercially harvestable quantities, and the United States is blessed with between fifteen percent and twenty percent of the world's productive continental shelves within its two-hundred-mile waters.

In a summarizing preamble to the final legislation, the drafters noted the ineffectiveness of existing international fishery agreements and declared: "Fishery resources are finite but renewable. If placed under sound management before overfishing has caused irreversible effects, the fisheries can be conserved and maintained so as to provide optimum yields on a continuing basis."

Government usually tries to take control when it legislates. In the case of fishery resources, some central control was appropriate given the multitude of sea creatures to be harvested and the varied interests of more than twenty coastal states and territories. The wonder of the bill was that it gave a portion of the authority back to the states. This reflected the tenacity of the bill's principal sponsors and drafters—Senator Warren Magnuson of Washington (for whom the bill was eventually named), Representative Gerry Studds of Massachusetts, Senator Ted Stevens of Alaska, Senator John Pastore of Rhode Island, Representative Don Young of Alaska, and their staffs.

The final bill, Public Law 94-265, signed by President Ford on April 13th, 1976, was divided into two distinct parts. The first took control of the seafood resources within two hundred miles of the coasts, as everyone expected it to do. The second provided a structure for managing the resources. This structure had as its cornerstone an entirely new form of national government that relied on the recommendations of regional councils.

The Magnuson Act established eight regional councils, gave them oversight responsibilities, and assigned them the duty of preparing management plans for every fishery in their area. Their makeup provides that, although members may have political roots and individual commitments, their allegiances lie within the region rather than in Washington, D.C. In practice, it was expected that the interests of industry, commercial fishermen, and recreational fishermen would all be represented.

The act withholds from the councils the ultimate power to pass regulations, leaving the final word to the Commerce Department's National Marine Fisheries Service, but it contains strong language directing that Commerce heed their recommendations. Thus, the councils have become a significant force in deciding the quotas and priorities of the American fishing industry.

Many of the fishermen who had stormed for congressional action assumed, during all the years of drafting and redrafting the Magnuson Act, that after the foreigners were removed from the grounds there would be an American open house on the stocks. In New England, fishing boat registration tripled during the first few years of the act's implementation.

Any study of the act's language as it evolved would have shown a different reality. Foreign nations were indeed forced to reduce their fishing effort, but they remained eligible to receive quotas through Governing International Fishery Agreements negotiated with the U.S. State Department. The foreign ships were to be banished only gradually as American fishermen proved capable of harvesting the stocks, and—meanwhile, hold on, buddy—the fish taken by anybody were going to be regulated closely by the councils to reflect long-term goals.

The surprised outrage exploded especially among New England fishermen who had traveled poor for years. It surfaced in my personal experience a year and a half after the act took effect, aboard a dragger out of New Bedford whose targets on Georges Bank were cod and flounder. Cod was still considered endangered enough from foreign overfishing to have had a strict weekly quota set on catching it. We reached our cod limit halfway through each trip that was to last a week. There we stood gutting fish for hours with frigid seas churning around our knees, convinced that such conditions entitled us to keep everything in the nets. And the fat, money-potential cod kept flopping aboard wherever we dragged! We tossed tons of it back over the side—most of it dead at that from the pressure within the trawl bag—while passionately bad-mouthing the politicians who had betrayed us.

The quotas may have been stingy. Those declaring them intended to err on the side of conservation so that the stocks could regenerate as quickly as possible. The new councils were feeling their way under a system never tried before. Whoever was right, fishermen threatened mass civil disobedience and eventually forced the three Atlantic coast councils to back off and withdraw the conservative quotas. "At that point, management began to go downhill," said one Commerce Department official in retrospect. "Now the fish just aren't there anymore."

The official was optimistic that the tide might be turned by a tough new multispecies groundfish plan approved at the council's recommendation by the National Marine Fisheries Service, effective in October 1987. It may take years to tell, while the disturbing truth remains that in New England the species considered to be the prime market fish—cod, haddock, redfish, and the yellowtail and blackback flounders—are running scarce under heavy American fishing pressure. On a positive note, fishermen have begun harvesting and selling species that they once scorned—squid, pollock, dogfish, and skate—all of which are good eating and should never have been wasted. Meanwhile, biologists warn that inshore fishermen in some areas, pushing on scarce stocks to make their trips, are working grounds that bring up too many juvenile fish in their nets, and are thus making a narrow present tradeoff on the future.

The Bitter Neighbors of Georges Bank

Declaring extended jurisdiction opened inevitable conflicts between North American neighbors, since two-hundred-mile lines extending from parts of United States coasts intersected Canadian and Mexican lines. In the Gulf of Mexico, fishermen from Texas, Louisiana, Mississippi, and Alabama lost many of their prime shrimp grounds to boats from Veracruz, Tamaulipas, and Campeche.

On the west coast, Canadian and American seiners had worked each other's shores routinely (not without rivalry) since salmon that spawned in the rivers of the two nations migrated freely, unconcerned with national borders. Fishermen of both nationalities lost salmon grounds and began to show less concern for immature salmon that came to areas where they were fishing other species. Canadians lost halibut grounds off Alaska that they had fished for more than a century.

But nowhere was the potential greater for hard feelings between Canada and the United States than on Georges Bank. At Georges, rich in seafood and expected to be rich also in oil, two-hundred-mile lines drawn from the coasts of Massachusetts and Maine overlapped two-hundred-mile lines from New Brunswick and Nova Scotia. Georges had been the backyard of New England fishermen for three centuries. Canadians, while relative newcomers who arrived in force only after World War II, now depended on Georges Bank also.

Contention began as far back as 1969, when the United States protested Canada's issuance of oil exploration permits on Georges Bank, but it remained at a simmer while the two neighbors resolved the threat of the foreign fleets. After two-hundred-mile jurisdictions became effective in 1977, the two nations began signing annual Reciprocal Fisheries Agreements while they negotiated a permanent pact on fishing rights. In June 1978, Canada abruptly terminated the next pending agreement and the United States followed suit immediately. The precipitating issue concerned salmon grounds in Pacific waters, but Georges Bank was the long-range issue.

[275]

On Georges Bank, fishermen of the two nations dragged for fish and scallops alongside each other. But Americans watched with disaffection as Canadian refrigerator trucks delivered increasingly massive loads of fresh fish to New England plants and markets to compete directly with U.S. catches on the same grounds at prices less than American boats could afford to charge. The Canadian government makes cheaper Canadian fish possible by providing a variety of aids to their fishermen (some call them subsidies) that relieve them, for example, of the heavy boat mortgages most American fishermen must pay.

The Canadians nursed their own burns. They had established a scallop fishery on Georges Bank, where Americans had once participated but had only re-entered in force after stocks closer to home became depleted. One day in Yarmouth, Nova Scotia, a major Canadian scallop port, I wandered innocently to the docks for an expected chat with fellow fishermen, quite unprepared for the angry, bitter blast I received when they learned I was an American. Indeed, the difference between the two fishery management structures made the sharing of grounds for whatever species highly difficult, since Canadians limited number of boats and size of catch, while Americans allowed all boats but regulated such variables as scallop count, minimum fish sizes, the mesh size of nets, and the periods that areas could open. Each set of rules seemed profligate and irresponsible to the other side's fishermen.

The road to a solution turned out to be a long one that bruised both sides. By 1979 (with the annual agreements deadlocked since 1978), negotiators had signed a tentative document to have the World Court fix the boundary but to allow each country access in perpetuity to each other's waters. However, New England senators, reflecting their constituencies, promised such a fight that the Reagan administration by 1981 decided it would be futile to submit the treaty to the Senate for approval.

Finally, the United States and Canada agreed to accept binding arbitration in the World Court. The state departments of both nations worked overtime for three years, preparing cases of indisputable logic that were reported to fill six feet of bookshelf space. The World Court delivered its decision in October 1984. It gave Canada the oil and fishing rights to a coveted area that might comprise only one-sixth of Georges Bank but which included a much larger part of its riches.

To the despair of many New England fishermen, the new Canadian territory included the Bank's most productive sea scallop beds, the major grounds of the U.S. swordfish fleet, and areas crucial to some American groundfish and lobster fishermen. The decision put many of them out of business at least temporarily, since the lost grounds were those to which they had committed themselves while areas further south that they tried to enter as newcomers were already overcrowded. Some of these fishermen now travel a thousand miles to a free-for-all zone at the Tail of the Grand Banks beyond any nation's two-hundred-mile limit, to compete with large foreign trawlers just as in the old days. Nor did all Canadian fishermen rejoice. Many suffered a similar loss of grounds they had developed. Ironically, some Nova Scotia fishermen lost their scallop beds.

The boundaries are now a fact of life, and the fishermen of both countries have made their adjustments. The executive director of the New England Fishery Management Council, Douglas Marshall, gave a realistic assessment in retrospect: "The U.S. lost good scallop grounds, but it got the Canadians off the rest of Georges Bank." American fishermen, in fact, began to explore new scallop beds, so that their scalloping fleet of seventy to eighty boats has remained the mainstay of the New Bedford fishing economy. But the pilot of a U.S. Coast Guard plane patrolling the "Hague Line" could tell me in 1989: "We never have to worry about Canadian boats crossing over here. They'd be fools. The fish are on their side of the line."

A Fishery Council in Action

The New England Council meets several times a year in a variety of locations throughout the area of its jurisdiction. At a February 1988 meeting held in Newport, Rhode Island, the agenda reflected the range of matters under the council's purview, and the ways that the jurisdictions needed to interact. Actions to be taken included a revised management plan for fluke (made with the Mid-Atlantic Council), a possible revision of penalties assessed against fishermen caught delivering undersized scallops, a management plan for the migratory billfish caught mostly by sport fishermen (made with the Caribbean Council), and a proposed change in the regulation on fish sizes that would allow Canadians to bring smaller fish to U.S. ports than Americans could deliver.

The New England Council also discussed the effects on the fisheries of the pending free trade agreement between the United States and Canada, and voted to register formal objection both to the practice of ocean dumping and to national budget cuts leveled against the Coast Guard that would reduce its ability to conduct fishery enforcement patrols.

The issue of Canadian fish sizes reflected the differences in fishing between the two nations. U.S. regulations prohibit possession anywhere in the United States of fish smaller than the minimum size in a fishery management plan. However, Canada bases its management (as noted above) on quota rather than size. Thus, Canadians could deliver smaller fish to U.S. processors than Americans were allowed to do. Fish often take longer to grow as water temperatures decrease, and mature fish caught on northern Canadian grounds might be smaller in the same year class than those regulated by size in U.S. waters. However, the U.S. catch, much of which went to the fresh fish markets in New York and Boston, could not supply fish in the volume needed by the domestic markets. The bottom line was that without deliveries of Canadian fish many of the processing plants in Massachusetts and Maine would be forced to close.

New England fishermen expressed no enthusiasm for a caveat the council was considering that favored the Canadian competition. However, their feelings were closer to grumbling than hostility. Processors gone out of business could buy nobody's fish. Within the council structure, commercial fishermen were only one of the interests represented.

Of greater concern to New England fishermen and processors was the pending free trade agreement with Canada that would eliminate all tariff and trade barriers between the two nations. While major portions of the domestic economy might be expected to benefit, the fishing industry saw itself as a clear loser. The pact, said worried processors, would give Canada free access to U.S. markets but would provide nothing in return. While the help that the Canadian government provides its fisheries would remain to give them a competitive pricing advantage, the domestic producers of such items as fish sticks and canned sardines would lose their tariff protection.

This was all new ground for the councils. The priority of the Magnuson Act had been to gain control of the fish and to manage them. "We related the text only to harvesting," according to James P. (Bud) Walsh, Senator Magnuson's staff aide on the Senate Commerce Committee during the drafting of the act. "There was a reluctance to tackle issues of the marketplace, nor did we address trade issues."

Regarding scallop penalties, on the other hand, the New England Council at its February 1988 meeting plunged into the sort of issue that fishermen can find words to address whether they influence the outcome or not. The U.S. regulates the scallop catch on its grounds by meat count: the number of shucked scallop meats per pound. An inspector takes a random pound-weight sample at the dock from a standard forty-pound bag of meats. The fishermen have already made the same check at sea, often under stormier circumstances. Since scallop sizes are not uniform, the bag sampled can contain a wide mixture. The count may depend on the chance of where it is harvested. Making the count becomes even trickier during the fall spawning season, when scallop meats shrink.

The law at this point (that is, the scallop management plan that had been recommended by the council, then approved and issued by the Department of Commerce) required an average count of thirty meats per pound but allowed a ten percent tolerance, which brought it to thirty-three. A boat delivering even a fraction over this became subject to catch confiscations and fines, which, even before they escalated with a larger penalty schedule, could represent thousands of dollars.

The council's Scallop Oversight Committee considered the matter in order to make recommendations to the full council later in the day on a possible modification of the rules. Committee members sat around a U-shaped table. Behind them, feet squarely on the floor and arms folded, sat seven scallop fishermen, the crew of the 190-foot boat *Hustler* who had moored their boat (thus suspended their income) and driven up from New Bedford to speak for themselves. Their spokesman was Jim Costakes, the forthright manager of the Seafood Producer's Association in New Bedford.

Costakes, an appointed member of the council itself, wore a dark suit at the shirtsleeve table. He leaned forward and spoke with the rumbling smooth-rough force of a grass-roots politician. "If you say we're supposed to adhere to thirty count, that is the law. But how would you like to bag up, and you know you've got thirty count in that bag. And a federal officer comes down and happens to take a sample with a smaller count. You are now a violator. You have now broken the law, yet you know the bag has met the standard."

The council lawyer, a sharp-voiced young man who appeared pale beside the bulky fishermen and their representative: "I understand what you're trying to explain . . ."

Costakes: "No, I don't think you understand. You understand what that piece of paper says. You don't know what it's like on Georges."

Lawyer: "I understand that the piece of paper was passed by Congress, and there's nothing I can do about that."

Fisherman Bob Britto, from the sidelines, a lean, articulate man: "It's like getting a speeding ticket for doing fifty-six. There's not many dinner plates |big scallops| left on Georges to beef up a bag. Go try and find yourself a fifty-year-old virgin, same thing as going out on Georges now and finding those big scallops. It's all little stuff coming in now."

A woman with the scallopers: "Fishermen are so up against it to pay their mortgages. Does the council understand this problem?"

Other scalloper: "We're out there, wind blowin' fifty-sixty, wit' a tin can . . . |Refers to taking a sample in a one-pound coffee can and counting the meats.| How many of you been out wit' a tin can to do it, blowin' fifty, sixty, tired, end of ya' watch?" He faced the committee members. "Twenny years ago you guys didn't *exist*, when we were fishin'."

After hearing the case, the full council recommended a new penalty schedule that would eliminate fixed fines (which was how men lost their boats), relax the graduated penalties for seizure of catches, and raise the count that triggered a violation to thirty-five meats. At best, it appeared an interim solution, a point in regulatory evolution. Some Americans present even admitted that Canada's quota system by total weight rather than size might be more realistic.

Issues vary within the councils. One of the most intense faced by them all involves allocations between recreational and commercial fishermen. The state fishery departments share this problem, since the states control waters within three miles of the coast. It often becomes a situation of classic triage, deciding where one man's ox must be gored to save another's. In the Gulf of Mexico, a major sports-commercial conflict rages over red drum, as all boats rush to cash in on the national fad for Cajun blackened redfish. The same tug of war exists on the West Coast over catching rights to the spirited salmon, which is a delight on the end of a pole but which has also been the base of a huge commercial fishery since the 1850s. Along the eastern seaboard, who is to allocate to satisfaction between anglers and gill-netters for the scarce runs of striped bass, or between party boats and workboats for the big billfish and tunas?

The sport fisherman's side is easy to understand. The old fishing hole is an American institution. Any pleasure that a commercial fisherman may feel for the sight of water and the feel of flapping fish is echoed in spades by the teachers and doctors and truck drivers who might dream of a larger commitment to seafaring, but settle for precious hours in a hired boat. There are also "recreational" fisher-man with low incomes, who cannot pay the high market price for commercial seafood and who fish when they can to put food on the table.

Lucy Sloan, a fighter for fishermen's interests since the drafting days of the Magnuson Act, is a small woman whose voice can penetrate a roomful of men as she knits doggedly throughout end-less hearings. She articulates what many fishermen have on their minds. "It's time," she declares on the sport fishing issue, with no attempt at impartiality, "that we distinguished between people who play with food and those who produce it."

Patrolling the New Fences

When I used to ride on fishery patrols to Georges Bank with the U.S. Coast Guard, in the mid-1970s before passage of the Magnuson Act, it was their mission by ship and plane to keep track of the foreign fleets and to make sure that they were not breaking domestic laws or international agreements.

When I flew again in 1989, the mission had changed to one of watching American boats to make sure they did not fish in certain areas closed to protect spawning stocks. It was late spring, and over the sea hung patches of low fog dense enough to hide a boat. The plane, like others on fishery patrol, left the Cape Cod base at an unannounced time so that its flight could not be predicted. The mood was different from that of the old days. The pilots of the earlier flights had dogged the big foreign ships with the zest of the chase, hoping to catch one in an illegal act that would lead to "hot pursuit" and capture. Now, tracking fellow Americans, they hoped to find no violators although they conducted their search as thoroughly as before. As noted above, they did not expect to find Canadian boats crossing the "Hague Line" drawn on Georges Bank by the World Court. It was more likely that Canadian patrols would pick up Americans slipping across through the fog, since more productive grounds lay on the Canadian side.

As a consequence of two-hundred-mile jurisdictions, the Canadian Coast Guard not only patrols the Hague Line on Georges Bank, but also two international lines on Canada's vast Grand Banks where portions extend beyond the two-hundred-mile boundary. The Banks have a shape resembling roughly the map of Africa. Beyond the boundary is a section to the south known as the Tail of the Bank which would correspond to the position of South Africa, and a smaller section to the east called the Nose of the Bank that forms a knob resembling Ethiopia and Senegal. Foreign ships can still fish with impunity on the Tail and the Nose, regulated only by the rules agreed to by their own nations.

The lack of total control over the Grand Banks gives the Canadians fits. It means they cannot manage the Banks as a complete ecosystem, since some of the fish that appear in maturity around major areas like the Virgin Rocks and Eastern Shoals pass early parts of their lives in places where fishermen need not answer to Canadian law.

One July evening, I flew over the Banks with an enforcement officer from the Canadian Department of Fisheries and Oceans. It was a routine unannounced observation flight from St. John's, in a small plane whose human leg room had been usurped by radar and camera equipment. For one person to move, another needed to remain immobile. Flying high over the Virgin Rocks, we noted on the radar's long-range scale a concentration of medium-sized trawlers, presumed Canadian and of no interest during this patrol. (Other Canadian patrols by sea and air monitored the activity of the domestic fleet.) At the two-hundred-mile line from shore, the radar showed four orderly blips in a row seven miles apart, ranged just a mile or two outside the line. The pilot descended to an altitude that permitted visual inspection as the radar operator switched to a closer scale.

All the talk above the noise of the plane was conducted by head-phone. Wayne Evans, the soft-spoken young fisheries officer in charge of the patrol, directed: "See if the captain's got any gold teeth, shall we, John?"

"Roger." John Lee, the pilot, swooped down for a pass as he noted, "Taking it on the right side. I think there's a name on the bow, near the waterline."

The cameraman readied for high speed photographs as everyone else peered through the small windows. The rapidly approaching ship had a green hull with scupper streaks of rust, and over the deck a trawler's typical high black "gallows" (a support structure for raising heavy weights). We swept past the ship on a crooked visual angle seen through the smudges of thick thermal glass, but practiced eyes noted the blur of a name on the bow. The ship's taut cables dipping into the water astern showed that it was towing a net.

"Gear in the water," said Evans and the pilot simultaneously, as Evans scribbled notes on his report. "*Santa Maria Manuella*, right? Portuguese." The radarman called the ship's exact position, and the plane continued to the next blip along the line.

During the flight, we logged twenty-four ships, most with gear in the water, all of them located on the international grounds within a mile or two of the Canadian boundary. We flew low to identify each, a job that sometimes necessitated two or three passes. Inside the cramped plane, someone passed out jelly donuts. The final count included eight Spanish ships, seven Portuguese, and four Cuban. Then there were two trawlers flying the Panamanian flag, which Evans noted from past experience carried Portuguese crews. He also knew that another flag-of-convenience ship with Cayman Islands registry had a Korean crew. He speculated that a single Soviet support ship was there to service the Cubans. We sighted only one American vessel, notably smaller than the others—a boat rather than a ship, without a gallows, geared with a mere drum astern. She looked vulnerable among the big ones, an echo of the New England fisher-man's life before the Magnuson Act. Yet the thousand-mile cruise from Gloucester still made the men aboard the closest crew to home among those fishing the Tail.

The low pastel lights of late day settled over the water below. With darkness, the visibility began to dim. The radarman announced a ship close to the line: "His heading's zero-one-zero. That's a good heading if you want to go inside the line." The plane made three passes in order to gather all the information possible in the waning light, and then, with fuel near the safety margin for the hour and a half return flight, we ascended to the high altitude again.

"A mile outside, he may be," said one of the Newfoundlanders aboard. "But now its nighttime and we're gone 'ome. A lot of ocean there, b'y."

The Next Dozen Years

After passage of the Magnuson Act, it came time to build a domestic fishing industry able to handle the seafood stocks that foreigners had proven could be exploited. It was a time of transition. The U.S. State Department under fishery ambassador Ted Cronmiller played a game it called "fish and chips." Cronmiller was credited with defining the policy and making it work. "We made it clear to the foreign fishing nations that if they wanted access to any surplus in our zone, they'd have to provides us with something in return by way of cooperation with our industry—either in providing export markets for our products, or providing for over-the-side sales in joint ventures."

Throughout most of the 1980s, the system called "joint ventures" enabled Americans and Canadians, each in home waters, to catch their quotas of fish and deliver them to foreign processor ships that had no quota. The arrangement provides a beneficial transition, allowing local fishermen to develop the capability to handle more fish than they had dealt with before, while giving foreign fleets with large investments the time to phase out in North American waters.

Americans made joint-venture agreements particularly with ships of Japan, Russia, and South Korea. Canadians contracted also with ships from Portugal, Bulgaria, and other countries that had formerly fished on the Grand Banks. It was to a Portuguese ship under a joint venture agreement that Max and Cyril Oxford of the longliner *Sealer* delivered their Labrador cod off Smokey while exchanging little personal gifts.

When he assumed the duty of U.S. fisheries ambassador in 1983, Edward Wolfe remembers telling the foreign fishing nations that, distressed as it might make them, they should anticipate the end of foreign allocations and even of joint ventures. This still came to pass sooner than anyone anticipated. In record time, Americans have developed new ships and shoreside plants to process their own raw material.

Now that there are no longer quotas to negotiate with foreign nations, the U.S. State Department's business turns toward pacts and concessions. Wolfe's efforts have involved opening Soviet grounds to Americans fishing for crab and other species in the Bering Sea; negotiating a treaty that involves development money and tuna fishing rights with sixteen South Pacific island nations spread over ten million square miles of ocean; clearing the way in China and South America for American investments in aquaculture; and drafting agreements with Japan, Taiwan, and South Korea to monitor and enforce the elements of their squid drift-net fishing that affect fish that migrate to American waters.

By the end of the 1980s, with virtually all foreign fishing in United States two-hundred-mile waters abolished as domestic fishermen proved their ability to harvest the entire sustainable yield themselves, the original intent of the Magnuson Act had been accomplished, and without international disaster at that.

Two-hundred-mile jurisdiction did not produce flowers without thorns. But in redefining the ocean part of the world's commons it established more realistically the rights of coastal nations to control their resources, and as advances in technology made development and exploitation possible as never before it enabled the owner nations to focus their management efforts.

In the reslicing of the world's seafood pie, the nations most hurt were some of the giants—Japan and Russia particularly—who had invested hugely in distant-water fisheries that harvested in other people's waters. The Portuguese lost their centuries-old cod fishery on the Grand Banks off Newfoundland. However, the new rules enabled other nations, India and New Zealand and Chile among them, to develop domestic fisheries and explore options in the world market never before considered. Some of the little places like Ghana suddenly found themselves in a bargaining position to lease their fishing rights. On the other hand, nations without a seacoast like Switzerland and Paraguay and Mongolia, which made an attempt through the United Nations' Law of the Sea to receive a share of the world's ocean wealth by declaring it common property, must look elsewhere in our time for equity.

[285]

As for the regional councils on which the probable future strength of the American fishing industry depends, they have been maturing, often by painful trial and error. "The real test of their effectiveness will be in the next few years," says Rod Moore, who as senior Republican staff member of the House Merchant Marine subcommittee on fisheries has helped draft and shepherd clarifying amendments to the Magnuson Act since its passage. "It was real easy, when you had a foreign fleet out there, to bash the foreigners and not to worry about internal squabbles. Now we don't have foreigners to bash any more. The councils are going to have to make some tough choices between competing domestic fisheries. That's going to be a real test of how good a job they can do."

2

Threats and Changes

F ishing has changed. There is no doubt about it. For every surviving fisherman who goes on the water in an open boat with no
bigger investment than a simple net, line, or hand tongs, there are
now a hundred of his brethren who can afford the latest that technology has to offer and must work like hell to pay for it. And men who
once could consider themselves independent, free to go hungry or
get rich as their luck and skill led them, now have learned to be wary
of more than the sea.

"Part of fishing today is not being the best fisherman, not being
out there the longest. Part of fishing today is spending a certain
amount of your time fighting for the right to fish." The speaker was
Larry Simns, a Chesapeake Bay waterman with a regional drawl and a
plain manner. Simns supports his family by clamming, and for a
salary that does not cover expenses he has served for several years as
president of the Maryland Waterman's Association.

Simns has a quiet tiredness about him, the long reserve of a man
who fights issues and bureaucracies. All commercial fishermen feel
encroached, but none have greater reason than those of Chesapeake
Bay, where the bounty of the sea comes into waters so accessible
that recreational fishermen compete as their right. Since "everyone
wants to live on the water," as Simns concedes, he has seen the rural
life of Bay watermen invaded, particularly by federal employees in the

Washington-Baltimore corridor whose salaries "for not doin' a day of work in their lives" far exceed anything a waterman could ever hope to earn. "Their numbers outrank us a thousand to one. So when you go to your elected officials and they start counting votes on you, you haven't got anything."

Chesapeake watermen have seen sewage treatment plants foisted on their small communities in the name of purifying the water, only to have the water become sterilized and devoid of sea life as the new amenities draw urban people who raise land values and usurp the working waterfront. They have seen zoning laws passed that appear to grandfather a waterman's rights but actually ease him out. Many of the sheltered wharves where they unloaded oysters and crabs now house cabin cruisers and require a membership fee for the privilege of mooring.

For a while in the late 1980s, it appeared that pleasure boat owners had persuaded the Maryland legislature to allot all the striped bass in' the Maryland part of Chesapeake Bay for recreation. Then, as the bill was being considered in committee, watermen led by Simns attended the hearing in such numbers that the politicians shelved the bill.

Simns may regard politicians warily, but he notes that at least they must run for re-election. The people to watch out for? "It's your regulators. Once they get that job, they've got it forever and they're going to keep it forever. They can't be fired, and they'll let you know that in a hurry. They've read something in a book that tells them how to manage fish, and. . . ."

They're Out to Get Us!

Simns might have revealed a fisherman's paranoia toward authority, but he had formed his opinion on the line. "The bureaucrats will almost *cause* you to have gear disputes, keep you fighting amongst yourselves, while you really don't know they're doing it. And then, they rule and regulate just as they want to without any interference from you."

Men who fish for a living often have reason to think that the rest of the world is against them. Animal welfare people do their bit by protecting marine mammals as an article of faith. With seal hunting stopped, there is no longer any control of their numbers. Seals now proliferate along the coasts of Norway and eastern Canada to compete with fishermen for the fish stocks. Through the parasites that seal overpopulations generate, the seals are threatening even the quality of fish that can be wrested from them. Other protected marine mammals raise different problems. American shrimpers in the Gulf of Mexico have been forced to include clumsy turtle excluder devices on their nets that reduce catches. American tuna fishermen are the only ones in the world held to relinquishing a harvest if their nets take in too great an incidental catch of dolphins. It is good to know—I am not being sarcastic—that America leads the way in animal protection. However, when foreign-caught shrimp and tuna can be delivered cheaper to the American consumer, he is not noted for extending his high moral requirements for others' conduct to the everyday matters of his own pocketbook.

Some encroachments, like pollution from dumping, pit fishermen against the whole of urban society. The unbelievable quantity of effluent from coastal cities must go somewhere, and it is more easily unloaded into the sea than into holes dug endlessly on expensive land. A continuous stream of barges, for example, tows the waste of New York and Boston over some of the great east coast fishing banks to designated deep-water dump sites. However, when the weather turns bad (loosely left to the discretion of the barge captain who may be simply weary of the trip), the barge can "short dump" along the way. How can they all be monitored? New England fishermen report tows that mix fish with such by-catch as bed frames, sheets, doctors' gowns, hypodermic needles, and rotting bandages.

Scientists are another suspect party, even though most fishermen sincerely assert their support for conservation. (If the resource goes, who's put out of business first? they say, but, like others of the human race, they would generally rather see someone else regulated.) Marine biologists who determine the health of fish stocks are regarded with particular suspicion.

When the cod stocks were being regulated closely on Georges Bank and Nantucket Shoals just after the Magnuson Act began to make fish available to Americans, fishermen pressed for a more generous quota. The regulators, at least, credit this pressure with discouraging effective management and thus perpetuating the continued decline of fish stocks. *National Fisherman*, a comprehensive magazine of the North American fisheries, in a 1986 editorial quoted a New England fishery biologist as blaming the decline on "a fifteen-year legacy of poor recruitment, the result of poor spawning stocks. When a good class year has surfaced, we and the Canadians have chopped its head off. . . ." The biologist continued, "We can't make fish. Only fish can do that. All we can do is protect a good year class when it comes along."

The fishermen have their own viewpoint. Two and a half years after the Magnuson Act became effective, I was visiting some Maine fishermen moored in Gloucester. The conversation concerned several fishery biologists who chartered a fishing boat to tag fish, follow their migrations, and determine their abundance. "Goddamned taggers'll screw you," a clean-cut young skipper warned in a pleasant voice, without heat. "What they do, what they did to us last year, after we took them tagging and everything . . . ? Went out with me last year, two biologists and two scientists. So they came again the other day and wanted to charter the boat for a couple of weeks."

He leaned back in a wheelhouse chair, pulled a cap over his eyes to shelter them from the setting sun, and propped his boots comfortably on the chart ledge. "We was out a while, six hours. They started telling us all the tags that we tagged last winter in January? They tried telling us the stock from here's mixed with the stocks over there. Well, you know how much fish was there, how everybody was doing good, and then they cut our quota right in half? They was the ones. And they did it on my own fuckin' boat. They never even told me. I got so pissed off I took 'em right back to the dock, their gear, their tubs, the whole damn works. I told 'em, I sez, we think we're doin' something for you guys, and look what you done to us. That's what happened here." The others in the wheelhouse agreed with a down-East snort of recognition. Those were guys you couldn't trust, biologists.

It may or may not be that times are changing. The incident happened in 1979. By 1988, Richard Roe, New England regional director of the National Marine Fisheries Service, could say, "New England fishermen are finally admitting that the resource is diminished. Up until now they might have known it from poor catches, but they never admitted it." He spoke bluntly on the strength of the new groundfish management plan approved in late 1987, which he felt offered a fresh chance at restoring the fish. "Now maybe we can stop managing fishermen, and get to the stocks."

One insidious problem for the fishing industry comes from within its ranks. The American penchant for litigation has reached a height, or depth, unequaled in any other country. Fishing boats with their inherent dangers have caught the brunt of it, as disastrously as the medical profession. In Norway, where the government has set a limit on any liability unless bad intent is proven, my shipmates on the Myre trawlers listened with fascination and disbelief to the possibilities under the American system of guilt. Crewmen injured ashore while carousing have successfully held their skippers responsible. In one case on the West Coast, the insurance company reneged and the owner had to sell his boat to pay. Such rulings, by judges and juries coaxed into vindictive pity, have raised the cost of fishing boat insurance more than five hundred percent in the past few years. Inevitably, the cost must be passed on in the price of fish.

The Strength of Numbers

Like the big spirit Gitche Manito in Longfellow's epic *Hiawatha*, Larry Simns of the Maryland Waterman's Association has seen enough to have a long view. The Manito counseled his warring Indian tribes (who did not know how endangered they were): "All your strength is in your union. All your danger is in discord." Looking beyond the Chesapeake Bay and its specific issues, Simns counseled fishermen from over the nation, at a Fish Expo seminar in Boston, to forgo their differences and stick together. "We can't do it if we're backbiting each other and saying that *your* gear's destroying this, *they* shouldn't catch this fish because I don't catch it, *my* gear's better, *this* fisherman shouldn't fish this way. That's the biggest enemy that the commercial fisherman has, being divided by fighting amongst ourselves. And we play right into the hands of the bureaucracies, and the sport fishermen, and the environmentalists, that want to do away with us by reducing our force. Divided you're not strong enough to make any difference to them."

American fishermen are mostly inclined to act on their own, like the young Maine skipper who put the fish biologists ashore. They have indeed organized, from time to time, after a fashion, but the regionality of their conditions makes them less likely than truck drivers or auto workers to have goals so much in common that they can unite across the board.

In the United States Lucy Sloan attempted to form a nationwide lobbying organization with the National Federation of Fishermen, and her work as a spokesman for fishermen made decisive contributions to national legislation during the first decade of the Magnuson Act. However, Sloan's base remained with East Coast fishermen despite members recruited from other regions. Eventually the organization could no longer support itself even at a Spartan level.

Local organizations have survived better, most on the strength of a single person who is also a fisherman but often also with the help of an articulate hired gun. The Maryland and the Virginia Watermen's Associations are examples among those on the U.S. East Coast (the former representing seventeen county associations), as are the Massachusetts Inshore Draggermen's Association (under respected fisherman Dan Arnold until recently), the Massachusetts Lobstermen's Association, and the Organized Fishermen of Florida (under former teacher and biologist Jerry Sansom, who must really compete, in a state heavily populated with sportsmen-retirees who have the wealth to clear the waterfronts of fishy odors permanently).

The concerns of the organizations cover many areas, with the stakes ranging from self-interest to economic survival. Dan Arnold's group once defeated a pending federal regulation mandating that fishermen maintain logbooks for public inspection, a requirement regarded by fishermen as simple public disclosure of their painfully earned fishing secrets. The Florida group battled a fuel tax increase. Gulf of Mexico groups have contested bitterly the inefficient turtle excluder devices, now required on shrimp nets even in areas where the turtles to be protected never appear. The Maryland group recently fought a state plan to lease oyster mariculture sites on public bars, which they maintained was the initial step to push watermen from all the remaining oystering sites. As noted above, the group also challenged pending Maryland law that would have given the entire striped bass harvest to sport fishermen.

Another form of American fishermen's organizations is the co-op and the marketing association. The dozen skippers in Gloucester with whom Joe Testaverde fishes had formed the latter. Among East Coast co-ops are the Belford Seafood Co-op Association of Belford, New Jersey, founded in 1953, and the Stonington Lobster Cooperative of

Stonington, Maine, founded in 1948. The classic New England co-op is that of Point Judith and the port of Galilee, Rhode Island, founded in 1947.

In a brochure the Point Judith Fishermen's Cooperative defines itself and co-ops in general:

> The purpose of a cooperative is to provide their users or customers with the goods and services that they need at the lowest practical cost and in the form those owners desire. The only way to be sure that this is done, is for the customers or users of the services to be the owners of the company providing the services. . . . By combining their catches the Co-op members can economically ship product to far away markets and achieve top prices and quick payment for their fish. The Co-op then uses these economies of scale to build and operate their own fuel and ice-making operations. Today the Co-op has over 80 vessels and 200 members and is recognized worldwide as a large supplier of quality seafood products.

Under fisherman Jake Dykstra (now retired), a man with a wild scraggly beard that made him look deceptively like an eccentric until he began speaking with calm logic, the Point Judith Co-op became a leading force in drafting and passing the Magnuson Fisheries Conservation and Management Act. Dykstra, credited with helping elevate the two-hundred-mile law beyond a mere stopgap to chase away the foreigners, was among the first to propose the idea of regional councils.

Newfoundland has a famous co-op on Fogo Island. After the 1949 confederation of Newfoundland into a province of Canada, the Canadian government decided to close down the remotest of the outport fishing communities in order to make its social benefit programs more manageable. Fogo Island seemed a natural target for evacuation. It could be reached only by boat in an area where ice often made this impossible, and its level of development included light furnished by lantern and water fetched from a community well.

However, the inhabitants had no taste for becoming refugees simply because a benevolent central government threatened to close the schools. The people had a history, and family graves lay in sight of their small houses. The islanders' forebears, from such villages as Fogo, Seldom-Come-By, Joe Batts Arm, Sandy Cove, and Tilting, had settled there for the proximity to cod and seals. In the century past, they had furnished many of the ships and crews of the sealing fleet, and were proud of it. The fish remained. Why would families who fished for a living want to leave?

With help and advice from sympathetic outsiders, the islanders formed a fishery co-op. A few lines cover years of work and imagination. The Fogo Co-op succeeded, to become a model of such organizations in underdeveloped regions. It provides markets and a stable price, fish plant jobs, and a gear store where purchases in quantity keep down the price. Incidentally, the schools there now are bright and clean, and the noisy gaiety in the yard at recess is that of kids at ease in their environment.

Unions have played only a minor role among American fishermen, but a form of them exists among the fishermen of Newfoundland and Norway. The principal exception in the United States is that of New Bedford, where fishermen have allied themselves since 1958 with the Seafarer's International Union (except for a five-year commitment to the Teamsters) while functioning autonomously.

In the 1960s, the New Bedford union, under Howard Nickerson, a former fisherman, claimed a ninety percent membership of the men on the boats. It earned a reputation for its ability to negotiate and for its strong medical plan and pension fund. But beginning in the late 1970s, under different leadership, the union continually lost members. It still had enough clout, however, to call a strike in early 1986 that kept the fleet in port. The union struck over the way in which crewmen were hired, and over the division of shares between boat and crew. The demand to alter the accepted share structure came at a bad time. Trips fishing on diminished stocks could return as "brokers" with barely enough gross to enable the skipper to pay the boat's fixed expenses including nightmarish insurance premiums. The issue pitted skippers against their crews, in an occupation whose dangers require teamwork.

During the strike, some ugly old-time union thuggery occurred from union outsiders shipped in for the purpose—threats, roughing-ups, windows smashed. The general outrage soon sent the hired persuaders back across the state line, but according to observers the way the strike was conducted weakened the position drastically of local organized labor. By the final settlement in February 1988, most boats had returned to fishing and disassociated from the union.

Fishermen throughout Newfoundland accept their single union as a welcome fact. The Newfoundland Fishermen, Food and Allied Workers Union represents a wide range of interests that includes both inshore and offshore fishermen as well as cannery workers, so that it focuses entirely on the regional fishing industry. Like the draggerman I encountered on the bus headed for Catalina to ride a trawler to the Grand Banks, Newfoundland fishermen credit the union with changing their lives. For the men who work on factory trawlers, it means a guaranteed wage in bad fishing times.

Richard Cashin, the head of the union which he helped organize and then charter in 1971, is a St. John's lawyer and former politician with the drive to confront and dig in. When he entered the scene in 1969—to see that fishermen received adequate compensation for fishing losses due to industrial phosphorus poisoning in Placentia Bay—Newfoundland fishermen were still a generation behind most of their brethren in the Western world. The fishermen of Myre and other ports along the Norway coast had long since reclaimed their souls from the company stores of the fish czars.

In Norway, the national fishermen's association, Norges Fiskarlag, has a voluntary membership that includes most Norwegian fishermen from both large and small boats. According to an official description, the organization is politically independent. However, it "works in close cooperation with the government authorities" to negotiate "on matters which concern economic conditions in the industry as a whole. . . . Because of the great importance of the fishing industry in Norway's coastal districts, Norges Fiskarlag have an important responsibility as regards the development of the society in these areas."

Reliefs and Stresses of Technological Wonder

The fishermen's co-ops, marketing associations, and unions are all products of social change, but it was technology that made the social changes possible. Engines and powered machinery freed fishermen from the worst of exhausting labors—the kind that produced iron men who became crippled by middle age—so that they had the energy left to speak up for themselves in some fashion.

Until about a century ago, the physical conditions of the fishing life had changed little since the apostle Peter's time in Galilee. The development of the mariner's compass in the fourteenth century did make it possible to sail the open sea even when bad weather blotted out the ancient standbys of sun, moon, and polar star. With compass and dead reckoning, Basque and Portuguese fishermen were soon routinely crossing two and a half thousand miles of open sea to hunt for whale and cod in the waters off Newfoundland. But the options opened by the compass, and subsequently by the sextant and chronometer in the eighteenth century, actually increased the hardship of the fishing life by freeing men from the need to return frequently to shore and home.

Technology always took a while to catch up with fishermen. The Industrial Revolution, which began in England before the American Revolutionary War, was by 1800 harnessing steam power on land. But a costly engine, for none but the largest fishing boats, had begun to appear only at the end of the nineteenth century. (The first came in 1881, on steam trawlers out of Hull and Grimsby in England.) This was twenty years after the first adaptation of steam in the 1860s to the running of ships. Winches powered from the engine were still a fishing deck luxury in 1913, and did not become universally common on smaller fishing boats until after World War II, while farmers had had tractors since the turn of the century to help absorb their heaviest labor. Modernity for the world's fishermen finally began in the mid-1950s, when several military products developed during World War II were redesigned to fit on boats at an affordable price.

The fish deck innovations of the 1950s affected four categories in particular: surface locating, machinery, underwater search, and materials. The most basic development was the compact marine diesel engine. These were slow to reach small fishing boats. In the early 1950s when I served aboard a Coast Guard cutter out of Ketchikan, Alaska, we often raced to help fishermen whose boats had exploded from the fumes of gasoline engines. As boat inspection officer, one of my chief jobs was to impress on fishermen the dangers of gassy bilges. But by the 1960s a boat of any size with a gas engine was considered antiquated in any prosperous world fishery.

In terms of effectiveness, the change in materials might appear the least of the four innovations since it relates less directly to production. Yet anyone who has ever worked hours of heavy, wet manual labor while encased in heavy cloth layered with linseed oil will appreciate the tough but pliable waterproof "oilskins" now manufactured from plastics that do not stink, crackle, leak, or rot. A fisherman can now work on deck in coveralls that will keep him afloat if he falls overboard. Sponge rubber survival suits that slip over deck clothing in a minute (with practice) now save lives routinely in all the northern fisheries where cold water kills quickly.

In running gear, nylon and other synthetic materials have replaced hemp, cotton, and linen for every fish deck fiber from rope to net. The resulting lines are smaller and lighter for the same load. They also coil more easily, and leave no needlelike slivers sticking in the hands. The old cotton fishing nets were not only heavier than nylon when dry, but they absorbed water to become leaden while they were being pulled into the boat. They required a regular soak in "bluestone," copper sulfate, to prevent them from rotting, which was a long chore at the end of a hard fishing week. Linen nets in the old Gloucester gillnet fishery were kept black from dips in tar to alleviate decay. To prevent rot, the gillnets needed to be dried for a day ashore after each night's soak, so that a boat needed double sets. Present nylon nets, partly translucent, come in light watery greens and blues that do a better job of fooling the fish, and they dry at once on deck.

Hydraulic devices now turn all manner of wheels to bring in lines and nets, and younger fishermen would be lost without them. In truth, their dads and grandads pulled smaller nets and lines, but they also worked in larger crews among whom to divide the shares.

The work, the crippling work that used to be! Listen to the reminiscence of a 1911 apprenticeship on a hand-powered gurdy in the halibut dory fishery:

Turning! It sounded so easy. But it is backbreaking, killing work, when the gear is full of fish, or the hooks are dragging up rocks and corals, often 150 fathoms down. . . . I was sitting forward [in an open dory] heaving on the gurdy, hauling good strong gear that could stand a lot of strain without parting. I would turn and strain until I was blue in the face; call upon what seemed to be the last ounce of strength and gain one more turn; then rest the handle of the gurdy across my thighs, which would serve as a sort of brake [In Alaskan Waters by Alfred Wolfe, published 1942].

[297]

This was Wolfe's continuous labor, except rowing, for a fifteen-hour day, sometimes with salt boils on his hands giving him near agony.

The invention in 1955 of the power block altered the entire scope of the world's net fisheries. Like those used on the menhaden and herring seiners, a power block is essentially a big hydraulically powered wheel with treads, which rotates to grip and pull in the net. The inventor, Mario Puretic, was an Italian-born tuna fisherman in California who decided one day to use his head instead of his back. Puretic told me that, being no mechanic, he hired a jobber to make him a prototype from his sketches (this cost him three hundred dollars) and then tried to interest a manufacturer. He had gained only polite attention when, at first sight of the new gadget, a young engineer starting a marine equipment company in Seattle, signed up with him on the spot. (Peter Schmidt still heads Marco Marine Construction and Design, which, thanks in part to the Puretic power block, is now one of the world's major fishing boat builders and fishing equipment manufacturers.)

For fishermen, all the power block needed was a few dockside demonstrations, and word could scarcely have traveled faster. Within two years, it had become a staple of all seine-type fishing boats, drastically altering the work pattern and raising the efficiency for catching salmon, tuna, herring, menhaden, mackerel, capelin, and other fish that school in large numbers near the surface.

Radar was the first electronic boon to fishermen. Developed by the military during World War II, it reached fishing boat size about a decade later. The change was particularly significant in places where rocks and shoals pepper the water. Before radar, no local fisherman with any sense traveled at night except in the most known, open waters. Now radar permits boats to move when they want. Ironically, this frees crews to be underway at night after an exhausting day or two of "clockaround" fishing, a freedom which exacerbates fatigue, considered to be the greatest cause of all fishing boat accidents.

Boats can now travel miles across open water and arrive within a hundred feet or so of a net or buoy marker. They do this with electronic navigating devices, particularly those using signals from Loran and from transit satellites.

Loran is a navigational system based on chart location at the intersection of two radio signals transmitted from different shore stations. Satellite navigation, which alone of the new seafaring technologies originated after World War II, employs several satellites in orbit six hundred miles above the earth. "Satnav" was developed by the Johns Hopkins University's Applied Physics Laboratory for the U.S. Navy following the Soviet's 1957 launch of Sputnik, and by 1967 had been made available worldwide for civilian use. However, until the late 1980s, only the largest fishing ships could afford satellite receivers because they were very expensive. Their cost is gradually reaching the deck level for smaller boats.

Fishermen must balance the greater accuracy of Satnav against certain drawbacks. Loran equipment (and that of another system called Decca that operates only in European waters) is cheaper, and it provides a reading at any time since Loran stations send a continuous signal. Satellite fixes require a spacecraft pass at a fifteen- to seventy-five degree angle from the ship to be effective, and these may occur only at intervals of an hour or more depending on the boat's location and the number of satellites (usually four) that are operative. Eventually, the world will have a U.S. Global Positioning System with a constellation of spacecraft, orbiting at a 1,200 mile altitude, to form a tight enough grid for continuous signals. When GPS becomes a reality, scientists predict that Loran, Decca, and every other ground locator system will become obsolete since satellites can transmit in complete independence of local earth conditions.

Steel hulls have supplanted wooden ones in most of the world's prosperous fisheries. They are stronger and require less maintenance, although there is still a word to say for the groaning accommodation of Joey Testaverde's caulked seams in a bouncing sea. Resilient fiberglass hulls, practical only for boats up to about fifty feet long, eliminate the biofouling and rust that plague other hulls. Among significant modifications in propulsion gear, there are variable pitch propellers, which Europeans accepted before Americans but which now appear as a feature on the newest fishing boats. They allow such maneuvering options as instant emergency back-off without the need to stop the shaft and then reverse it.

When fishing gear changes, so must the designs to place it on deck for easier, safer operation. Crew comfort was the least consideration of all during any fishing time before the present, but fishermen of the Western world now have better expectations. The individual cabins and bathrooms aboard *Myrefisk-One* in Norway make its crewmen the envy of the fleet, while the bilge bucket for a toilet aboard the

Chesapeake Bay skipjacks and many of the wooden inshore draggers of New England may help account for heavy crew turnover on all but family boats. An article in *Commercial Fisheries News*, a monthly newspaper devoted to the affairs of New England waters, speculated just this. It noted that despite the grand new plotters and fish finders in the wheelhouse, the old wooden vessels usually have an antiquated deck layout that invites gear snags, and requires extra labor which newer boats have eliminated with more efficient layouts. Fishermen may be proud of their ability to tough it through the necessary hardships, but they pass on the fireside romance when it comes to unnecessary ones.

The technological bonanza is heating up. Displays at the annual Fish Expos sponsored by *National Fisherman* magazine (which occur alternately in Boston and Seattle) show enough imaginative new products each year that fishermen find it worthwhile to tie up their boats and come to town from ports up and down the coasts. Sometimes the congestion of wool shirts and tractor caps around a booth hides the product being demonstrated, whether it be an automatic baiting machine, the latest inflatable life raft, an improved diesel engine, a filleter for on-board processing, a new fish hook (there has been an absolute revolution in the design of fish hooks), or the newest color display using phased array radar or navigation satellites.

By 1987, the color plotters that had been a marvel of the 1982 Expo in Boston were standard equipment on fishing boats from Oddmund Bye's grand *Myrefisk-One* to Joey Testaverde's venerable wooden-hulled *Peter & Linda*. Color itself had been a marvel way back in 1980. What next? Nevertheless, while the microchip boxes may have increased man's advantage over fish, a wheelhouse full of gadgets does not automatically make a highliner. The usefulness of electronics is proportionate only to how well the fishing skipper understands them. Like the commanding officer in the Combat Information Center of a modern naval warship, the skipper must learn to think in the three dimensions reported by his displays, which in fishing involve the relative but constantly changing positions between boat, fish, and gear. Without sea sense, he still might as well stay ashore.

And he must still be a man-of-all-work to survive. For fishermen in the old days, this meant mastering marlinspike seamanship as well as skills like carpentry. A fisherman still routinely ties knots, splices rope, mends nets, and drives a nail straight. But with the coming of engines, he needed to become a mechanic also, since he could seldom afford professionals to fix his breakdowns—which might occur at sea in a current taking him toward rocks with no mechanic handy. As equipment became more sophisticated, most fishermen taught themselves such new basic skills as welding and hydraulics repair. Now, however, the new plethora of electronic gear with its microchip circuitry has begun to leave him behind. This dependence on skilled repairmen is no more healthy for a fishing fleet, which must be self-sufficient, than it would be for a modern navy with ships that have weapon systems that can be serviced only by Ph.Ds.

The situation is leading to a change beyond equipment and advantages. The fisherman has lost some of his independence. As one young fisherman I know—Helge Johansen of Sommarøy village in Norway—learned when the possession of a splendid new longliner "stressed" him more and more until he sold it, the cost of the new tools may keep a fisherman in heavy debt, and thus more driven to work longer for larger catches. But if he fails to invest in the minimum new gear for his fishery, he often cannot make even a subsistence living because the local catch is taken so efficiently by others around him. And then the new efficiency tempts governments to step in more and more, which adds an escalating burden of regulations that requires a fisherman to become an accountant or hire one.

Farming in the Water

The wealth of the sea is not the infinite cornucopia that people considered it as recently as the 1950s, before high-volume fishing made possible by gear technologies had thinned the life in many waters. The men of the Soviet trawlers that ravaged the eastern Atlantic stocks actually put to sea with the good feeling that they were helping to feed a hungry world. When Jake Dykstra of the Point Judith Co-op looked back on the first decade of the Magnuson Act and mused on the new American drives, he declared, "I didn't think we had the fishing power to harm the stocks."

Working to catch the most product from the seas—even wresting a share from marine mammals—is not all greed. As the human world overpopulates, the demand and need for protein increases. And seafood is the most direct protein food of them all. Beef is wastefully indirect, a luxury for nations rich in tillable land, since to produce it requires nearly a ten-to-one ratio of feed grain to harvested meat. There seems one logical way around the depletion of native fish. More and more learned experts predict that the seafood of the future will be mass-produced in the manner of chickens, with fish in the wild becoming a curiosity like moose and buffalo meat.

The Chinese and Japanese have farmed certain passive fish and other sea creatures for centuries. In China, I have waded with everyone else into one of the big ponds of a fish culture commune near Wuhan on the Yangtze River, to help pull in a beach seine full of fat silver carp. The meal that night was splendid, as it was another night in the village of Tsinda on the southwestern coast of Taiwan after we had casually netted some farmed milkfish. In the Dominican Republic, the farmed "centolla" king crabs, herbivores fed by villagers with algae grown on screens in the water (part of Smithsonian project augmented by Peace Corps volunteers) provided another gourmet meal. In Japan, I stayed in villages that had specialized, some for generations, in growing such single sea products as oysters, seaweed, and yellowtail.

In the mid-1960s, Norwegians entered the field of aquaculture with notions of farming salmon, a migratory and therefore most unpassive species of fish. The project raised angry passions in Norwegian fishermen, who feared competition that would put them out of business. The passions have now found their way to North America, where similar fears are being realized as successfully raised Norwegian salmon penetrate the world market, and North American entrepreneurs commission the Norwegian technology for aquatic farms of their own.

Norwegians raise salmon by keeping them in pens throughout their life. This requires feeding and aquatic housekeeping. Resembling small farms on land, sea farms can be run by an individual and his family. The ones I saw in Norway, like that of my old Lofoten deckmate Torstein Sandholm, were just this, involving ten or twelve pens in the water and a regular feeding schedule.

Salmon can also be ranched—raised in fresh water, then released into the sea at the migration phase with the hope that they will return to their mother waters at spawning time as do wild salmon. Weyerhaeuser, the timber giant, started a salmon ranch in Oregon, but abandoned the project in the early 1980s when it decided the

[302]

At a meeting of the
New England Fishery
Management Council,
scallop fishermen
line the wall while
members consider a
regulation that affects
their work directly.
Speaking up for the
scallopers, center in
dark suit, is Jim Cos-
takes of the New
Bedford Seafood Pro-
ducer's Association.

Larry Simns, fisher-
man and president of
the Maryland Water-
man's Association,
protests provisions of
a fishing ban on
striped bass (rockfish)
in the Chesapeake
Bay. Behind him
waiting to testify
are a state senator
and state resource
officials.

Watermen attend the
hearing to support
Simns, above. Sign in
photo, cropped short,
reads in full "DNR
(Maryland Depart-
ment of Natural Re-
sources) Creates
Rockfish Decline."

Net handled on the double aboard a seine boat fishing for menhaden in the Virginia portion of the Chesapeake Bay. Despite summer heat, the man under the net wears oilskins to avoid the painful stings of seanettles. His attitude still seems to agree with a sign in one wheelhouse: "The worst day of fishing is better than the best day of work."

small return from the sea failed to compensate for local resentment engendered by the project. On the other hand, the fishermen of Prince William Sound in Alaska have developed a successful co-op hatchery-ranching operation for their specific waters. The Alaska project has produced good fish for nearly two decades despite outside fears that artificially raised salmon might infect the native wild fish with diseases and may perhaps even alter their gene structure.

The objections to aquaculture do not hang merely on the fear of competition. It seems that interference with nature simply cannot be done without a price. Critics say that fish kept in pens, where despite ambient currents they live with their own collective excrement and dead, fall prey to insects and funguses, and that they become prone to ills not suffered by fish in the wild. The caged fish attract marine mammal predators who add to the general effluent. Reports from Norway indicate that penned fish can even become "psychotic." Farming fish requires the use of pesticides, fungicides, antibiotics, herbicides (against plant growth that forms on the equipment), and sex hormones (to keep them from breeding too soon). Of course, we raise chickens this way, and they would not be so cheap at the counter if we did not.

Advocates of fish farming maintain that diligent care keeps all these problems small, and that none of the problems can override the advantage of being able to kill a fish right alongside the equipment that will process it, without any of the hook rips or net burns that occur with boat gear. The fish can also be kept until the market price is right. In remote coves of Norway, I watched big, healthy-looking salmon—the kind that made you yearn for a rod and reel—taken directly from their circular pens to a small, sanitary butchering trough. Within the hour, they were being packed in ice and loaded into a truck for an hour's drive to the nearest quick-freeze plant or a two hours' trip to the airport and the world market.

Out There on the Water

Fishing will never become an elegant profession, dealing directly as it does with the mess of living creatures, but as an occupation it has the most honorable of histories. The Encyclopaedia Britannica's

[303]

speculation that fishermen's dugouts were the earliest boats, the progenitors of all the world's navies and merchant fleets, leads to the conclusion that the fishing occupation prepared the way for sea trade, civilization, and the high destinies of coastal nations.

Yet until recent decades fishermen have been among the lowliest and least protected of workers. Over the centuries, it has seemed a truth of human societies—those existing long enough to support an aristocracy or at least a merchant class—that the rougher and messier an occupation the less prestige and security are given those who practice it. The fisherman's wife in the famous old fable of greed truly occupied the bottom end of the social scale, and had reason to yearn for something better when the magical fish offered it, however much she became carried away. Fishermen in general still have not struck it rich. However, with luck, and with longer hours than office and factory people know, they now can earn enough to hold their own in most societies.

Fishing resembles no other means of livelihood. It is a form of hunting. And it has something in common with farming, since together fishing and farming provide most of the world's food while both remain dependent on the forces of nature. But land, once cleared, has been tamed. The sea remains as wild as when the first Viking sailed with hook and line from the protection of a fjord, and the work of making a living from it remains chancy despite the wonders of engines and microchip boxes. The land-based hunters have all been absorbed into the society, which now grows its meat in pens and has no need of their services. That leaves fishing to be the last of man's hunting occupations to survive as an industry. And a hunt it remains.

The great maritime hunting grounds were finally contracted when nations enclosed the ocean commons with their two-hundred-mile jurisdictions. Does that mean that fish farming, which appears wonderfully practical, will eventually put the ocean hunters out of business? More likely, it will only crowd them and drive them away in some places, since unless pollution destroys us entirely, the sea will continue to generate renewable food resources in global quantity for the taking.

The sad truth is, however, that the resource is simply no longer there for anybody's taking. It must be managed because there are too many candidates for the harvest.

In New England waters, there is never enough to go around, and scarcity becomes exacerbated when the young fry of future harvests becomes decimated as they converge on grounds where nets are dragging for mature fish. There is no way around the need to regulate with a tightness that independent fishermen abhor.

Fishing pays for itself readily in some areas of marine abundance—at least for the most able—yet needs constant help to survive in others no matter what the fisherman's talent. Newfoundlanders, whose harbors ice solid for three to eight months of the year, cannot support themselves year-round at the minimum standard of a prosperous Western nation without government unemployment checks each winter, especially with the loss of sealing incomes during the ice months. Norway has a strong coastal fishing economy, but this is so because the government poured in money for processing plants and roads to keep the strategic coasts populated.

Journalists may sentimentalize the salty fish-puller, but fishermen and their work are not always understood except in communities of their peers. With irregular hours and independent ways, they tend to remain outside the social mainstream. Nonfishermen have nonfishing priorities, even those glad to order fresh scrod or salmon from a menu. Said an acquaintance of mine, discussing the Maryland watermen's fight to keep a commercial quota of striped bass, when sports fishermen lobbied to keep it all: "It's time the state stopped spending money to protect a dying breed who want to keep living in the nineteenth century at the expense of everybody else."

I think that there will always be men who fish for a living. The abundances and beauties of the sea are too great for those of a certain adventurous calibre to ignore them because of mere hardship. Nobody need call fishermen a dying breed. But only the most primitive will fish unchanged.

Even a century ago, fishermen were locked into change, so apparently change itself will not doom a life on the boats. In The Last of the Vikings, one of Johan Bojer's characters, from the final generation to rely on sail and oar, ruminates disapprovingly that "the modern motor fisherman is an industrial workman of the sea, who smokes cigarettes and is a member of a trades union." The 1880s' fishermen whom Bojer described chewed their tobacco—as do many small boat fishermen still, since you can't keep tobacco lighted with water slapping you in the face and tobacco is the only creature comfort around—but their country mixture would probably have eaten the membrane from modern fishermen's throats.

With the availability of engines, hydraulic gear, electronic boxes, and synthetic fibers, the equivalence today of iron men in wooden ships is only relative. Yet, as attested by the wreath below the Gloucester fisherman's statute and the cenotaphs in the New Bedford Seaman's Bethel, men have not stopped going into the sea from fishing boats. They still toll a bell every year in Gloucester, one stroke as the man's name is read, followed by a heart-stopping silence, for each fisherman drowned during the year. With strong marine engines, foam-rubber survival suits, and emergency Mayday devices, the names are more likely to number two or three than two hundred, but fishing remains the most dangerous occupation in the world. According to Department of Labor statistics, it loses two and a half times as many men as mining, the next most dangerous occupation.

In a Gloucester bookstore, the proprietor, a bearded, healthy-looking young man who might have been a waterman himself in this town of boat harbors, discussed the work of James Connolly, who wrote movingly a generation ago about New England fishermen. "Nice stuff, Connolly's," he said, "but unrealistic. A grown man rowing across Gloucester Harbor with dead fish slopped around his feet, singing happily at the top of his voice? Now come on." But only the day before, a half dozen miles down the road at Rockport, I had been talking with the retired lobsterman Frank Mackay over a bowl of clam chowder, when he volunteered, "You get out there and you yell and swear and sing, and get all your frustrations at the world out of you. It's hard work, damned hard, but it's satisfaction."

During the times I have gone fishing around the world, often in mean weather with nothing of physical comfort available, I have seen regularly (not always) the same responses to the sea that Bojer described in his fishermen a century ago. At least some men setting off today for weeks on Georges Bank, or Grand Banks, or the Labrador, or the Newfoundland ice, or the Lofotens, or the Barents Sea, would recognize the Norwegian author's description of the old-time fishermen as they sailed out gravely from home:

God was in the wind and on the sea, and . . . they would soon be on their way to meet Him. The familiar shore on which their cottages stood disappeared. . . . A wave beat against the bow and sent a shower of water into the fore part of the boat. Both hull and rigging trembled. The men looked at one another, wiped the water from their beards, and laughed. . . . They stood with legs apart, chewing tobacco and enjoying life. The boat rocked beneath them, and the wind sang in the rigging; they were out of the reach of tradesmen and banks, they were on the sea once more, they were free men.

It could be that fishermen, despite conflicts of gear and territory, can feel more brothers among themselves nation to nation than with others of their own countrymen in different walks of life. They have in common their self-sufficiency and independence, bought at a hard price although the details of the reckoning may have changed.